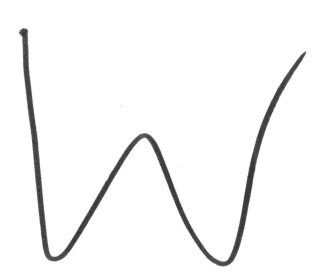

The Birth o

The Birth of Industrial Britain:
Social Change, 1750–1850

Second edition

Kenneth Morgan

Longman
is an imprint of

Harlow, England • London • New York • Boston • San Francisco • Toronto
Sydney • Tokyo • Singapore • Hong Kong • Seoul • Taipei • New Delhi
Cape Town • Madrid • Mexico City • Amsterdam • Munich • Paris • Milan

PEARSON EDUCATION LIMITED

Edinburgh Gate
Harlow CM20 2JE
United Kingdom
Tel: +44 (0)1279 623623
Fax: +44 (0)1279 431059
Website: www.pearsoned.co.uk

First edition published in 2004
Second edition published in Great Britain in 2011

© Pearson Education Limited 2004, 2011

The right of Kenneth Morgan to be identified as author of this work has been asserted by
him in accordance with the Copyright, Designs and Patents Act 1988.

Pearson Education is not responsible for the content of third-party internet sites.

ISBN: 978–1–4082–3095–4

British Library Cataloguing in Publication Data
A CIP catalogue record for this book can be obtained from the British Library

Library of Congress Cataloging in Publication Data
Morgan, Kenneth, 1953–
    The birth of industrial Britain : social change, 1750–1850 / Kenneth Morgan. – 2nd ed.
        p. cm.
    Includes bibliographical references and index.
    ISBN 978-1-4082-3095-4 (pbk. : alk. paper)   1. Great Britain–Economic conditions–
1760–1860.   2. Industrialization–Great Britain–History.   3. Industrial revolution–
Great Britain–History.   4. Industries–Great Britain–History–18th century.
5. Industries–Great Britain–History–19th century.   I. Title.
    HC254.5.M635 2011
    330.941'07–dc22

                                                                2011007459

10   9   8   7   6   5   4   3   2   1
15   14   13   12   11

Set by 35 in 10/13.5pt Berkeley book
Printed and bound in Malaysia, CTP-PJB

Introduction to the Series

History is narrative constructed by historians from traces left by the past. Historical enquiry is often driven by contemporary issues and, in consequence, historical narratives are constantly reconsidered, reconstructed and reshaped. The fact that different historians have different perspectives on issues means that there is also often controversy and no universally agreed version of past events. *Seminar Studies in History* was designed to bridge the gap between current research and debate, and the broad, popular general surveys that often date rapidly.

The volumes in the series are written by historians who are not only familiar with the latest research and current debates concerning their topic, but who have themselves contributed to our understanding of the subject. The books are intended to provide the reader with a clear introduction to a major topic in history. They provide both a narrative of events and a critical analysis of contemporary interpretations. They include the kinds of tools generally omitted from specialist monographs: a chronology of events, a glossary of terms and brief biographies of 'who's who'. They also include bibliographical essays in order to guide students to the literature on various aspects of the subject. Students and teachers alike will find that the selection of documents will stimulate discussion and offer insight into the raw materials used by historians in their attempt to understand the past.

Clive Emsley and Gordon Martel
Series Editors

To Leigh, Ross and Vanessa Morgan

Contents

Acknowledgements

We are grateful to the following for permission to reproduce copyright material:

Maps 1, 2, 3 and 4 adapted from Langton, J. and Morris, R. J., *Atlas of Industrialising Britain* (Routledge 1986), reproduced by permission of Taylor & Francis Books UK.

Plate 1 courtesy of Calderdale MBC Museums; Plate 2 photo © Philip Mould Ltd, London / The Bridgeman Art Library; Plate 3 courtesy of Ironbridge Gorge Museum, Telford, Shropshire, UK / The Bridgeman Art Library; Plate 4 © Bettmann / Corbis; Plates 5 and 7 courtesy of the Mary Evans Picture Library; Plate 6 courtesy of Manchester Art Gallery, UK / The Bridgeman Art Library; Plate 8 from Private Collection / The Bridgeman Art Library.

In some cases we have been unable to trace the owners of copyright material, and we would appreciate any information that would enable us to do so.

Chronology

1748

18 October   Treaty of Aix-la-Chapelle ends War of Austrian Succession.

1752

2 September   Last day of the Julian calendar in Britain.

14 September   First day of the Gregorian calendar in Britain.

1754

March   Duke of Newcastle becomes prime minister.

1756

17 May   Britain declares war on France.

20 June   The Nawab of Bengal imprisoned 146 British captives in a prison cell at Fort William (the Black Hole of Calcutta).

29 August   Seven Years' War begins in Europe.

October   Duke of Newcastle resigns as prime minister.

1757

23 June   Bengal passes into British control after the Battle of Plassey.

July   Formation of the Pitt-Newcastle administration.

1759

13 September   General Wolfe's victory over the French at the Plains of Abraham, Québec.

1760

8 September   Montreal surrenders to Britain. Virtual loss of Canada by France.

25 October   Death of George II and accession of George III to the throne.

1761

9 March Riot against the Militia Act, Hexham, Northumberland.

October Resignation of the Elder Pitt. Formation of the Bute-Newcastle administration.

1762

4 January Britain declares war on Spain.

1763

10 February Paris peace treaty between Britain, France and Spain ends the Seven Years' War.

30 April John Wilkes arrested for his attack on the King's speech in No. 45 of the *North Briton*.

1765

22 March The Stamp Act passed.

1766

18 March Repeal of the Stamp Act.

1768

10 May 'Wilkes and Liberty' riot in London.

1769

February Formation of the Society of the Supporters of the Bill of Rights.

1770

31 January Lord North becomes prime minister.

1771

August Richard Arkwright began building Cromford Mill, Derbyshire.

1772

April–June Food riots mainly in East Anglia and the West of England.

1773

16 December Boston Tea Party.

1775

19 April The War of American Independence begins at Concord, Massachusetts.

1776

4 July   Declaration of American Independence.

1777

17 October   General Burgoyne defeated at the Battle of Saratoga, New York.

1778

17 June   War declared between Britain and France.

1779

July   The Penitentiary Act authorised the building of one or more national penitentiaries.

1780

8 February   Presentation of the Yorkshire petition for parliamentary reform to the House of Commons.

2–9 June   Gordon (anti-Catholic) Riots in London.

1781

19 October   Lord Cornwallis surrenders to George Washington after the Battle of Yorktown, Virginia.

1782

20 March   Lord North resigns as prime minister.

27 March   Formation of the Home Office.

1783

April–December   The Fox-North Coalition ministry.

3 September   Treaty of Paris ends the War of American Independence.

19 December   William Pitt the Younger becomes prime minister.

1786

26 September   Anglo-French commercial treaty (the Eden treaty) signed.

1788

18 January   First fleet of convicts reaches Botany Bay.

1789

January   The Regency Bill passed to deprive the Prince of Wales of power.

14 July   Storming of the Bastille, Paris marks the beginning of the French Revolution.

1790
November Edmund Burke publishes *Reflections on the Revolution in France*, warning of the dangers of the French Revolution.

1791
2 March Death of John Wesley, the main founder of Methodism.

March Thomas Paine publishes *Rights of Man*, part one.

14–17 July 'Church and King' riots in Birmingham against Dissenters.

1792
25 January Formation of the London Corresponding Society, the first artisan-based political society in Britain.

February Thomas Paine publishes *Rights of Man*, part two.

1793
1 February France declares war on Britain and the Netherlands.

1794
October–November Thomas Hardy, founder of the London Corresponding Society, and other radicals acquitted of high treason.

1795
December Seditious Meetings Act restricts public meetings and political lectures.

1797
February The Bank of England suspended specie payments.

16 April–15 May Naval mutiny at Spithead.

12 May–16 June Naval mutiny at the Nore.

1798
23 May–12 October Irish Rebellion, the largest popular Republican rising in Irish history.

1799
12 July Combination Act passed.

1801
1 January Act of Union, creating the United Kingdom of Great Britain and Ireland, came into effect.

16 February William Pitt the Younger resigns as prime minister.

10 March The first national census in Britain.

1802

17 March   Peace of Amiens temporarily ends hostilities between Britain and France.

1803

16 May   War resumes between Britain and France.

1805

21 October   Nelson defeats the Franco-Spanish fleet at the Battle of Trafalgar.

1806

23 January   Death of William Pitt the Younger.

1807

25 March   An act to abolish the British slave trade passed.

1811

March   Beginning of Luddite disturbances in the Midlands.

1812

January   Luddite disturbances spread to Yorkshire and Lancashire.

8 June   Lord Liverpool becomes Tory prime minister.

19 June   The United States declares war on Britain.

1814

24 December   War between Britain and the United States concludes with the Treaty of Ghent.

1815

20 March   Parliament passes the Corn Law.

9 June   Treaty of Vienna ends the Napoleonic wars.

18 June   Defeat of Napoleon at the Battle of Waterloo.

1816

2 December   Spa Fields riots, Islington, London.

1817

28 January   Mobbing of the Prince Regent's coach, London.

10 March   March of the Blanketeers gathers in Manchester.

9 June   Pentrich rebellion, Derbyshire.

1819

16 August   Peterloo Massacre, Manchester.

1820

29 January   Death of George III. George IV becomes king.

23 February   Apprehension of the Cato Street conspirators.

1824

21 June   Repeal of the Combination Acts.

1825

September   Opening of the Stockton and Darlington railway.

1827

9 April   Lord Liverpool resigns as prime minister.

1828

9 May   Repeal of the Test and Corporation Acts.

1829

24 March   Catholic Relief Act grants Catholic Emancipation.

29 September   Formation of the Metropolitan Police by Robert Peel.

1830

26 June   Death of George IV. William IV becomes king.

August–October   'Swing' Riots against agricultural machinery.

15 September   Opening of the Liverpool and Manchester railway.

22 November   Earl Grey becomes Whig prime minister.

1831

October   Reform Bill demonstrations and riots at Nottingham, Derby and Bristol.

1832

7 June   Great Reform Act becomes law.

1833

29 August   Factory Reform Act passed.

1834

February   Foundation of the Grand National Consolidated Trades Union (GNCTU) by Robert Owen.

18 March   Six Dorset farm labourers (the Tolpuddle martyrs) sentenced to convict transportation to Australia for trade union activities.

1 August   Slavery abolished in most of the British Empire.

14 August   Poor Law Amendment Act passed.

1835

9 September   Cruelty to Animals Act passed.

21 October   Municipal Corporations Act passed.

1836

26 June   London Working Men's Association formed.

1837

20 June   Death of William IV. Accession of Queen Victoria.

1838

6 August   The People's Charter adopted at a mass rally in Birmingham.

1839

7 May   Presentation of the 1st Chartist petition to Parliament.

4 July   Riots at the Bull Ring, Birmingham.

4 November   Rebellion at Newport, Monmouthshire.

1841

30 August   Sir Robert Peel becomes Conservative prime minister.

1842

2 May   Presentation of 2nd Chartist Petition to Parliament.

10 August   The Mines Act passed.

August   'Plug' riots in the Midlands, Scotland, Yorkshire and Lancashire.

1844

7 June   Factory Act passed.

1846

25 June   The House of Lords repeals the Corn Laws.

29 June   Sir Robert Peel resigns as prime minister.

1848

10 April   Presentation of 3rd Chartist petition to Parliament.

1851

May–October   The Great Exhibition at the Crystal Palace, Hyde Park, London.

Who's who

Arkwright, Richard (1732–1792): Industrialist and inventor. Originally from Lancashire, he patented the water frame in 1769 to speed up the mechanisation of cotton spinning. He was the proprietor of Cromford mill, near Matlock, Derbyshire, the first major cotton factory in Britain.

Bell, Andrew (1753–1832): Inventor of the 'Madras' system of education in which the older, clever pupils taught younger pupils under a monitorial system. This was adopted by the National Society for Promoting the Education of the Poor in the Principles of the Established Church, founded in 1811.

Bentham, Jeremy (1748–1832): Utilitarian philosopher and social reformer, Bentham wanted reforms that brought in the greatest happiness for the greatest number of people. He made numerous important contributions to ideas about legal and prison reform. His advocacy of centralised bureaucracy, efficient administration and inspection influenced the operation of the New Poor Law.

Birkbeck, Sir George (1776–1841): Doctor, philanthropist and academic. Pioneer of adult education for the working man who founded mechanics' institutes for the advance of scientific knowledge.

Brougham, Henry (1778–1868): Scottish Whig lawyer, politician and statesman who became Lord Chancellor between 1830 and 1834. He was an opponent of the slave trade, and promoted the education of the poor and legal reform.

Chadwick, Edwin (1800–1890): Social and legal reformer. A disciple of Jeremy Bentham. He played an important role in formulating social policy in Britain between 1832 and 1854, when he retired. He made important contributions to poor law provision, public health and factory reform.

Crompton, Samuel (1753–1827): Lancashire-born inventor of the 'mule', a spinning machine used in cotton factories from 1779 onwards that achieved greater productivity than Arkwright's water frame.

Eden, Sir Frederick, 2nd baronet (1766–1809): Writer on poverty and social investigator. His *State of the Poor*, 3 vols (1797) gathered comprehensive information on the labouring classes in England.

Engels, Friedrich (1820–1895): German social scientist, author and political theorist, closely associated with Karl Marx, with whom he co-authored the *Communist Manifesto* (1848). He was the author of *The Condition of the Working Classes in England in 1844*, based on his experience working for a textile firm in Manchester in the early 1840s.

Fielding, Henry (1707–1754): Combined the roles of lawyer, magistrate and author of plays and novels. He was Justice of the Peace for Bow Street from 1748, where he tried to reduce crime and disorder.

Fielding, Sir John (d. 1780): Magistrate and half-brother of Henry Fielding. Active in tackling robbery and other types of crime in London.

Frost, John (1784–1877): Welsh Chartist and leader of the Newport Rising in 1839. Found guilty of high treason and transported as a convict to Australia. He was eventually pardoned.

Fry, Elizabeth (1780–1845): Quaker who was active in the reform of London's prisons, paying particular attention to the relief of women prisoners and to educational and religious schemes for inmates.

Gilbert, Thomas (1720–1798): Poor Law reformer and MP. He promoted legislation in 1782 (Gilbert's Act) which permitted two or more parishes to unite to form poor law unions.

Gordon, Lord George (1751–1793): Politician who became President of the Protestant Association. The anti-Catholic Gordon Riots (1780) are named after him. After these riots, lasting six days, he was tried for treason and acquitted.

Graham, Sir James, 2nd baronet (1792–1861): Politician and statesman. Originally a Whig, he joined the Conservatives in 1837. Home Secretary between 1841 and 1846 in Sir Robert Peel's Conservative government.

Grey, Charles, 2nd Earl (1764–1845): Whig leader and prime minister in 1830–34. His main achievement was to steer the Great Reform Bill through Parliament in 1831–32, which redistributed some parliamentary constituencies and extended the franchise while retaining aristocratic influence.

Hanway, Jonas (1712–1786): Philanthropist who founded the Marine Society, London, in 1756. This helped poor boys from the metropolis to enter a naval career. Involved in other reform initiatives, including support for the Foundling Hospital.

Howard, John (?1726–1790): Sheriff in Bedfordshire and prison reformer. His visits to gaols formed the basis of his influential indictment of prison conditions in *The State of the Prisons in England and Wales* (1777).

Hunt, Henry (1773–1835): Radical reformer known as 'Orator' Hunt because of his ability to address large open-air crowds effectively on the need for parliamentary reform. Advocated universal manhood suffrage, annual Parliaments and use of the ballot box at general elections.

Kay-Shuttleworth, Sir James, 1st baronet (originally James Phillips Kay) (1804–1877): Educationalist and politician. Trained as a doctor, he worked in the factory districts of Lancashire and later became an important contributor to factory reform and to popular education. He jointly founded in 1839–40 the first British training college for school teachers in Battersea, London.

Lancaster, Joseph (1778–1838): Educationalist and nonconformist. Established a school in Southwark, London in 1798 which was free for those unable to pay. His monitorial system was widely adopted in non-denominational schools throughout the nineteenth century, particularly under the auspices of the British and Foreign School Society.

Liverpool, Lord, Robert Banks Jenkinson (1770–1828): Tory politician and prime minister between 1812 and 1827. Opposed to radical agitation and parliamentary reform, his administration brought in repressive measures to counteract popular protest in the difficult peacetime years immediately after the end of the Napoleonic wars.

Lovett, William (1800–1877): Chartist leader. Founder of the London Men's Working Association in 1836, Lovett is best known for his Chartist activities. He was a 'moral force' Chartist who advocated the spread of literacy and political education for the poor and their children.

Lowery, Robert (1809–1863): Chartist based on Tyneside. Originally a tailor who opened a political bookshop in Newcastle, he travelled widely as a radical politician. He advocated teetotal Chartism.

Malthus, Thomas Robert (1766–1834): Social thinker, clergyman and population theorist. Malthus published numerous works on political economy but is best known as the author of an *Essay on the Principle of Population as It Affects the Future Improvement of Society*, first published in 1798 and revised in 1803. Malthus was the first notable thinker to explain mortality and fertility in relation to wages and food prices.

Marx, Karl (1818–1883): German philosopher, social theorist and political economist who wrote influentially on class consciousness, capitalism and class struggle. Author of *Capital*, 2 vols (1885, 1894) and co-author, with Engels, of the *Communist Manifesto* (1848).

O'Brien, James Bronterre (1805–1864): Irish-born Chartist leader, reformer and journalist. Favoured a militant approach to Chartist campaigning but eschewed the use of violence to gain political representation for the working class.

O'Connor, Feargus (1794–1855): Irish Chartist leader and journalist. Advocated 'physical force' Chartism and a Land Plan for settling working class families on rural plots. Founded the radical newspaper the *Northern Star*, based in Leeds. The only Chartist ever elected as an MP.

Oastler, Richard (1789–1861): A Yorkshireman who was a leader of the factory reform and anti-poor law movements. He fought for the rights of working children in the Factory Act of 1847.

Owen, Robert (1771–1858): Entrepreneur and social reformer. Co-owner of New Lanark mill, a model cotton factory in Scotland, and involved in many labour, cooperative and communitarian experiments. Active in the factory reform movement, the early trade union movement and public campaigns for poor relief and popular education.

Peel, Sir Robert (1788–1850): Politician, founder of the Metropolitan Police and Conservative prime minister in 1834–5 and 1841–46. Peel led the transition from the Tory to the Conservative Party. His main political concerns were the Irish situation, finance and commerce, ecclesiastical policy and law and order.

Pitt the Younger, William (1759–1806): Politician, statesman and prime minister in 1783–1801 and 1804–6. Called himself an 'independent Whig,' but some historians characterise him as an independent or as a Tory. Oversaw the restoration of the nation's finances after the end of the American Revolution and steered Britain through the difficulties of war, radicalism and the French Revolution.

Place, Francis (1771–1854): Radical social reformer with interests in organised, public education, the political representation of the working class and Malthus's views on population growth. Active in the agitation that led to the Great Reform Act of 1832.

Priestley, Joseph (1733–1804): Chemist, political theorist, millenarian and clergyman who discovered what was subsequently called oxygen. His open support for the French Revolution contributed to a mob burning down his house, library and laboratory. He eventually emigrated to the United States.

Raikes, Robert (1736–1811): English philanthropist and evangelical Anglican layman. Proprietor of the *Gloucester Journal* and a pioneer of the Sunday school movement.

Ricardo, David (1772–1823): Political economist. A prolific writer and economic theorist whose key text was *On the Principles of Political Economy, and Taxation*. His writings on profits, value and income distribution were widely influential in his time.

Russell, John, 1st Earl (1792–1878): Whig politician, statesman and prime minister between 1846 and 1852 and in 1865–6. Responsible for the preparation of the Reform Bill in 1832.

Salt, Sir Titus, 1st Baronet (1803–1876): Manufacturer, politician and philanthropist. His textile mill at Saltaire, near Bradford, was part of an industrial community with workers' houses, a hospital, almshouses and churches.

Senior, Nassau (1790–1864): Political economist. A member of the Royal Commission into the Poor Law in 1832 and the Handloom Weavers' Commission in 1837. He published extensively on economic theory.

Sharp, Granville (1735–1813): Civil servant, lawyer and antislavery campaigner. He chaired the Committee for the Abolition of the Slave Trade from 1787 and established the African Institution to establish legitimate commerce with Africa.

Simeon, Charles (1759–1836): Evangelical leader, vicar of Holy Trinity, Cambridge, between 1786 and 1836, and a founder member of the Church Missionary Society in 1797.

Smith, Adam (1723–1790): Economist and moral philosopher. Author, principally, of *An Enquiry into the Nature and Causes of the Wealth of Nations* (1776) in which he presented a critique of mercantilism, recognised the potential productivity of capitalist markets and advocated free trade as a creator of wealth.

Stephens, Joseph Rayner (1805–1879): Methodist minister and champion of the working class of south-east Lancashire and north-east Cheshire. A radical supporter of Chartism.

Vincent, Henry (1813–1878): Active in early working men's associations and a popular Chartist orator and leader. Promoted universal manhood suffrage and welfare benefits for the working class.

Wellington, Arthur Wellesley, 1st Duke of (1769–1852): Soldier and prime minister between 1828 and 1830. Wellington's fame rests mainly upon his exploits as an army field commander, which climaxed in his victory over the French at the Battle of Waterloo (1815). As prime minister he agreed to Catholic Emancipation in 1829 but later opposed the Great Reform Act of 1832.

Wesley, Charles (1707–1788): Brother of John Wesley and a fellow Methodist preacher. Renowned as a writer of over 7,000 hymns.

Wesley, John (1703–1791): Founder of Methodism. Brought up in an Anglican household, Wesley became a leading religious figure. Arminian in theology and concerned with saving souls, he preached the gospels wherever he found a receptive audience and made important contributions to Methodist organisation.

Whitbread, Samuel (1758–1815): An MP from a prominent Bedfordshire brewing family. He championed religious and civil rights, campaigned against slavery, and admired Napoleon's reforms in France and elsewhere in Europe.

Whitefield, George (1714–1770): Methodist preacher, originally from Gloucester, who inspired large open-air audiences with his fiery evangelical preaching. His Calvinism led him to split from the Arminian-based theology of his fellow Methodist leader, John Wesley.

Wilberforce, William (1759–1833): Politician, philanthropist, evangelical and campaigner against the slave trade. MP for Hull, Yorkshire. He had a long parliamentary career, and was the main spokesman in the House of Commons for the anti-slave trade cause.

Wilkes, John (1725–1797): Politician and radical campaigner. A rakish MP who left a significant imprint on popular politics. He criticised the legitimacy of parliamentary elections, political corruption and the freedom of the press. Twice imprisoned. Spent several years in political exile on the continent.

Glossary

Act of Settlement (1701): Legislation that provided the basis for the Hanoverian Succession. It stated that the heir to the English and Scottish throne should be Protestant. In particular, it provided that on the death of Queen Anne, the crown should pass to her nearest Protestant relative, Sophia, Electress of Hanover, a grand-daughter of James I, or her descendants.

Arminian theology: Named after the Dutch religious reformer Jacob Arminius (1560–1609). Arminianism embraced the notion of free will and the belief that all people could be saved. It therefore opposed the Calvinist notion of predestination and only the elect being saved. Arminianism was the dominant theology of the Church of England and of the Wesleyan Methodists.

Baptists: A nonconformist group that comprised two denominations, the General Baptists, who were Arminian, and the Particular Baptists, who were high Calvinists. The Baptist Union was formed in 1813, and served as a meeting ground for both denominations. Baptists selected their own ministers and believed in adult baptism. Baptists were also opposed in principle to the connection of church and state.

Bible Christians: A group, also known as the Bryanites, that separated from the Methodists in 1818. They were formed by William O'Bryan as the Bible Christian Society in 1815, and were based particularly in Devon and Cornwall.

Birmingham Political Union (BPU): Founded in 1830 by Thomas Attwood, Member of Parliament for Birmingham between 1832 and 1839. The BPU agitated for parliamentary reform. In April 1837 the BPU drew up a National Petition calling for sweeping changes in the economy and system of parliamentary representation.

Bloody Code: A term applied by historians to the series of criminal statutes enacted by eighteenth-century British Parliaments, many of which prescribed the death penalty. There were over 200 capital statutes by the end of the eighteenth century.

British and Foreign School Society (BFSS): Established in 1804 as a society that embraced the monitorial system and non-denominational elementary schools that were established in south London in 1798 by Joseph Lancaster (1778–1838).

Calvinist theology: Named after the Genevan religious reformer John Calvin (1509–64). Calvinism was a belief in the predestination of souls either to salvation (the elect) or damnation (the non-elect). It was associated especially with the Puritan wing of the Church of England.

Catholic emancipation: From the 1770s onwards penal laws against Roman Catholics were repealed on a piecemeal basis. The Catholic Emancipation (Relief) Act of 1829 removed all remaining disabilities to Catholic worship throughout the United Kingdom.

Clapham Sect: An Anglican evangelical group that met regularly at Holy Trinity Church, Clapham, London, in the 1790s. Members engaged in philanthropic, missionary and other collective religious activities, and were known as the 'Saints'. Among their members were William Wilberforce, Zachary Macaulay and James Stephen.

Combination Acts (1799, 1800): A government attempt to prohibit workmen's organisations. The 1799 legislation consolidated Acts passed since the 1720s against workers' combinations in specific trades into a general statute banning all such organisations. The 1800 Act superseded it and provided for arbitrators to settle disputes over work or wages. The Acts were repealed in 1824 and 1825 following a campaign against their restrictive nature.

Common Pleas: The Court of Common Pleas was a common law court that generally met at Westminster. Its business came to centre on disputes between private individuals and on the registration of land transactions.

Common rights: Communal rights on the land that were important to the labouring poor. Such rights could include the right to glean corn after the harvest, to collect furze from hedgerows, and to keep poultry and tether livestock on common land. Parliamentary enclosure eroded some of these common rights.

Congregationalists: A nonconformist denomination that objected in principle to the connection between church and state and also rejected all church hierarchy. Each local Congregational church was voluntarily constituted and depended directly on Christ as its Head. During the eighteenth century, Congregationalists were often known as Independents. The Congregational Union of England and Wales was formed in 1831.

Corn Laws: Protective duties on corn were first introduced in 1804. The Corn Laws refer to two protectionist measures: the Corn Law of 1815, which prevented the import of foreign grain until the domestic price reached 80 shillings per quarter, and another Corn Law of 1828, which introduced a sliding scale of tariffs. Both statutes were intended to protect the landed interest, following the collapse of artificially high grain prices after the end of the French Revolutionary and Napoleonic Wars.

Crompton's mule: A cotton textile machine perfected by Samuel Crompton in 1785. It spun many scores of thread at once and produced a soft, firm yarn suitable for either warp or weft threads.

Enclosure: The privatisation of land by parliamentary statute, though sometimes private enclosure awards occurred. Usually the land concerned was previously subject to communal rights. Many schemes for parliamentary enclosure were passed from 1604 onwards. Parliamentary enclosure was particularly prominent during the reign of George III (1760–1820).

Exchequer of Pleas: The oldest of the common law courts. Originally intended to adjudicate matters pertaining to the royal revenue, its case load increased in the seventeenth and eighteenth centuries in common law and equity by accepting fictitious pleas of suitors that they were debtors of the crown.

'Gagging' Acts: The six Acts passed in 1819 after the Peterloo Massacre. They allowed magistrates to search premises for arms; permitted seizure of seditious writings; prohibited meetings of more than 50 people; prevented military drilling; increased newspaper duties; and accelerated judicial proceedings.

Game Laws: A set of laws passed between 1671 and 1831 to protect landed proprietors against the hunting of game, especially pheasants, partridges and hares. The Game Laws were frequently modified to discourage particular forms of poaching.

General warrants: Warrants issued for the arrest of unspecified persons under the provisions of the Licensing Act of 1662 for use against the authors, publishers and distributors of seditious publications. They became controversial in the years 1763–65 when they were issued against those responsible for publishing issue no. 45 of Wilkes's weekly paper the *North Briton*, which attacked the King's speech to Parliament.

Grand National Consolidated Trades Union (GNCTU): Begun by Robert Owen in 1834 as an exception to small, localised trade unions that were then characteristic in Britain. Owen hoped to link all British trade unions to his cooperative and socialist movement. The GNCTU had 16,000 members, mainly in London, but it failed to appeal to cotton operative and cloth workers and collapsed in 1835.

Habeas corpus: A Latin phrase meaning 'you have the body'. This was the common law writ that could obtain the release of those imprisoned without charge or not brought to trial. A Habeas Corpus Act of 1679 defined its use. Parliament temporarily suspended the Act in times of emergency in 1715, 1794 and 1817.

Hungry forties: A phrase that evokes the deep depression, widespread unemployment and popular discontent of the 1840s, a decade that witnessed Chartist protests, the Irish potato famine, the campaign against the Corn Laws and mass emigration from Ireland.

Jacobinism: Derived from the followers of the Jacobin Club (1790–94), who were radical followers of Robespierre in the French Revolution. Jacobinism was a term used in the French Revolutionary Wars to refer to British radicals whose political ideology was similar to their French counterparts.

Jacobite: A name given to supporters of the exiled James II, his son and grandson, based on their hereditary claim and divine right to the dual throne of England and Scotland and (after 1707) of Britain. The Jacobite movement existed mainly from the Glorious Revolution (1688) until the Battle of Culloden (1746).

Justices of the Peace (JPs): The most important officers in local government from the fourteenth to the nineteenth centuries. They presided at quarter sessions and dealt with minor charges before the law. They were also involved with the poor relief system.

King's Bench prison: A high court prison that catered for those imprisoned for debt. Inmates were held on civil rather than criminal charges and were allowed considerable autonomy in their living conditions. Debtors were often kept in the King's Bench prison at their creditors' expense.

Labour aristocracy: A distinct upper stratum within the working class characterised by higher incomes, better living standards and more regular employment than the majority of working-class people. Most men among the labour aristocracy were skilled workers affiliated with craft unions.

Laissez-faire: An approach to economic affairs that arose among certain economic writers of the late eighteenth and early nineteenth centuries. Its advocates believed there should be an absence of direct attempts by the government to control and regulate the nature and direction of economic development. Adherents of laissez-faire views nevertheless believed there were still areas where the government should act to protect the weaker members of society.

Latitudinarianism: A pejorative term, used with reference to the later seventeenth and early eighteenth centuries, to denote clergy in the Church of England who gave little priority to ecclesiastical organisation or liturgical practice.

London Corresponding Society (LCS): Formed in January 1792 to promote the cause of universal manhood suffrage and annual Parliaments and to maintain links with other corresponding societies. Its founder was Thomas Hardy, a shoemaker. Most members were artisans and working men. The Society was suppressed by government statute in July 1799.

Lumpenproletariat: The lowest rung of the unskilled working class.

Malthusian crisis: A crisis where the growth and size of a population outstrips available food resources. Named after the population theorist Thomas Robert Malthus.

Methodism: A Protestant denomination that began in the 1730s as an adjunct to the Church of England. Among its founders were John Wesley and George Whitefield. Most Methodists followed an Arminian theology, but there were also Calvinist Methodists. The Methodist movement separated from the Church of England in 1795.

Militia Act: Three Militia Acts were passed in the early years of Charles II's reign (1661–63). These statutes established the legality of the militia under the ultimate authority of the monarch. Militia service was carried out on a voluntary basis, except in times of threatened invasion when a ballot might be called, as happened with the highly unpopular Militia Act of 1757.

Moral economy: A phrase popularised by E. P. Thompson, referring to the collective behaviour of lower-class people based on notions of custom and community rather than on capitalist market relations. It is usually applied to pre-industrial Britain, where, it is suggested, a moral economy involved the use of 'fair' wages, 'just' prices and 'honourable' market practices.

Municipal Corporations Act (1835): Provided for the creation of town councils to be elected on a wide franchise. Many new industrial towns, formerly without self-government apart from vestries or improvement commissions, took advantage of the Act to secure incorporation (grant of powers of local self-government by an elected corporation).

National Society for the Education of the Poor in the Principles of the Established Church: Founded in 1811 as an Anglican society to promote monitorial teaching in elementary schools. Its first superintendent was Andrew Bell, who had devised the 'Madras' system of education, in which much teaching was done by older, able pupils.

New Poor Law: Refers to the poor relief system in operation after the passing of the Poor Law Amendment Act (1834). It was characterised by greater centralisation in the organisation of poor relief, by the principle of 'less eligibility' applied to able-bodied paupers, and by attempts to erect more workhouses. The system was not dismantled until the arrival of old age pensions marked a shift in policy under the Liberal government of 1906–14.

Normal schools: A name given to early Victorian teacher training colleges.

Old Poor Law: Refers to the poor relief system in operation until the Poor Law Amendment Act (1834), established under Elizabethan statutes dated 1597 and 1601, though an earlier Act dated 1552 contained elements of the system. Justices of the Peace had overall responsibility for maintaining poor relief locally. Individual parishes had their poor rate administered by overseers of the poor, who were appointed annually.

Political economists: Practitioners of the theoretical science of the laws of production and distribution. Political economists examined the processes whereby finite resources were allocated among various social classes and the operation of various factors that constrained wealth and productivity.

Poor relief: A parish-based system of relief payments for various categories of paupers, given formal establishment under two Acts passed in 1597 and 1601. Poverty was widespread and poor relief continued to be significant until the early twentieth century.

Presbyterian: A Calvinist nonconformist denomination that accorded no special hierarchical status to individuals. Ministers (presbyters) had equal status in making decisions together in councils (presbyteries or synods). Presbyterianism flourished particularly in Ulster and lowland Scotland.

Primitive Methodist Connexion: Established in 1812 by Hugh Bourne and William Clowes and based on revivalist meetings using dramatic missionary methods. Attracted mainly humble followers.

Privy Council: A body that emerged from Henry VIII's royal council. It was a leading executive body until Charles I's reign. It still exists and advises the sovereign on the approval of orders-in-council and the issue of royal proclamations.

Rebecca riots: A crusade against toll gates, and to a lesser extent against workhouses, that occurred in Wales in 1843–44. The protests were organised by the Children of Rebecca, named after the biblical precedent of Rebecca, daughter of Isaac.

Religious Society of Friends: Founded in the 1650s by George Fox and usually referred to as Quakers. Friends shun liturgical and sacramental worship and spend their time in meetings 'waiting on the Lord'. They eschew a professional ministry. They seek God's 'inner light' in the individual.

Scottish Free Church: Formed in 1843 after a major split in the Church of Scotland. The Scottish Free Church sought spiritual independence from civil interference and attracted evangelical clergy in particular.

Social control: A term used usually with regard to bourgeois reformers in the period *c.*1830–60 who tried to instil the virtues of sobriety, orderliness, punctuality, thriftiness, godliness, and obedience to authority among the lower orders. Historians have found more examples of the intentions of social control than they have of social control in practice.

Society for Effecting the Abolition of the Slave Trade: Founded in 1787 as the first national society devoted to the abolition of the British slave trade. Ten of the original 13 members were Quakers. The Society immediately embarked on a public campaign against the slave trade.

Statute of Artificers (1563): Established procedures for fixing maximum wages by JPs and regulated the system of apprenticeship and entry into trade crafts.

Swing riots: Named after the mythical Captain Swing, whose name was often appended to threatening letters, these were riots that occurred throughout much of rural southern and eastern England in 1830–31. The main tactic of the protesters lay in the breaking up of threshing machines.

Tractarianism: A mid-nineteenth century name for the Anglo-Catholicism of the Oxford Movement, which began in the Church of England in 1833. Tractarianism as a sobriquet stems from the published theological series *Tracts for the Times*.

Unitarians: A Protestant denomination that rejected the Trinity and the divinity of Christ in favour of the unity of the Godhead. The first Unitarian chapel was opened in 1774 in London. Many Presbyterians converted to Unitarianism in the late eighteenth century. Unitarians were often educated, intellectual people who favoured discussion of religious principles.

Utilitarians: Followers of Jeremy Bentham who believed that political and reform activity should be devoted to the greatest happiness of the greatest number of people. Often referred to as Philosophical Radicalism, it was a branch of moral philosophy that exerted great influence on British political, economic, social and legal thought during the nineteenth century.

Water frame: A water-powered machine, patented by Richard Arkwright in 1768, that speeded up the spinning process in the textile industry. It incorporated rollers that produced for the first time a cotton thread strong enough for use in the warp of the cloth.

Wilkes and Liberty: The famous chant of the British and American supporters of the would-be political reformer John Wilkes in the decade after 1763. There were 'Wilkes and Liberty' petitions, banners and teacups.

Yorkshire Association: Formed in 1779 with the aim of shortening Parliaments and campaigning for a more equal representation of the people at general elections. The Association promoted economic reform, the addition of an extra 100 county MPs, and triennial Parliaments. It ceased activity in April 1785 without achieving its objectives.

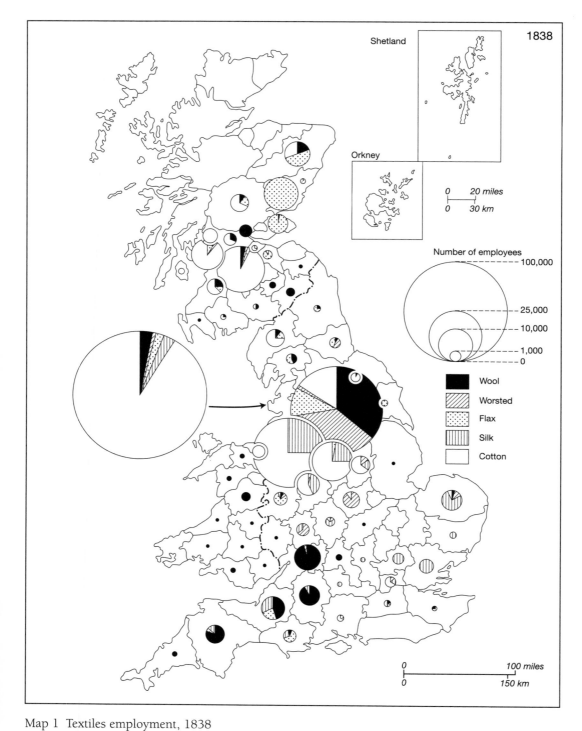

Map 1   Textiles employment, 1838

Source: Adapted from Langton, J. and Morris, R. J., *Atlas of Industrialising Britain* (Routledge 1986), reproduced by permission of Taylor & Francis Books UK.

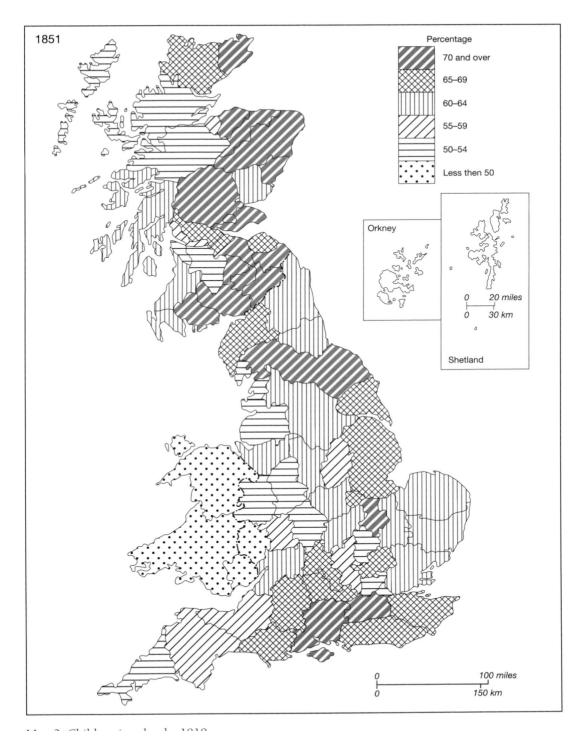

Map 2 Children in schools, 1818

Source: Adapted from Langton, J. and Morris, R. J., *Atlas of Industrialising Britain* (Routledge 1986), reproduced by permission of Taylor & Francis Books UK.

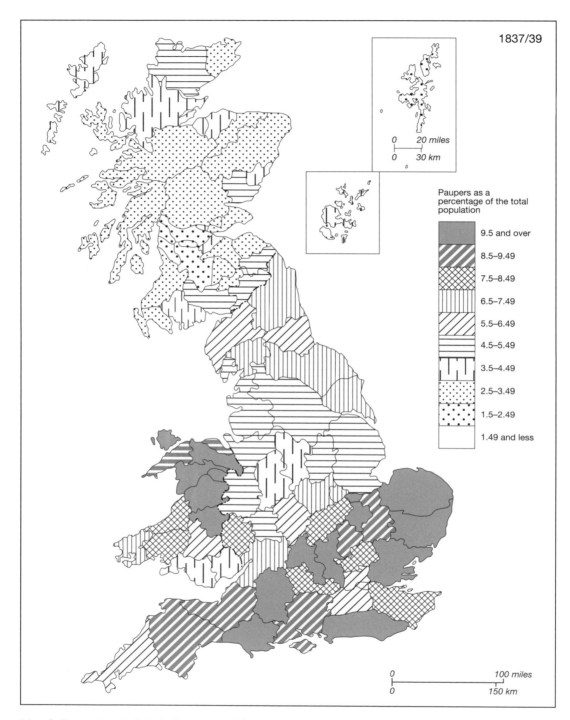

Map 3 Pauperism in Britain by county, 1837/39

Source: Adapted from Langton, J. and Morris, R. J., *Atlas of Industrialising Britain* (Routledge 1986), reproduced by permission of Taylor & Francis Books UK.

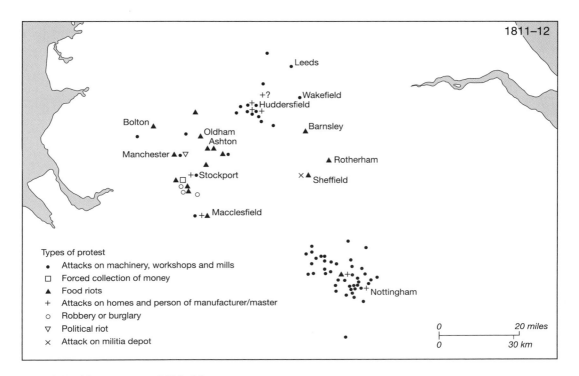

Map 4 Luddite protests, 1811–12

Source: Adapted from Langton, J. and Morris, R. J., *Atlas of Industrialising Britain* (Routledge 1986), reproduced by permission of Taylor & Francis Books UK.

Part 1

INTRODUCTION

1

The Birth of Industrial Britain

This book serves as a companion to *The Birth of Industrial Britain: Economic Change 1750–1850* (1999). In that volume the main contours of Britain's economic development were charted during the century that witnessed the most significant structural economic changes in modern times. After *c.* 1760 Britain gradually achieved rates of economic and industrial growth that reached a 2–3 per cent annual increase by the early nineteenth century. These growth rates point to a slower transition to a capitalist industrial economy than the metaphor of a 'take-off' into self-sustained growth once implied, yet they were still sufficient, according to economists' criteria, for an industrial revolution to be under way. During the century after 1750 the nation was also transformed from a country where most people lived in rural areas and worked on the land to one where increased work in towns and cities became the norm. High wages in England and abundant supplies of capital and cheap energy stimulated the demand for new technology. A wave of macro-inventions – notably the steam engine, cotton spinning machinery, and iron smelting by coke – resulted from this mix of factors. Britain's success in global trade in the early modern period directly affected the wage and price structure in the English economy, and this created the demand for new technology (Allen, 2009). Though British industrialisation was incomplete by 1850, the main sectors of the economy had experienced significant structural growth and change since the mid-eighteenth century.

The Birth of Industrial Britain: Economic Change 1750–1850 analysed changes in population growth, agriculture, industry, finance and capital, foreign trade and internal transport. It concluded that the dynamics of change in the economy outweighed evidence of continuity. There was still much traditional rural labour and domestic industry in the mid-Victorian era, and margins of the nation where time had stood still. There were areas of deindustrialisation, labour immobility and poverty. Representative political participation lagged behind economic improvements and social change. Yet by 1850, compared with the situation a century before, important changes in the economy outstripped signs of stasis: Britain had several large industrial cities with flourishing hinterlands, a vastly improved internal communications network, more efficiently organised agriculture, more sophisticated business techniques in overseas trade, developing financial institutions, continuing evidence of inventiveness and technological ingenuity, more intensive economic development in regions with good fuel resources and raw materials, and a reputation for producing quality manufactured goods at prices cheaper than most of its competitors. Small wonder that Britain was hailed as 'the workshop of the world' at the Great Exhibition held at the Crystal Palace, Hyde Park, in 1851: economic improvements had led to important changes in the social fabric of the nation.

The current book looks at the social consequences of these economic changes. Though it discusses areas of continuity, it is particularly concerned with the impact of social change on the mass of the population affected by rising industrial and economic growth. A fair amount of attention is given to the role of Parliament and the middle classes in promoting legislation concerning changes in social policy. The ideas of major reformers who had a significant impact on social change are examined. The institutional contexts of British society are dovetailed into the analysis. But the main focus is on the mass of working-class people who experienced changes in agricultural and industrial work, alterations in patterns of leisure, shifts in living and health standards, improvements in educational provision, wider choice in religious worship, amendments in poor law policy, and changes in crime and the law. That these changes in British society were accompanied by discontent in some regional areas and opposition among certain occupational groups is traced through patterns of popular protest. Some themes that would form an essential part of a general account of British history in the Georgian and Victorian periods are omitted because they throw little light on the experiences of the working population. Thus the book has virtually nothing to say on the growth of Tractarianism or nineteenth-century public schools, on genteel leisure pursuits and aristocratic lifestyles. Consideration is given, however, to themes where the behaviour, ideas and power of the middle and upper classes did impinge on workers' lives.

Our study begins with a consideration of the variety of working practices in early industrial Britain, focusing on changes in agricultural and industrial work, notably in relation to the rise of factories and trends in female and juvenile labour. These themes take up the first half of Chapter 2. The remainder of that chapter charts the time and space constraints on working-class recreational pursuits during the century after 1750. Chapter 3 examines different ways of gauging changes in working-class living and health standards, concentrating on problems associated with evidence on housing and environmental conditions, wages and prices, family incomes, and height and nutrition. Chapter 4 underscores the importance of Christianity to people's lives in the period of early industrialisation, examining the position of the Anglican church and the growth of Protestant nonconformity. Evangelical religion is accorded its place in the spectrum of religious change that occurred in Britain in the century after 1750. Chapter 5 traces the slow growth of popular education for the masses, showing the spread of monitorial education and explaining the cautious entry of the state into educational provision for working-class people. Chapter 6 discusses the provision of poor relief and shows that a moral and economic critique of the Old Poor Law led to the implementation of a harsher New Poor Law in the 1830s. Chapter 7 shifts the focus of the study towards patterns of popular protest. It documents the range of demonstrations that broke out in Georgian and early Victorian Britain and assesses the causation and consequences of breaches to the peace. Chapter 8 concludes the book with an account of changing patterns of crime and the main changes in justice and punishment in early industrial Britain.

Part 2

ANALYSIS

2

Work and Leisure

Changing patterns of work are an essential component of social change in early industrial Britain because agricultural, industrial and economic growth rates were sustained through labour productivity during the transition to industrialisation. For the mass of the population – men, women and children aged over six – long hours of work were common on six days of the week: only the Sabbath was sacrosanct and free from toil. Most work consisted of manual labour in which stamina and dexterity were necessary: small wonder that the early industrial workforce provided an 'industrious revolution' (De Vries, 1994). Over time, work practices were subject to increased specialisation, regularity, time discipline and wage labour, all characteristics of a burgeoning capitalist society. Family cooperation and family earnings were necessary for ordinary folk to live at anything better than a relatively poor subsistence level. Yet there were opportunities, with the diversification of industrial and urban work, for manual workers to acquire skills that led to better wages, a higher artisanal status, and possibly social and geographical mobility. Leisure time was at a premium for most people in early industrial Britain, more so as the factory system spread and regular working hours increased. Recreational activities altered as much from the control exercised by the middle and upper classes as from the initiatives of workers. By 1850 work and leisure had changed significantly from the patterns characteristic of a century earlier. The main features of that transformation are outlined below.

Until *c.* 1820 most work in Britain was undertaken in the agricultural sector, on farms growing cereals or tending livestock, in market gardens, and in seasonal fruit and hop picking. But since Britain had a relatively large industrial sector before it underwent the structural transformation to an industrialised economy, dual occupations in industrial and agricultural work commonly existed on a seasonal basis. No national breakdown of the proportion of people engaged in particular occupations is possible for the eighteenth century. Data become available with the arrival of national censuses from 1801 onwards. According to the 1811 census, 33 per cent of full-time employees in Britain were engaged in agriculture, forestry and fishing; 30 per cent in manufacturing and mining; almost 12 per cent in trade and transport; a further 12 per cent in domestic and personal employment; and 13 per cent in public, professional and other jobs. Over the next 40 years this distribution altered: the manufacturing and mining sector became more prominent, agricultural work declined, and public and professional workers also experienced relative decline. The 1851 census showed that manufacturing and mining was the largest employment category, accounting for 43 per cent of the full-time workforce, followed by agriculture, forestry and fishing with 22 per cent, trade and transport with 16 per cent, domestic and personal employment with 13 per cent, and public, professional and other jobs with 6 per cent.

AGRICULTURE

There was little long-term change in absolute employment in English and Welsh agriculture in the period of early industrialisation: the total size of the agricultural labour force comprised *c.* 1,553,000 workers in 1700, 1,405,000 in 1800 and 1,524,000 in 1851. Yet this decline over time in agricultural work was relative to a rising national population. Agriculture remained an important sector of the economy in Georgian and early Victorian Britain, though it declined in relative terms vis-à-vis industry and as a proportion of total employment. There was also a clear shift in the composition of the rural labour force. Between 1700 and 1850 the share of adult males increased from 38 per cent to 64 per cent; the proportion of adult male labourers employed continuously over the year declined; and, correspondingly, the number of day labourers in agriculture increased significantly. Thus agricultural work during early industrialisation became more geared to adult male labour but also became more precarious as a source of regular income.

Agricultural work varied by region and function but many common tasks were found on farms. Arable land needed to be ploughed, harrowed and planted. Weeds and stones had to be dug up. Manure was spread to improve soil fertility. Reaping, mowing, threshing and gleaning were part of the annual cycle in cereal agriculture. Draught animals had to be tended. Dairying required the production of milk, butter and cheese and the marketing of those goods. And there were more specialised aspects of agricultural work such as hedging and ditching, market gardening and fruit picking. These tasks had been carried out for centuries, of course, but in early industrial Britain many of them experienced significant modifications. The nature of agricultural work changed even though labour on the land by 1850 was still largely carried out by muscle and draught animal power, simple hand tools and limited use of technology.

Already in the eighteenth century England had achieved a considerable comparative advantage in agricultural labour productivity. This is best illustrated by comparison with France. By 1750 England had experienced a 20 per cent gain in agricultural labour activity compared with the level for 1700, whereas France had only a 3 per cent increase in the same half-century. This trend continued. In 1800 England's gain in labour agricultural productivity was 26 per cent above the 1750 figure; in France the rise was only 4 per cent. By 1850, as noted above, agriculture provided just over one-fifth of England's labour force whereas one-half of labourers in France and over a half in Germany and the USA still worked on the land. The release of agriculture to industry and the towns was therefore an important feature of the working patterns experienced by labouring people in early industrial Britain. After the mid-nineteenth century, further contraction of the agricultural sector of the British economy was counterpoised by the growth of workers in the service or tertiary sector.

The shedding of agricultural workers in early industrial Britain led to changes in the range and organisation of agricultural work. Farm servants and labourers comprised between 15 and 38 per cent of rural labourers in different parts of the country in the 1831 census, but their absolute numbers were declining as a result of greater specialisation in grain growing, the rising costs of feeding 'living in' servants and, in some areas, a cutback in poor relief for mobile workers without a parish settlement. The increased use of the scythe rather than the sickle at harvest time, the growth of enclosure and the presence of many draught animals aided the shedding of agricultural labour. The scythe speeded up the harvesting of grain, enabling fewer labourers to be employed than previously; it also contributed to a gender division in the allocation of work, as discussed below. The acceleration of parliamentary enclosure in George III's reign provided more short-term employment for hedging and ditching the fields but contributed to the attrition of agricultural labour in the long term. The exceptionally large number of animals of burden, especially horses, when compared with most European countries, harnessed draught power as an energy input for ploughing and harrowing, increased the supply of manure to improve the soil, and released labour into industry and services. The consolidation of estates and creation of large tenanted farms, coupled with labour productivity, also helped to shed rural labour. These developments led to the creation of a large, landless rural proletariat, often working at very low wage levels. Most farm workers, once they received regular work, were reluctant to move to new forms of employment because this would mean losing their low-rent 'tied' cottages. Many agricultural labourers tolerated low earnings for this reason; but this meant that, as a group, they were less mobile than the landless rural proletariat that sought work in industry in towns and factories.

DOMESTIC INDUSTRY AND THE FACTORY

Industrial work in the century after 1750 continued the rhythms and practices of domestic industry found in the pre-industrial economy, but also incorporated the new discipline of the factory. It is incorrect to see textile mills supplanting cottage industry before the middle of the nineteenth century. Both cottage industry and the factory coexisted in early industrial Britain; they complemented rather than competed with each other. Thus until the 1820s it was common for cotton spinning to occur in mills while weaving of fabrics still continued in cottages on an outwork basis. By 1850 factory work was prominent in Lancashire, Cheshire, parts of the West Midlands, parts of central and lowland Scotland, and the West Riding of Yorkshire. But in many other industrial districts, notably Birmingham and the Black Country, domestic industrial practices still prevailed and small workshops and outwork were common. A similar situation obtained among the cutlery trades in Sheffield.

Industrial work patterns outside the factory had certain common characteristics. Most domestic industrial work arose from seasonal underemployment in the British economy up to c.1830. Labouring people in rural areas and small towns had enough agricultural work to fill up only part of the working year, notably in sowing crops and harvesting. At other times, particularly during winter months, agricultural work was difficult to find on a permanent basis, a problem that intensified with the growth of parliamentary enclosure and the shedding of labour. To compensate for underemployment, workers acquired skills in domestic industry to enable them to meet year-round subsistence requirements. This was the most common form of employment for able-bodied people wishing to avoid claiming poor relief. In the textile industries, spinning and weaving served families as a prime source of domestic employment. This combination of agricultural and domestic industrial work was only partly based on wages: sometimes farm labour was rewarded by payment in kind, such as lodging or gifts of food and clothing, rather than by daily or weekly wages. And the work was usually carried out in family groups: mothers, fathers and children worked cooperatively to support family needs.

The pace of domestic industrial work was flexible, since people were usually working in their own cottages. The task orientation of work enabled workers to set their own pace to a large extent. Nevertheless, when production schedules had to be met, the work speeded up and fathers, as heads of families, could demand extra sweat and longer hours to ensure that tasks were completed on time. Although a time dimension operated in domestic industry, it was much more flexible than the tick of the clock in factories. Usually the pressure and intensity of domestic industrial work increased during the week for a deadline on Friday and then several days of leisure followed. In accordance with these rhythms of work, Monday was 'sanctified' as Saint Monday – an additional day for leisure before serious work began again on Tuesday morning. Domestic industrial workers used simple machinery and hand tools, sometimes supplied by employers and their agents: most work was done by hand and there was no need for elaborate machinery. The work was carried out in order to meet market demands from outside the home, as in the classic example of the putting-out system in the West Riding woollen industry. Whether labourers in domestic industry only did sufficient work to cover immediate needs or worked harder to acquire additional income and savings is still debated by historians, but the consensus is that cottage industry was mainly a non-acquisitive form of work.

Factory work had many features that differed from domestic industrial labour in the textile industries. Instead of working at times of slack agricultural employment, factory-based labour meant regular employment throughout the working year. It was of course entirely wage labour: workers toiled for their weekly wage packet, paid in coins or by truck methods. The family nature of domestic industrial work did not survive in the same form in the mills. Factories were divided into separate floors and workers undertook various tasks and might deal with only one part of the production process: mule spinners were distinct from weavers, and other specialised workers included carders, reelers, winders, frame cleaners and roller coverers, all of whom had specific skills. Factories operated on the basis of the classic division of labour that Adam Smith described in *An Inquiry into the Nature and Causes of the Wealth of Nations* (1776). Members of families might be employed in the same mill but rarely on the same floor or with any direct connection to each other's allotted tasks.

The pace and hours of factory labour differed from those found in cottage industry. Workers kept pace with the demands of machinery and foremen, and had set hours in shifts throughout a regular working week. Saint Monday disappeared from the textile districts, though not without resistance. In areas such as the Midlands, where factories were slower to spread, the practice continued up to 1850 and beyond. Labour-saving technology and the presence of the clock were equally characteristic of the factory environment. Indeed, the time orientation of factories was at odds with the task orientation of domestic industry: bells and clocks punctuated work shifts in a way unheard of in cottage industry. The new time discipline of the factories has been viewed as part of the transition of work relations towards a more capitalist system, with relentless demands made upon workers' stamina. The nature of employer–employee relations altered in the mills from what had been experienced before: the agent who visited weavers' homes from the master manufacturer in the putting-out system was replaced by the factory owner organising production schedules to maximise profits.

Factory discipline of the workforce was instilled not just by the regularity and observance of clock time but also by a mixture of incentives and punishments. Inducements might include additional cash payments on a piece basis, awards made for the best workers after adjudication by foremen, and the provision of housing for workers near the factory. Modest rows of cottages surrounding the mill were pioneered by Richard Arkwright at Cromford, Derbyshire, in the 1770s. They later became quite common as factory villages, where workers' dwellings were supplemented by a shop and sometimes a pub. The apogee of the factory village, albeit on a grand scale, was the woollen manufacturer Titus Salt's model industrial town of Saltaire on the River Aire near Bradford, Yorkshire, begun in 1851 and intended to house 3,000 workers. These carrots were combined with sticks, such as docking workers' wages for insubordination or pilfering; corporal punishment on occasions for recalcitrant children; and the ultimate threat of dismissal, for drunkenness and other offences. The unpleasant behaviour of factory managers has often illustrated accounts of Britain's industrial revolution, but there was a more humane side, too. This is exemplified by New Lanark mill in upper Clydesdale, where great attention was paid to the morals and diet of workers **(Doc. 1, p. 114)**. When that cotton factory came under the control of Robert Owen, social idealism came to the fore. Corporal punishment was forbidden and financial provision was made for different religious sects (with none of whose teaching Owen agreed). In Scotland schooling was frequently provided in industrial parishes around cotton and flax mills, but in England and Wales this was rarer.

WOMEN'S WORK

Women's work played a significant, possibly vital, part in sustaining economic growth in early industrial Britain; but examining trends in female labour market participation are difficult to pin down because it was not until the 1851 census that women's full-time employment was enumerated. In that cumulation, females aged 15 and above comprised just under 30 per cent of the paid workforce but only a quarter of wives were engaged in full-time employment – presumably a reflection of their domestic roles and duties. The most prominent female occupation in 1851 was domestic service, accounting for 1,027,000 women in full-time employment (37.3 per cent).

This was followed by 508,000 women in textiles (18.5 per cent), 494,000 in the dress trades (18 per cent) and 213,000 in agriculture (7.7 per cent). Thousands of women worked on a part-time basis, combining work with family chores, but these were not counted by the census makers. Seasonal work in agriculture would have included hop picking, market gardening and haymaking. In dairy farming women often played a significant part in making butter and cheese and milking cows. In industry a range of tasks were traditionally associated with women's labour, especially in the textile industries: making yarn, stockings and clothes for family use were female tasks for many centuries before the Victorian period. Altogether, a very diverse labour market existed for women in early industrial Britain.

The absence of national statistics on women's employment has not prevented historians from analysing the extent and nature of women's work in early industrial Britain. One influential hypothesis claimed that women's work experienced growth in the decades from 1780 to 1820 as the burgeoning industrial economy provided extra job opportunities in industry, within and outside the factory. It also suggested that the subsequent period from c. 1820 to 1850 was one in which female employment prospects diminished with the structural transformation of the economy and the growth of railways, engineering and construction, all of which were male preserves (Richards, 1974). This interpretation has been modified, however, because the continued persistence of women's work in domestic service and cottage industry is now more fully appreciated than it was a few decades ago: even if women did not contribute labour to 'heavy industry', they still continued to work at other tasks demanded by the industrial economy.

Women's work in early industrial Britain in fact experienced different trends over time according to the type of employment. In agriculture, women's work followed specific trajectories according to whether they were working in the pastoral or cereal sector. In pastoral agriculture a change occurred in the contributory level of women to work in 1850 compared with a century earlier: work in the dairy increasingly fell under the control of male managers rather than farmers' wives. This development coincided with the introduction of the largely male preserve of scientific methods of production. In cereal agriculture, change also occurred. In the mid-eighteenth century women worked alongside men, sowing and planting crops in the spring and gathering in the harvest. But increasingly over the period 1750–90 women were replaced by men in most of these activities. This was partly because the main harvesting tool became the scythe, a larger, heavier implement than the previously used sickle, and one which, it was thought, needed male muscle power to ensure a swift, productive gathering of the harvest. In addition, wages were traditionally at their highest seasonal rate during the harvest and, with demographic growth and rural underemployment, men became more concerned than before to secure the best wages for themselves. Women's work in cereal agriculture gradually withered away apart from customary gleaning, picking up the waste or leftover crop after the harvest. Instead, women were shunted into poorly paid drudgery such as weeding, stone-picking and so forth. Reports from Bedfordshire in the 1830s suggest that women were able to secure these types of jobs only in cereal agriculture. Generally, women's work in agriculture became marginalised and poorly paid: by the early nineteenth century they usually only earned between one-third and three-quarters of male wages.

In domestic industry, it seems that women's employment was largely stable throughout the century after 1750. Female workers dominated numerous small crafts, such as glovemaking in Oxfordshire, Dorset and the Welsh borders; button making and straw plaiting in south Bedfordshire and north Hertfordshire; lacemaking in north-east Bedfordshire; and silk manufacture and metalworking in the West Midlands. The spinning of yarn was tradi-tionally a female task, especially when based in the home and using a spin-ning wheel. Many of these jobs were poorly paid but necessary for women earning supplementary wages to support family incomes. But these forms of employment did not disappear with the growth of heavy engineering and structural change in the British economy; they continued to demand workers and women largely provided the labour on fairly low wages. In the 1790s, for instance, female domestic spinners in Essex, Norfolk, Leicestershire and Yorkshire were paid between 1s. 6d. and 3s. per week whereas male agricul-tural labourers could earn a weekly wage of 8s.

Women's labour in the textile mills exhibited yet another trend. Factory reports of the early 1830s showed that 65,000 women were employed in cotton mills compared with 60,000 men. But there was an uneven spread of female adult workers. Only a quarter of women working in cotton mills were married and three-quarters of the female labour force in these factories comprised young, single women aged between 15 and 21. The low propor-tion of married women in the mills suggests that they dropped out of the factory workforce to look after their families. Given the high average family size in early industrial Britain, it is not surprising that they could not reconcile regular paid work in factories with domestic duties. The adolescents who dominated the female workforce in cotton factories earned independent wages, but since they mainly lived at home, according to studies of mill towns such as Preston, their wages contributed to their parents' family budgets rather than being spent independently.

Certain aspects of women's work in early industrial Britain were transformed by the arrival of factories and machinery in the textile industries. In the cotton mills women found that, though they were a majority of the workforce, their labour was confined to low-skilled and menial tasks. In domestic industry it was customary for women to carry out the spinning of cloth in the home and for men to work the weavers' loom. Once new machinery was installed in the cotton mills to spin the fibre – Arkwright's **water frame**, say, or **Crompton's mule** – men monopolised fine cotton spinning, while women often took up weaving in the home. Spinners were the best paid workers on the factory floor in the cotton districts. Men assumed this reversal of work roles in the transition from domestic industry to cotton mills because they wanted to earn the best wages as breadwinners. In addition, handling machinery was considered a masculine form of employment. The same gender division of labour arose in the hosiery industry in the East Midlands after *c*.1825. This was the time when large framework knitting machines were installed in workshops in cities such as Leicester and Nottingham. Once that happened, the working of the knitting machines became exclusively a male preserve, while women in the hosiery industry gained employment stitching and seaming garments at much lower wage levels. Employers assumed this gender division of labour was justified by the physical effort involved in operating wide frames and by the desire to confine women's work to finishing garments in the home. In the cotton and hosiery industries, therefore, male work and female work became separate entities in early industrial Britain.

Generally, women's ability to pursue independent waged work was severely restricted in Britain in the century after 1750. Yet female supplementary earnings helped to sustain family budgets, as Chapter 3 shows. By 1850 male attitudes played a large part in constraining women's employment opportunities: men commonly thought they should attract jobs with the best wages; the introduction of women into particular crafts and trades was known to depress wage levels; and women were often stereotyped as best suited for paid and unpaid work in a domestic setting. By the 1840s patriarchal concern for the protection of women (and children) meant that disapproval of working women was common. This was based on humanitarian concerns about the protection of women and the possibility that working-class women could succumb to immorality. The culmination of this process was the Victorian elevation of the home as a woman's proper abode, the notion that men and women operated in 'separate spheres' and that housework was a feminine activity. Given that ideology, it is unsurprising to find that domestic service employed such a large number of women by the time of the 1851 census and continued to do so for generations until well into the twentieth century (**Doc. 2, p. 115**).

Water frame: A water-powered machine, patented by Richard Arkwright in 1768, that speeded up the spinning process in the textile industry. It incorporated rollers that produced for the first time a cotton thread strong enough for use in the warp of the cloth.

Crompton's mule: A cotton textile machine perfected by Samuel Crompton in 1785. It spun many scores of thread at once and produced a soft, firm yarn suitable for either warp or weft threads.

CHILD LABOUR

Juvenile labour was common in Britain throughout the eighteenth and nineteenth centuries but its scope and distribution can be estimated with a degree of precision only in the 1851 census. This showed that 28 per cent of children aged between 10 and 15 were working. It also recorded some 42,000 children aged under 10 as being at work. These statistics underestimate the extent of child labour because, as with adult work, they fail to account for casual and part-time employment and they probably list children engaged in household production inadequately. Whether over the century before 1851, child labour was a steady, increasing or decreasing part of the total employment pattern is difficult to determine from scattered evidence. It is possible that child labour declined during the first half of the nineteenth century, even though it was still at a considerable level by later standards. The reasons suggested for the decline include parents putting greater emphasis on schooling for young children and having a wider choice of schools to which to send their off-spring, combined with less use of domestic industrial labour in the home after *c.*1820. Against these views, however, one could note that increased schooling did not always bring regular attendance and many manufacturing and agrarian tasks still demanded child labour in the early nineteenth century.

Child labour was most extensive in agriculture, even as late as 1851, as the census figures for that year show. Children also found employment as textile workers, in road and water transport, in coal and copper mines and (usually only for girls) in domestic service. Charles Kingsley's *The Water Babies* (1862) popularised the image of children as chimney sweeps but they were just as common in trades such as pinmaking. Child labour in the fac-tories drew much contemporary criticism on account of its exploitative nature and disruption to family life **(Doc. 3, p. 117)**. It is therefore unsurprising that industrial legislation in the first half of the nineteenth century affected children who were mainly working outside the home, such as apprentices and factory workers.

LEGISLATION ON LABOUR PRACTICES

Only limited legislation was passed by Parliament to protect workers in early industrial Britain. The most frequent statutes concerning employment dealt with factories and, in particular, with child employment and hours of work. The first law to protect mill workers was Robert Peel's Health and Morals of Apprentices Act (1802). It tried to ban night-time work for children and to limit pauper apprentices to working a 12-hour day, but it lacked enforcement machinery. A long hiatus followed in industrial legislation. An Act of 1819 banned the employment of children aged under 9 in cotton mills and stipu-lated that those under 16 could only work for 12 hours a day. Once again, however, no enforcement procedures were implemented. It was not until a

Whig government passed the Factory Act of 1833 that further improvements were made to working hours. This law introduced factory inspectors for the first time and set up factory schools, which will be discussed in Chapter 5. Under its provisions, children under 9 were excluded from all textile mills except silk manufactories; and those aged from 9 to 13 were to receive some schooling each day. Nightwork was prohibited for those aged under 18.

The factory movement, which attracted a number of paternalist Tory and Conservative campaigners, put pressure on government to introduce legislation to protect workers from dangerous machinery and to gain a maximum ten hours working day. The fencing of machinery was introduced as a result of the Factory Act of 1844, which also fixed a maximum 12 hours' work per day for women and children. But it took 16 years of campaigning until the ten hours' movement achieved its goal in the Factory Act of 1847. Outside the factories, the other main type of work that attracted parliamentary legislation was mining. The Mines Act (1842), based on an illustrated report depicting the dangerous conditions existing in coal mines, stipulated that henceforth women and children under 10 were not allowed to work underground in the mines; they could, however, still undertake work at the pit-head.

The relative lack of legislation to protect workers stemmed from the **laissez-faire** policies of various early nineteenth-century governments, from the influential lobbies of factory masters opposed to regulation, and from the fact that effective laws on social policies only really became common with the Whig governments of the 1830s. For most of the century after 1750, trade unionism existed in only a rudimentary form and was unable to influence governments that did not wish to support laws for protecting workers' conditions and rights. But the trade union tradition was not entirely ineffective. Workers' combinations existed in some quantity during the eighteenth century when over 50 such unions are known to have existed. They were craft associations, such as those connected with London tailors, country weavers, journeymen hatters and so on. Skilled artisans were the backbone of these craft unions. They often had success in resisting wage cuts by employers, maintaining customary practices and insisting on the enforcement of apprenticeship in their trades. Craft unions moved from domestic manufacture into the factory in the late eighteenth century, and cotton spinners were the first such group to form a factory workers' combination. But they came under severe pressure during the French Revolutionary and Napoleonic War years. From 1799 until 1824, when the **Combination Acts** were in effect, trade unions (i.e. combinations of workers) were illegal, but these laws were rarely enforced. In 1814 the Elizabethan **Statute of Artificers** of 1563 was repealed; the apprenticeship clauses of that act were abolished, and it became more difficult for workers to challenge employers over their regulations.

Laissez-faire: An approach to economic affairs that arose among certain economic writers of the late eighteenth and early nineteenth centuries. Its advocates believed there should be an absence of direct attempts by the government to control and regulate the nature and direction of economic development. Adherents of laissez-faire views nevertheless believed there were still areas where the government should act to protect the weaker members of society.

Combination Acts (1799, 1800): A government attempt to prohibit workmen's organisations. The 1799 legislation consolidated Acts passed since the 1720s against workers' combinations in specific trades into a general statute banning all such organisations. The 1800 Act superseded it and provided for arbitrators to settle disputes over work or wages. The Acts were repealed in 1824 and 1825 following a campaign against their restrictive nature.

Statute of Artificers (1563): Established procedures for fixing maximum wages by JPs and regulated the system of apprenticeship and entry into trade crafts.

Trade unionism continued to struggle after the Combination Acts were repealed. Artisans and skilled workers began to develop a trade union consciousness as carpenters, shipwrights and sawyers in different areas forged links with one another, but unions found it difficult to contest wage reductions by employers in the adverse trade conditions in the late 1820s. Nevertheless, groups such as cotton spinners and building workers began to develop notions of national and general unionism. London artisans also became interested in cooperative production and formed the backbone of the **Grand National Consolidated Trades Union (GNCTU)** in 1834, the most striking attempt at general unionism to that date. But individual trades disagreed over the aims and tactics of the GNCTU: there was no working-class solidarity to bind together the skilled with the unskilled, and the union collapsed by August 1835. The new reformed Parliament after 1832 was determined to attack the spread of trade unionism. The Tolpuddle martyrs, the six Dorset farm labourers sentenced to transportation in 1834, were victims of the zeal to root out the spread of unionism. In the following decade, craft unions pursued their aims cautiously, trying to uphold apprenticeship and focusing on patient wage bargaining and moderation in dealing with employers and government.

Grand National Consolidated Trades Union (GNCTU): Begun by Robert Owen in 1834 as an exception to small, localised trade unions that were then characteristic in Britain. Owen hoped to link all British trade unions to his cooperative and socialist movement. The GNCTU had 16,000 members, mainly in London, but it failed to appeal to cotton operative and cloth workers and collapsed in 1835.

LEISURE AND RECREATION

For the middling orders in British society, the eighteenth and early nineteenth centuries witnessed an efflorescence of recreational activities. Many of these were connected with the metropolis, where newspapers, coffee houses and clubs flourished, and theatres and pleasure gardens also catered for those comfortably off. Middle-class leisure extended through the spa towns that arose in the eighteenth century, where an organised social round of activities, fine architecture and the medicinal properties of taking the waters flourished at Bath, Harrogate, Tunbridge Wells, Leamington Spa and, later, Cheltenham. Patronage of seaside resorts such as Weymouth and Brighton, though stimulated initially by the visits of royalty, became popular among the middling orders by the early nineteenth century. In most of these leisure activities there was a fair amount of commercialisation, with the promotion of recreational and sporting activities that helped to fill the coffers of the service industries.

Leisure activities for the lower orders were largely separate and distinct from the forms of bourgeois entertainment outlined above. Over the course of the century after 1750 plebeian leisure changed markedly. This stemmed partly from constraints on time and space. The introduction of a regular working week, taking up five-and-a-half days, meant that wage labourers in full-time employment had less time to devote to recreation than in the long centuries when underemployment in the rural economy was the norm for many people. During the long hours devoted to work, most labourers were standing on their feet and consequently were tired at the end of the working day, so leisure was confined to one or two hours on weekdays and to occasional holidays. Space constraints came with the movement of many workers from countryside to towns and cities in the early period of industrialisation and from the privatisation of common land through enclosure. But the middling orders and educated classes also influenced the pattern of working-class leisure. They were able, to a large degree, to channel plebeian leisure to fit the new time and space constraints of early industrial Britain, and to promote respectable recreation at the expense of rough amusements associated with the coarser end of the working class.

Contemporaries, and some modern historians, have dubbed this desire to control the behaviour of the working classes as 'rational recreation' – an attempt to make the lower orders adopt the more sedate behaviour of the respectable middle classes. Such an impulse was related to the fear of working-class resentment stirred up by radical societies, trade unionism and the Chartist movement. It can be seen in the provision of lyceums, clubs, parks, botanic gardens, museums, concerts and organ recitals, all of which flourished by the early Victorian period. It also underlay the growth of fêtes and parades, with banners associated with churches, chapels and trade unions. These forms of recreation received strong support from the temperance movement, which pursued zealously the need to combat the roughness and drinking of the public house. Open spaces where people could stroll and picnic in a genteel way were regarded as ideal places for rational recreation. When Regent's Park was opened in 1841, *The Times* encouraged this new oasis of greenery in London as inculcating 'the redemption of the working class through recreation' (Reid, 1980: 52).

In 1750 the lower orders had a series of seasonal leisure activities related to traditional rhythms and holy days of the church and agricultural calendars. Revels, wakes and feasts lay at the heart of 'days off' given over to festivities. Mummers' plays acted in village streets between Christmas and New Year were followed by wassailing of the trees in January and by other activities such as Shrove Tuesday football matches, May Day dances around the maypole, the beating of the parish bounds at Rogationtide, harvest home festivals and suppers, and celebrations on Guy Fawkes night (Bushaway, 1982). Great hiring fairs for agricultural labourers occurred in the spring at Candlemas and in the autumn at Michaelmas, which marked important junctures in the agricultural calendar; such holidays were associated with courtship as much as the search for labour. Revels, wakes and feasts also took place. They lay at the heart of 'days off' given over to festivities and provided scope for communities to enjoy their leisure pursuits in the open air. They were particularly appropriate for rural communities and small towns where people knew each other on a face-to-face basis, where life's rhythms were not entirely determined by time constraints and space was available for staging these occasions and festivities.

Besides the leisure activities linked with the church and agricultural calendar, lower-class folk also had games and rude sports to provide entertainment. Football was commonly played throughout England, but it often involved people running through village streets in an unruly manner rather than being confined, as usually today, to a pitch with two teams, goalposts, a set time and nationally agreed rules. Cricket was played on village greens. Cockfighting, bull-baiting, badger-baiting, prize fighting, wrestling, cudgelling, and so forth were among the ruder pastimes. Bull-baiting was probably the most widespread of these rough amusements. It was a cruel sport that involved setting dogs on to bulls attached to a post with rings, accompanied by betting and prizes awarded to those who backed the dog which attacked the bull with most success (i.e. drawing blood) (Griffin, 2005). Calendrical customs and the more uncouth leisure pursuits were often patronised by the gentry, and served the useful purpose of binding communities together despite differences in social rank.

All these recreations increasingly came under attack from the mid-eighteenth century onwards; some gradually disappeared and many others became attenuated in their observance by 1850. Church festivals in villages were more difficult to mount when mobility took workers away from their home communities to towns in search of work. Many industrial employers frowned upon festivities as unnecessary interruptions to the working week. The gentry began to withdraw its support for celebrating calendrical customs by local communities, a trend observable in the early part of the nineteenth century. Football was restricted by many local officials through concerns about chaos and disorder. Rough sports came under attack from the educated classes, with their dislike of leisure activities associated with cruelty and bloodshed. Often middle-class observers had an intellectual aversion to inflicting pain and were worried about the potential disorder caused by gambling at such activities. The Society for the Prevention of Cruelty to Animals was founded in 1824. Its major achievement was to persuade Parliament to ban bull-baiting, badger-baiting and dog-fighting in the Cruelty to Animals Act of 1835, followed seven years later by making cockfighting illegal. The gentry, who had often turned a blind eye to the pursuit of rough sports, now condemned them as uncivilised. As Robert Malcolmson put it succinctly, 'a solid barrier had developed between the culture of gentility and the culture of the people' (Malcolmson, 1973: 165). Despite class differences over popular recreation, however, by 1850 holidays and festivals remained important safety valves for individuals and communities inured to the daily grind of urban industrial life **(Doc. 4, p. 119)**.

Evangelical religion, especially the spread of Methodism, played an important role in influencing working-class communities to tone down their leisure activities in order to inculcate a spirit of industriousness, sobriety, discipline and piety among the workforce. Such evangelical persuaders promoted the pursuit of rational recreation from the 1830s onwards. They sponsored railway excursions, Sunday school outings, temperance meetings and church parades rather than boisterous games or cruel sports. The latter activities were regarded by middle-class do-gooders as degrading, sinful and disorderly. This desire to spread rational recreation spilled over into the provision of libraries, local lectures and working men's institutes for the artisanal class, discussed in Chapter 5. The main recreational area of working-class leisure that proved difficult to control was the world of the alehouse and pub. By 1853 around 70 per cent of working men spent their evenings in pubs. The public house was a focal point for male working-class leisure that proved difficult to discipline – an interior enclave that stretched beyond the reach of middle-class reformers. After 1850 working-class leisure expanded into different areas such as seaside holidays and the music hall, which showed respectively how ordinary people could imitate the world of their social betters and create a recreational niche that was initially not influenced by the respectable classes.

3

Living and Health Standards

The living and health standards of the labouring population in early industrial Britain have long attracted analysis, but they are usually treated as discrete subjects. In this chapter, these two important features of working-class life are brought together to determine the extent to which socio-economic change in the first industrial revolution benefited the people whose productivity helped to sustain economic growth. In looking at living standards, historians have long been influenced by their political predilections. Broadly speaking, more right-wing historians, who endorse the beneficial effects of adjustment to a capitalist economy, have discerned signs of economic improvement for working-class people in terms of their real wages, family incomes and prospects for advancement through acquiring a wider range of skills in a more diversified market economy. Historians of the left, however, have offered more pessimistic assessments. Working on the assumption that the period of early industrialisation (1780–1850) brought hardship, difficult economic adjustments and periodic industrial slumps, they have argued that workers' real wages improved only marginally, that deskilling was rife in many industrial and agricultural tasks, and that a fully fledged market economy eroded the **moral economy** and customary nature of pre-industrial life. These issues are still widely debated. The difficulty of marshalling evidence to support either an optimistic or pessimistic inter- pretation has led to 'the standard of living controversy' becoming the most widely discussed topic concerning early industrial Britain.

Moral economy: A phrase popularised by E. P. Thompson, referring to the collective behaviour of lower-class people based on notions of custom and community rather than on capitalist market relations. It is usually applied to pre- industrial Britain, where, it is suggested, a moral economy involved the use of 'fair' wages, 'just' prices and 'honourable' market practices.

Investigations of living and health standards have to consider different types of data to provide a convincing analysis. Qualitative material is relevant to the subject, though discussions of socio-economic conditions in literature, parliamentary papers, diaries, reports and memoirs tend to dwell on the more adverse circumstances with which people contended. This is not to say that qualitative material should be ignored, for it can illuminate how ordinary workers lived and either suffered or prospered; and few historians would equate living standards entirely with cash rewards. It is rather to say that qualitative discussions can form only part of the answer: they need to be integrated with harder data. During the heyday of the 'new' economic history, in the 1960s and 1970s, the quantitative dimension was often treated in a historical vacuum and crucial aspects of living standards – such as the role played by women and families – tended to be glossed over; but this is no longer the case.

Though historians have long accepted that quantitative indicators are necessary to give precision to the study of living standards, there are limits in the historical record about what can be measured. Some potentially quantitative indicators, unfortunately, are unavailable. The major statistical item lacking is the extent of national unemployment, which was not recorded for any year until 1856. Underemployment was characteristic of pre-industrial Britain and industrial slumps and lack of protection against hard times at vulnerable periods of the life-cycle – while raising young families, during illness and in old age – were perennial problems for most people in early industrial Britain. But it has proved difficult for historians to pinpoint secular trends in unemployment as opposed to years of particular difficulty in the job market. Another lacuna exists in the distribution of income. Contemporary estimates for 1803 suggest that the top 2 per cent of families held 20 per cent of national income. Convincing data on the distribution of income are more difficult to find: it is still unclear whether income shifted towards investment and away from consumption in early industrial Britain. Statistics on rent are still to be collated properly, making it difficult to estimate how far rent impacted on family budgets. Two types of hard data are available, however, to provide material on living and health standards. One consists of trends in real wages, the main type of data deployed by economic historians to examine living standards. The second, treated thoroughly only in recent years, comprises data on people's height, which are relevant for looking at health and well-being and, by extrapolation, living standards.

It is futile to resort to one particular type of data in order to demonstrate whether living standards were rising or falling in early industrial Britain. Clearly, real wages have to be included in any discussion because they are the single most demonstrable quantitative indicator of the standard of living. But determining trends in real wages tells us nothing about consumption unless one assumes that virtually all of a household's earnings were channelled into life's necessities. Better real wages, for example, were not necessarily related to improved nutrition: much depended on expenditure of income. Thus one cannot assume that greater disposable income of workers was spent primarily on better food and shelter rather than on less responsible consumption. Other variables must also be considered, and so the discussion below also covers such facets of living and health standards as family budgets, height and health, nutrition, housing and the environment, and demographic factors.

In some of these areas, as we shall see, working-class living standards improved better than in others. Moreover, social and cultural factors leading to changes in living standards, illustrated in qualitative material, are just as problematic to weigh up as the quantitative measures that bear upon living and health standards. Analysis of living standards during Britain's industrial revolution will remain contentious, and subject to numerous revisions, precisely because many indicators need to be considered and the different variables do not 'suggest a uniform direction of change' (Voth, 2004: 269).

THE DEMOGRAPHIC CONTEXT

Demography is central to an understanding of life in early industrial Britain. Population growth was rapid in Britain in the century under consideration. The population of England and Wales rose from 5.7 million in 1751, to 8.7 million in 1801, to 16.8 million by 1851. The Scottish population also increased, but not so markedly, from 1.25 million in 1751 to 2.89 million a century later. How did demographic growth affect people's living standards? The answer is a mixed one. Mortality declined, fertility rose significantly and life expectancy increased. Crude death rates in England and Wales fell from 26 per thousand in the 1750s to 22 per thousand a century later, with most decline coming after 1800. The fall was more impressive than these figures suggest because the urban death rate was normally higher than that in rural areas, hence savings in mortality were achieved as the country became more urbanised. Legitimate fertility increased from 34 new babies in every thousand of population in 1751 to a peak of 41 per thousand in 1821 before falling to 36 per thousand in 1851. Most people born in England and Wales in the 1750s could expect to live for 36 or 37 years. There was little gain in the second half of the eighteenth century, but thereafter improvements occurred. By 1838–54 life expectancy reached mean figures of 40 years for men and 42 years for women. These are young ages of death compared with the Western world in the twenty-first century, where people live on average into their late seventies, but they still represented an improvement over the course of early industrialisation in Britain.

Killer diseases were still rife, however, by the mid-Victorian period. Smallpox was the one major disease where an effective vaccination was available from the early nineteenth century, though it was not enforced on a mass level until nearly 1900. The etiology of all other life-threatening diseases, such as measles, tuberculosis, typhus, yellow and scarlet fever and cholera was not fully understood, and therefore not curable in most cases until well into the twentieth century. All these diseases had a high incidence in nineteenth-century Britain and some, such as cholera in 1832 and 1848, reached epidemic proportions. A polluted environment, discussed below, contributed to many cases of respiratory disease among the working classes. Some diseases, notably typhus, measles and chronic gastroenteritis, had severe effects upon young children, contributing to high levels of infant mortality. Thus increased life expectancy was still accompanied by many intimations of mortality in industrial Britain.

Improvements in agricultural production, achieved at a social cost, meant that there was no **Malthusian crisis** in Britain during early industrialisation. The living standards of British workers never faced a catastrophe on the scale of the Irish potato famine of the mid-1840s. Yet there were few major improvements in diet for working-class people in the early industrial revolution. Most households consumed tea, wheaten bread and potatoes by the 1840s, but the provision of vegetables, fruit and fresh milk to urban centres was difficult before the railway spread throughout provincial Britain. Food and drink bought by the working class were widely adulterated in the nineteenth century; for example, a mineral salt, alum, was often added to bread to make it look whiter. Workers' diets were deficient in fruit and vegetables. Thus two sample family budgets, taken from a survey by Sir Frederick Eden in 1794, show that a Banbury widower, with three children to support, bought no fruit or vegetables with his yearly expenditure, and that a Wolverhampton spectacle frame maker, living with a wife and four children, spent less than a tenth of his yearly earnings on vegetables and nothing on fruit (**Doc. 5, p. 119**). This does not mean that families ate no fruit and vegetables, because some produce was acquired in kind or through barter, but it does suggest that ordinary people found it difficult to purchase these food items. In the countryside farm labourers did not have plots large enough to grow crops for their families, and in urban areas allotments spread widely only in the 1880s. Widely disparate findings on food consumption for British workers do not permit a more sophisticated analysis at present. It is probable, however, that adult working men had a more varied diet than women and children in nineteenth-century England, and that they ate more meat. This reflected decisions made in households about ensuring that the male breadwinner had sufficient nutrients to build up energy for long hours of manual labour.

Malthusian crisis: A crisis where the growth and size of a population outstrips available food resources. Named after the population theorist Thomas Robert Malthus.

HOUSING AND THE ENVIRONMENT

People's living standards in early industrial Britain were affected by environmental pollution in what has aptly been called 'an age of smoke and smells'

(Clapp, 1994: 13). Some environmental blights long preceded industrialisation; others were increased by its impact. Coal production left behind waste products in the form of ash, soot and slag, along with waste gases. The smelting of metals and the use of kilns in the Potteries left fumes and dross. Steam engines in industrial plants demanded stoking and produced clouds of smoke when furnaces were working full blast. Chimneys deposited sulphur compounds. Dust was found everywhere. Bad smells were part and parcel of industrial and urban life. Sodium carbonate, produced through alkali manufacture, emitted acid. Water pollution was common on river and canal-bank sites. The 'dirty trades' included slaughterhouses where the blood and guts of animals were regularly washed out onto streets. Smells also emanated from overcrowded urban graveyards where rotting corpses were dug up to make way for new ones. Edwin Chadwick's *Report on the Sanitary Condition of the Labouring Population of Great Britain* (1842) argued that atmospheric impurities from decomposing substances plus damp, filth and overcrowded buildings aggravated diseases for many widows and orphan children claiming poor relief **(Doc. 6, p. 121)**.

Standards of sewerage and drainage also left much to be desired. Water closets were introduced in many homes by the mid-nineteenth century, but bucket privies, dung carts and cesspits were more common in our period for disposing of human waste: Leeds, for example, had three privies and cesspits for each water closet by the 1860s. Main drainage and piped water systems were installed in British towns and cities largely after 1850. Thus Bristol (apart from the wealthy suburb of Clifton) relied on water from public and private wells, often tainted by contact with cesspools, until this date. Urban households smelt from human excrement, bones, fat, peelings and ashes. Galvanised dustbins were not used until the 1880s. Parliament did virtually nothing to alleviate unpleasant environmental factors until after 1850, though two select committees inquired into the smoke problem in the 1840s.

Between 1801 and 1851 urban growth rates were between 23.7 and 29.1 per cent per decade, a rapid increase by any standard. Increasing residential density in towns and cities led to urban congestion. Thus overcrowding and tenement housing were ever-present features of urban life in early industrial Britain. In 1840 Chadwick's investigations into the condition of labourers found ample evidence of overcrowding, notably in the metropolis. In the poor parish of Marylebone, for example, he found that 159 families and 196 single people had only part of a single room each and 382 families and 56 single persons had a whole room to themselves, but few people lived in more space. In London and other large cities innumerable seedy lodging houses existed where tramps, drifters, casual labourers and Irish immigrants stayed. The worst housing conditions were in cellars, backstreets, narrow courts and lanes. Municipal provision of working-class housing did not occur until the late Victorian period, after most adult males had been enfranchised. Instead, during the first half of the nineteenth century speculative building of back-to-back terraced houses, with poor sanitation and little privacy, was common in large industrial cities in the Midlands and the north of England. Two-thirds of Birmingham's population in the middle of the nineteenth century, for instance, was housed in back-to-back properties. Bradford, Halifax, Leeds and Sheffield still bear the visible remains of such housing.

Chadwick's reports on overcrowding and sanitation among the working population were influential in bringing public health onto the government's agenda for social policy. But his desire to see public health improvements met with much opposition from town ratepayers, factory owners and Tory MPs opposed to a centralised act governing public health. Only the approach of a major cholera epidemic in 1848 swayed public opinion and convinced doubters that action was necessary. The Public Health Act passed in that year was the first law that tried to deal with health problems on a nationwide basis. It established a General Board of Health, comprising three members, and brought in superintending inspectors and the possibility of appointing local boards of health. This legislation laid down general regulations for sanitation and required all new houses to have water closets or privies and ashpits. Older houses within 100 feet (30 metres) of a public sewer were to have a drain connected to it. The duties of local boards of health with regard to sanitation were laid down. It proved difficult, however, to enforce local rules on overflowing sewers, slums and dung heaps. The implementation of these public health procedures was slow and uneven, though at least they made a start in tackling the poor environmental conditions of industrial Britain.

Qualitative evidence on sanitation, housing, water supply and public health paints a grim picture of living conditions for working people in early industrial Britain. Yet how far contemporaries weighed up disamenities in the quality of life against generally better wage rates in urban occupations and industry, rather than agriculture, is difficult to say. The same is true if one tries to balance the longer hours of factory labour in dirty surroundings with the reward of regular wages: once again, it would be presumptuous to argue that contemporaries suffered because of the environmental factors. Statistical tests have been made to estimate what wage premiums were necessary for urban workers to offset poor material and environmental conditions, but these are rather artificial abstract constructs.

REAL WAGES

Data on wages as a proxy for living standards need to make use of real wages rather than money wages, which do not take account of price fluctuations. Estimating real wages for the labouring population requires gathering data on money wages for various occupations and adjusting for inflation, and providing indices on wholesale prices for goods consumed. Generating such statistics for the nation as a whole is fraught with technical difficulties. First, wage rates varied by region and by occupation. Around 1770, London and Kent craftsmen earned about a third more in wages than labourers, and the wages for London were about a third higher than in Kent. By the early nineteenth century, agricultural labourers in the north of England were able, as a result of industrialisation, to command better wages than rural workers in southern England. Second, the range of goods consumed by most people is open to discussion. A number of competing price indices are available to historians, none of which is ideal in its coverage of commodities and prices. Information on how household consumption changed over time is difficult to acquire, and the selection of particular price indices very much influences real wage calculations.

A third problem in generating real wage data is that prices fluctuated markedly over time. An index of the annual average price of British wheat shows, for the first half of the nineteenth century, the wide fluctuations in the single most important foodstuff in people's diets **(Doc. 7, p. 122)**. Prices for goods and services were obviously high in times of dearth and during and after harvest crises. They tended to fluctuate significantly in the long wars with revolutionary and Napoleonic France, when rapid inflation was common. Because of swings in prices, it is unwise to search for trends in real wages by taking the beginning of the nineteenth century as a starting point and 50 years later as an end point, as one classic discussion of this topic did: 1800 was probably the year of highest prices in the first half of the nineteenth century, while 1850 was a year of rather modest prices (Hartwell, 1963–4). Thus there is, fourth, the problem of the beginning and end points for investigation. Most analyses of living standards in early industrial Britain have selected different periods of time over which they measure trends. For our purposes here, however, the data presented start in either 1780 or 1790, when the structural transformation of the economy had begun, and continue down to the cut-off point for this book, 1850, though this is not intended to imply that the industrial revolution had 'finished' by then.

It is generally agreed that real wages showed little signs of progress for Britain in the period from 1750 to 1790. Thereafter trends in real wages are much disputed. According to one index of real wages, money wages and commodity prices for the period 1790–1850, using 1840 as the base year, real wages fell during the 1790s by 0.9 per cent annually (O'Brien and Engerman, 1981: the data in this paragraph are taken from this source). This decline in real wages is unsurprising given that the nation was at war for virtually all of the decade after 1793 and that several years in that period (1795, 1796 and 1800) had disastrous harvests. Real wages appear to have improved in the latter part of the war years with France, rising relatively swiftly between 1810 and 1816, before falling slightly in the next four years. The decline in real wages between 1816 and 1820 is more modest than one would expect from the well-known dislocation of the economy after the end of the Napoleonic Wars and the spate of working-class protest that occurred in these years, described in Chapter 7. Real wages improved somewhat during the 1820s, only to drift downwards in the 1830s. The 1840s brought rapid gains in real wages: levels in 1850 were almost 40 per cent above those for 1840. This is a little surprising at first sight, given the industrial slump of 1842 that led to loss of jobs and protest in industrial northern England, but it must be remembered that the estimates do not measure unemployment.

Overall the estimates cited suggest that real wages fluctuated considerably between 1790 and 1850 and that there were periods of notable slump (especially the 1790s) and of considerable increase (1810–16 and, more notably, the 1840s). The data indicate that real wages increased by 2.1 per cent over the period 1790–1850, but the real gains for the working classes came after 1840 (O'Brien and Engerman, 1981). This is, of course, only one example of many real-wage indices that have been prepared by economic historians. It should not be regarded as a definitive answer. Another attempt to recalculate real earnings for manual workers in early industrial Britain has argued in favour of a more modest increase in the period 1780–1850. According to this view, sustained advances in real wages for the English working classes did not materialise until the late 1850s and therefore little advance occurred in workers' living standards during the century covered in this book, though, equally, there is no evidence of a long-term deterioration in real earnings (Feinstein, 1998). Whichever compilation of data on real wages one selects, the trends, despite short-term fluctuations, do not point to a sustained decline in real wages over the decades from 1780 to 1850; the debate is centred upon whether real wages over this period improved only modestly or rose more rapidly. Allowing for unemployment and short-time work, real wage growth was probably less than 30 per cent between 1780 and 1850 (Voth, 2004: 273).

REGIONAL AND OCCUPATIONAL WAGE VARIATIONS

Wage levels for the working classes in early industrial Britain varied considerably by regions and occupations. In terms of occupations, there was a hierarchy of skill, status and wages ranging from craftsmen down to casual labourers, vagrants and street sellers; from what the Victorians referred to as

Labour aristocracy: A distinct upper stratum within the working class characterised by higher incomes, better living standards and more regular employment than the majority of working-class people. Most men among the labour aristocracy were skilled workers affiliated with craft unions.

Lumpenproletariat: The lowest rung of the un-skilled working class.

the '**labour aristocracy**' down to the Marxist notion of a '**lumpenproletariat**'. At the top of the working-class wage ladder were craftsmen such as blacksmiths, printers, joiners, cutlers, fine cotton spinners, engineers and engine drivers. These aristocrats of labour could earn between 50 and 100 per cent more than unskilled labourers. But John Rule has estimated that they accounted for only 15 per cent of the working-class population. Most manual workers – the remaining 85 per cent – continued to work for relatively low rates of pay throughout early industrialisation in Britain (Rule, 1986: 37–38).

The range of workers' remuneration can be seen by reference to textiles. Male factory workers could earn between one and three times the wages paid to northern farm labourers in early industrial Britain. At the end of the eighteenth century fine cotton spinners had wages of about 33s. per week and handloom weavers earned about 25s. weekly. But the earnings of handloom weavers declined within a few decades. The rapid growth of population flooded the weaving trades, and by the 1830s handloom weavers, some quarter of a million people, received only around 5s. a week. Their wages plummeted further and so did their numbers as machinery was introduced into the weaving of textiles. Only 23,000 handloom weavers were left in England and Wales 1856, earning paltry weekly wages of a couple of shillings. In Scotland handloom weavers saw their real wages cut in half between 1790 and 1840, and in the 1840s their numbers fell by 70 per cent.

Wage rates in other working-class occupations varied considerably according to skill levels, the nature of the job, and whether the work was based in town or the countryside. In the early nineteenth century weekly wages for London skilled artisans were between 25s. and 40s., a reasonable rate of pay, whereas unskilled industrial workers earned about 18s. per week and male agricultural labourers received between 8s. and 10s. Most out-workers, such as tailors, makers of boots and shoes, and cabinet makers, earned a few shillings per week. Regional wage differentials were common. Weekly wage rates for agricultural workers in 1794–5 averaged 6s. in Aberdeenshire, 8s. 1d. in Norfolk, and 10s. 1d. in Lancashire. Between 1833 and 1845 weekly wages paid to rural labourers were 9s. 6d. for Aberdeenshire, 10s. 7d. for Norfolk, and 12s. 5d. for Lancashire. In the period 1750–90 real wages for bricklayers in London declined whereas the money wage index for bricklayers in the Potteries rose by three-quarters. Regional and occupational differences in wages cast doubt on the extent to which a national index of real wages and commodity prices is meaningful for the century from 1750 to 1850. Indeed, it may be that the difficulties in calculating meaningful national indices mean that an impasse has been reached in this approach to living standards.

FEMALE AND CHILD LABOUR, FAMILY BUDGETS AND ENTITLEMENTS

Compared with adult men, female employees and labouring children gained significantly less monetary rewards for whatever type of job one cares to cite. The low comparative level of women and children's wages is shown in some sample average weekly wages in secondary industry for the years 1849–51. These rates also indicate that in each type of industrial employment the highest paid tasks undertaken by women offered lower wages, usually considerably so, than the lowest paid tasks done by men. Thus in the Birmingham brassmaking trades women earned between 7s. and 10s. per week and girls were paid between 4s. and 7s. whereas men received between 15s. and 50s. The highest paid female task (lacquerer) earned 5s. per week less than the lowest paid male job (brass thimble maker). In the Potteries male wage rates were between 20s. and 50s. per week and female wage rates ranged from 9s. to 12s. Both men and women worked as painters in this industry, but whereas male painters could earn a minimum of 20s., female painters could earn a maximum of only 12s. Wage rates for the South Staffordshire coal and iron industry, the Derbyshire lace industry, the Leicester hosiery industry, the Yorkshire woollen and worsted industry, and the Lancashire cotton spinning industry show the same disparity between male and female wages (**Doc. 8, p. 123**). In short, women's work was concentrated, with few exceptions, in low-paid trades.

Relatively low wage levels for women resulted, as Chapter 2 has shown, from the increased equation of male work with the notion of a 'breadwinner', from gender distinctions about the type and skill level of work, and from the widespread opinion that women's entry into various industries and trades brought down overall wage levels. Women's wages were viewed as supplementary earnings to help family budgets. The same was even more true of children's paid labour. The need to boost family incomes was an important aspect of life in early industrial Britain. Most children among the lower orders were expected to contribute to their family's income before their tenth birthday: child labour and female work in a household system of production were often the best means of staving off poverty during slumps in the employment cycle, coupled with access to poor relief. It is likely that as the highest average family size in modern British history was reached in the 1810–30 period, when parents commonly had five or six children, juvenile labour was necessary to support extra dependants at a time of relatively low incomes for most workers. Much child labour earned low wages subsumed under family wages – for example, in domestic spinning and weaving. But in cotton factories children were separately waged. In both cases, however, children normally handed wages to parents, who decided how the additional money should be used for family purposes.

However modest the earnings of women and children in early industrial Britain, they were vital in supplying additional cash to maintain family budgets and a decent competency in living standards. In 1790 at Corfe Castle, Dorset, for instance, 30 per cent of labourers' family budgets were provided by female and juvenile earnings, and in 1848 at St George's parish, in the East End of London, women and children contributed 23 per cent of family incomes. The ability of women and children to bolster family budgets nevertheless varied according to the main occupations available in particular areas. Thus employment in textile factories or domestic industry could provide wages for men, women and children, but in areas where jobs in heavy industry predominated – such as engineering, shipbuilding and railway navvying – the work was restricted to adult males, who perforce assumed the role of the breadwinner.

'Exchange entitlements' were also important for family earnings (Daunton, 1995: 423–25). Until the early nineteenth century many ordinary people did not survive entirely within the nexus of a cash economy, although, as industrialisation and urbanisation proceeded, they had greater necessity to do so. Instead, families relied on certain payments in kind, such as food, clothing, board and lodging; on perquisites arising from their jobs, such as taking home loaves of bread or collecting spilled sugar and tea from ships and wharves; and on customary rights, such as foraging in the hedgerows on common land or gleaning corn after the harvest. These exchange entitlements were gradually eroded over the course of the century after 1750 by changes in work patterns and changes in the law. Chapter 2 has shown that the decline of 'living-in' agricultural servants and dual occupations, coupled with the emergence of precise clock time and shifts in factories and the erosion of **common rights** through enclosure, served to reduce entitlements in lieu of cash. Chapter 8 discusses the creation of crimes by new laws that led to poaching being stigmatised under the **Game Laws** and pilfering being redefined as embezzlement. But entitlements still persisted as part of working-class remuneration, though the rewards varied according to price levels: employers granting extra perks took account of prevailing prices, thereby allowing negotiation between employers and employees to enter into arrangements for entitlements.

Common rights: Communal rights on the land that were important to the labouring poor. Such rights could include the right to glean corn after the harvest, to collect furze from hedgerows, and to keep poultry and tether livestock on common land. Parliamentary enclosure eroded some of these common rights.

Game Laws: A set of laws passed between 1671 and 1831 to protect landed proprietors against the hunting of game, especially pheasants, partridges and hares. The Game Laws were frequently modified to discourage particular forms of poaching.

HEIGHT AND HEALTH

Body height, weight and biomass are anthropometric measures that can help to quantify nutritional status. Measurements of height have been analysed in recent years to investigate the state of working-class living and health standards in early industrial Britain. The conceptual basis for using these data lies in the known links between nutritional status and the average height of a population. Put simply, the higher the mean height of a given population, the better the nutritional status. Individual well-being is connected to various factors, including genetic inheritance, susceptibility to disease, and environmental conditions; but height is a good quantitative indicator of whether a population is experiencing good living standards. Thus the average height of people in Third World countries today is significantly less than that of populations throughout the Western world. The mean height of an average adolescent boy of the late eighteenth century was shorter than 97 per cent of today's teenagers. There is a class dimension to height, namely that, where measurements can be made, people from a higher social class will have a higher mean height than those from lower down the social scale. A widely known feature of human biology, moreover, is that the greatest period of growth in height comes with adolescence, between roughly the ages of 13 and 18; once a person reaches adulthood his or her height tends to remain static until old age, when it can diminish through bodily infirmities.

These general observations are relevant to living and health standards in Britain's early industrialisation because data have been collated and analysed from the archives of the Marine Society to investigate heights in the period from 1770 to 1870. The Marine Society was a London-based charity established in 1756 by the philanthropist Jonas Hanway. It recruited boys for service in the navy, initially because extra manning was needed in the Seven Years War, but also because it provided useful employment for poor, ragged London adolescents from slum backgrounds. To determine which boys were fit enough to withstand the rigours of a life at sea, the Marine Society recruited entrants only above a certain average height. The records of the Society contain over 50,000 individual citations of heights. The fact that the height of the rejects was not recorded is not problematic because human biologists have established that the height of a population over a lifespan follows a normal bell-shaped distribution. Thus, the lifetime trajectory of heights can still be worked out through establishing the mean and standard deviation of the whole distribution. Since the recruits were all taken from the working classes, the Marine Society data afford an opportunity to look at living standards for a large sample of ordinary adolescents from the metropolis in late eighteenth- and nineteenth-century Britain.

These records show that the average height of recruits into the Marine Society was lower than the average height of recruits into the Royal Military Academy, Sandhurst, drawing on boys from a higher social background; and that boys in the Marine Society were shorter than in Britain today. These comparisons reinforce the point made above about class dimensions in height distribution. The Marine Society data suggest that the nutrition of those recruited increased noticeably in the early period of industrialisation. The average height of recruits aged 13 rose from 51 inches (130 cm) in 1750–65 to 54 inches (137 cm) in 1810–25. The mean height of 16-year-old recruits grew from 59^1/$_2$ inches (151 cm) to 61 inches (155 cm) between the same two time periods. These findings suggest, therefore, that the living standards of the recruits, and, by extension, the working classes in London, increased in the early decades of Britain's industrialisation. Similar records are unavailable for analysis outside the metropolis. But since London was a leading industrial city, it was not immune from the changes that increased urbanisation and industrialisation brought to the British economy. The most detailed study of these data suggests that they support an optimistic view of working-class living standards in Britain in the late eighteenth and early nineteenth centuries (Floud, Wachter and Gregory, 1990).

However, two important caveats should be noted about using data on height to determine living standards. First, the same study has shown that working-class heights began to fall in the late 1820s and only began to recover after the 1860s. Presumably this reflects other factors, such as environmental problems, that impacted on a population experiencing increasing urbanisation, with all the accompanying disamenities, after c.1820; if this were not the case, it would be difficult to reconcile the decline in height with evidence of improving real wages after that date. Second, another study of the lower segments of society, namely English convicts transported to Australia, has shown that before 1815 there was no improved height such as that achieved by the Marine Society recruits. This analysis, in fact, indicated the opposite: rural English convicts born in 1813 were nearly 1 inch (2.5 cm) shorter than the cohort born in 1780, and urban convicts were more than 1^1/$_2$ inches (4 cm) shorter in 1802 than the cohort born in the late 1770s (Nicholas and Steckel, 1991). These variations in the trends of height among different working-class cohorts suggest that anthropometric measures have not yet produced conclusive results about living standards in the industrial revolution.

Demonstrating that one working-class cohort experienced increased height and that the other cohort declined in stature means that more data and analysis are needed before height can be used as a measure for increased working-class living standards in early industrial Britain. The same could be said about other approaches to living standards: there is still a lack of consensus among historians about how to weigh the various factors that can be measured, and much disagreement about the types of evidence, the regional differences and fluctuations over time in estimating the standard of living of the working classes in Britain before 1850.

4

Religion and Society

Religious worship was a far more important phenomenon in Britain in the Industrial Revolution than it is in today's predominantly secular society. Most of the population, of whatever social rank, attended religious services and Christianity had a significant impact on social and political life. Most Britons in the century after 1750 lived in a society framed by an emphasis on orderly Christian behaviour. The Bible was the most frequently published book in Britain; it served as a code-book and encyclopaedia by which life as a whole was to be controlled. Hymnals appeared in print regularly. Prayer books could be found among many cottage dwellers *c*. 1830, a reminder of the importance of private worship in many households. Sunday was regularly observed as a day of rest and worship – many forms of recreation were frowned upon on the Sabbath. Society in early industrial Britain cannot be understood without appreciating the biblical frame of mind that permeated many people's lives.

The official state religion since Henry VIII broke with Rome in 1534 has been the Church of England, symbolised by the monarch as titular head of the established church, the archbishops of Canterbury and York, and 27 English and Welsh bishops at the apex of the Anglican church's structure of authority. The 39 articles of the Church of England, established at the Reformation, were the official test of loyalty to the political regime and the social order. The links between church and state, consolidated by the **Act of Settlement (1701)**, guaranteed for the future that the British monarch would be a practising member of the Church of England, a situation that still obtains. The Anglican church was dispersed over thousands of parishes in England and Wales, many of which were in rural areas and had served as the centres of local communities for centuries. In Scotland the established church was the Presbyterian Kirk until 1843, when the **Free Church of Scotland** was formed.

Though the Church of England was always the main forum for Christian worship, dissenting groups gained more adherents in the century after 1750.

Act of Settlement (1701): Legislation that provided the basis for the Hanoverian Succession. It stated that the heir to the English and Scottish throne should be Protestant. In particular, it provided that on the death of Queen Anne, the crown should pass to her nearest Protestant relative, Sophia, Electress of Hanover, a granddaughter of James I, or her descendants.

Scottish Free Church: Formed in 1843 after a major split in the Church of Scotland. The Scottish Free Church sought spiritual independence from civil interference and attracted evangelical clergy in particular.

Baptists: A nonconformist group that comprised two denominations, the General Baptists, who were Arminian, and the Particular Baptists, who were high **Calvinists**. The Baptist Union was formed in 1813, and served as a meeting ground for both denominations. Baptists selected their own ministers and believed in adult baptism. Baptists were also opposed in principle to the connection of church and state.

Calvinist theology: Named after the Genevan religious reformer John Calvin (1509–64). Calvinism was a belief in the predestination of souls either to salvation (the elect) or damnation (the nonelect). It was associated especially with the Puritan wing of the Church of England.

Congregationalists: A nonconformist denomination that objected in principle to the connection between church and state and also rejected all church hierarchy. Each local Congregational church was voluntarily constituted and depended directly on Christ as its Head. During the eighteenth century, Congregationalists were often known as Independents. The Congregational Union of England and Wales was formed in 1831.

The Church of England, though not as moribund as was once thought, still failed to meet the religious needs of the whole community. In the early eighteenth century old dissenting groups, originally established mainly during the Civil War and Interregnum, regularly held meetings; they included **Baptists**, **Congregationalists** and **Presbyterians**. The **Religious Society of Friends** (i.e. the Quakers) also flourished in this period, though its numbers were relatively small compared with other nonconformist groups. These denominations had various differences; all, apart from the Quakers, were broadly Calvinist in theology, and all were in decline by the 1720s as their early flowering of enthusiasm waned. The evangelical revival in the late 1730s was part of an international efflorescence of nonconformity and a reaction to the perceived deficiencies of the Anglican church that led to an upsurge in Protestant worship outside the confines of cathedrals and parish churches. The emergence of Methodism, originally not a dissenting movement, was perhaps the most striking feature of this change. But the existence of Protestant Dissenters and Methodists indicates that the Church of England did not have a monopoly in the eighteenth century; religious pluralism was found throughout society.

By the first half of the nineteenth century, nonconformity became numerically stronger, chipping away at the dominance of the Anglican church. This was realised by the Archbishop of Canterbury in 1809 when he noted that 'the fact was, that our population had, particularly in some large towns, far exceeded the machinery by which the beneficial effects of our church establishment could be universally communicated' (Walsh, Haydon and Taylor, 1994: 18–19). The number of nonconformist congregations increased tenfold between 1773 and 1851. The growth in the number of dissenting chapels was equally striking. Between 1801 and 1851 the Congregationalists (or Independents) increased the number of their chapels from 914 to 3,244; the equivalent figures for the Baptists were 652 and 2,789, and, for the Wesleyan Methodists, 825 and 11,007. All these sects also had an upsurge of sittings in the first half of the nineteenth century. The growth of Protestant dissent, as shown below, was clearly related to the urbanisation and industrialisation of the British economy.

Britain was predominantly a Protestant nation during the phases of early industrialisation. Roman Catholics comprised a tiny minority of the population, though in some areas, notably Lancashire, there were higher concentrations of those loyal to the Roman church. Because Catholics were relatively small in number and marginalised in England since the Reformation, a strong streak of anti-Catholicism pervaded English society. Papists were considered superstitious, clinging onto the fallacies of medieval Christianity, including a belief in transubstantiation or the literal transformation of Christ's body and blood into the communion bread and wine. Catholics were viewed as a political threat because of their allegiance to the Pope. Britain's principal enemy during this period – France – was predominantly a Roman Catholic nation. Catholics had been associated with absolutism on the European continent in the late seventeenth century, and during the French revolutionary era they were suspected of Jacobinism or support for republicanism. They were ritually humiliated each year on 5 November when bonfire parties with effigies of Guy Fawkes reminded people of the association of Catholics with plots against the monarchy. The Gordon riots of 1780 were a major public disturbance in London connected directly to anti-Catholic prejudice, as Chapter 7 shows. The number of Catholics increased in Britain after the wave of Irish immigration that followed the potato famine of the 1840s, but in 1851 there were only 597 Roman Catholic churches and 826 Roman Catholic priests in England and Wales. The Irish Catholic diaspora to mainland Britain grew more rapidly in the second half of the nineteenth century.

Anglicans were entitled to hold all types of government office, to enter Oxford and Cambridge universities, and to become Members of Parliament. Dissenters and Catholics, however, faced legal discrimination for many decades after 1750. Under the Test and Corporation Acts of 1661 and 1673 Dissenters were debarred from holding government and municipal office; and they were to leave the doors of their meeting houses open so that their services could be monitored for signs of sedition. Many nonconformists surmounted these difficulties by practising occasional conformity, which involved taking Anglican communion once a year. Those who followed such a practice, and thereby pledged allegiance to the Crown, could qualify themselves to sit in Parliament. In terms of worship, Dissenters, and indeed all Protestants, had freedom to conduct their services as they saw fit provided they believed in the Trinity of Father, Son and Holy Spirit. Various indemnity acts passed regularly after 1726 gave pardons to those who had not yet conformed. In 1813 Parliament extended toleration to **Unitarians** – relatively small in numbers – who believed in God but not in the Trinity.

Catholics faced greater discrimination than Dissenters. They could not serve in the armed forces or enter universities; nor could they hold government office or sit on corporations. Both nonconformists and Catholics eventually won their battles against discrimination, but only after a long struggle. Attempts to repeal the Test and Corporation Acts in 1787, 1789 and 1790 foundered. A Catholic Relief Act of 1778 met with intense opposition and was abandoned. A later Relief Act of 1791 removed most religious discrimination against Catholics, except that they were still barred from Parliament and other civil offices. The Younger Pitt's hope that **Catholic emancipation** could be granted in the wake of the Irish rebellion of 1798 collapsed because of the political expediency of concluding the Act of Union with Ireland in

Presbyterian: A Calvinist nonconformist denomination that accorded no special hierarchical status to individuals. Ministers (presbyters) had equal status in making decisions together in councils (presbyteries or synods). Presbyterianism flourished particularly in Ulster and lowland Scotland.

Religious Society of Friends: Founded in the 1650s by George Fox and usually referred to as Quakers. Friends shun liturgical and sacramental worship and spend their time in meetings 'waiting on the Lord'. They eschew a professional ministry. They seek God's 'inner light' in the individual.

Unitarians: A Protestant denomination that rejected the Trinity and the divinity of Christ in favour of the unity of the Godhead. The first Unitarian chapel was opened in 1774 in London. Many Presbyterians converted to Unitarianism in the late eighteenth century. Unitarians were often educated, intellectual people who favoured discussion of religious principles.

Catholic emancipation: From the 1770s onwards penal laws against Roman Catholics were repealed on a piecemeal basis. The Catholic Emancipation (Relief) Act of 1829 removed all remaining disabilities to Catholic worship throughout the United Kingdom.

1801. The United Kingdom was thereby created without conceding political power to the Irish Catholic majority. Only with the Repeal of the Test and Corporation Acts (1828) and the granting of Catholic emancipation by Wellington's Tory government (1829) did political and religious discrimination against nonconformists and Catholics disappear from the statute book. These reform measures showed that the Church of England was losing some special privileges it had long enjoyed. The Church's role in British society was further modified by state involvement in its practices, exemplified in 1836 by compulsory registration of births, marriages and deaths and the gradual abolition of church tithes. In the 1830s the Church of England became attracted to the **Tractarianism** of the Oxford Movement. But this enrichment of sacramentalism and renewal of high church practices only gradually penetrated to the grass roots of the Anglican church.

Tractarianism: A mid-nineteenth century name for the Anglo-Catholicism of the Oxford Movement, which began in the Church of England in 1833. Tractarianism as a sobriquet stems from the published theological series *Tracts for the Times*.

The religious census of 1851 recorded the distribution of religious allegiance in England, Wales and Scotland. This computation took place on Sunday 30 March of that year, and is the only such exercise ever conducted in Britain. Based on returns from 34,467 places of worship, the census demonstrated the significance of nonconformity in early Victorian religious life. Dissenters provided nearly half the religious accommodation in England and Wales, plus 40 per cent of those worshipping in the morning and afternoon and two-thirds of those attending evening services. The census revealed that 5,288,294 potential worshippers did not enter a religious service on the day the count was taken. This suggests either that religious indifference was substantial or that many ordinary people had never received religious instruction and felt uncomfortable attending a church or chapel. A contemporary assessment of the response of different social classes to religious services suggests that the latter was the case (**Doc. 9, p. 125**). There were higher levels of religious attendance in Scotland and Wales than in England. In Wales the established church had a weak position: Methodism and other nonconformist groups were far stronger. These findings point to the pluralism of Christian worship in Britain in the early Victorian period; to the erosion of the monopoly of the Church of England; to the greater religious attendance found in the Celtic parts of the nation; and (as indicated by the non-attenders) to the emerging secularisation of society.

THE CHURCH OF ENGLAND

Most worshippers in England and Wales owed their allegiance to Anglicanism in the century after 1750. The established church was strongly linked with the state. Thus in 1790 Edmund Burke wrote that the English 'do not consider their Church establishment as . . . something . . . they may either keep or lay aside, according to their temporary ideas of convenience. They consider it as the foundation of their whole constitution, with which, and with every part of which, it holds an indissoluble union' (Clark, 2000: 254–55). One influential modern assessment has argued that the connections between church and state led to the existence of a 'confessional state' – an *ancien regime* sustained until the late 1820s. In this interpretation, the authority of the state was underpinned by theology: there was one national church that maintained its hegemony with its 'one confession of faith'. The divine authority of Christ filtered down the social scale via the Anglican clergy, acting as agents of state within their parishes, and this was buttressed by patriarchalism. Thus Britain resembled an *ancien regime* polity in which the twin pillars of established church and state commanded the loyalty of most people (Clark, 2000).

Whether the bulk of the population subscribed to these notions is questionable, however, during a period of rapid social change. And despite the hegemony of the Church of England, religious practice in Hanoverian and early Victorian Britain was, as suggested above, characterised by pluralism and the proliferation of different sects. It was common for people to attend both Church of England services and those offered by other Protestant groups; indeed, this was the pattern of worship that John Wesley hoped to inculcate among his Methodist followers. The Church of England did not have 'either the internal unity, the legal monopoly, the enforcement powers or the absence of rivals that might have rendered England into something as absolute as a "confessional state"' (Corfield, 1995: 15).

It is not just the nature of religion's impact on the state that has stimulated debate. Historians have also disputed the character of the Church of England during the eighteenth century. For some, it was a static institution resting on its laurels and becoming moribund in areas of population growth and rising industrialisation in the second half of the eighteenth century. Critics point to weaknesses in its pastoral and administrative arrangements and to religious indifference among the lower orders. To others, writing from a revisionist viewpoint, the Church of England showed signs of resilience in the face of an efflorescence of alternative Protestant worship, and was by no means as neglectful of its duties as was once thought to be the case.

Certainly, the Church of England had problems in ministering to the population at large in early industrial Britain. There were probably as many Anglican worshippers in the 1830s as in 1750, but the population of England and Wales had virtually trebled in that period and many non-Anglican religious groups had flourished. Church building and the number of parish clergy did not keep pace with population growth and industrialisation.

Latitudinarianism: A pejorative term, used with reference to the later seventeenth and early eighteenth centuries, to denote clergy in the Church of England who gave little priority to ecclesiastical organisation or liturgical practice.

In London and several northern industrial cities – Bradford, Manchester, Liverpool – private pew holders dominated parish churches, making seating for working-class people difficult to attain. Satirical prints in the era of Hogarth depicted examples of clerical gluttony and greed, a penchant for good living, worldly comforts and materialism, highlighting the lack of piety among many ordained ministers. The **latitudinarianism** of the early Hanoverian church persisted in some quarters into the later eighteenth century, giving an impression of preaching that merely went through the motions of services on the Sabbath, with a particular aversion to religious 'enthusiasm'. Many ordinary clergymen survived on pitifully small stipends in poorer parishes or, as was frequently the case, in circumstances where tithes collected went to laymen rather than the parson.

Non-residence of clergy and pluralism were singled out by contemporaries as deficiencies of the established church. In 1807 there were only 4,412 resident incumbents for 11,164 parishes. A parliamentary inquiry of 1812 found that over 1,000 parishes were unattended by Anglican ministers, suggesting that non-residence and pluralism were still rife decades after they had been identified as a problem. Church attendance appears to have declined in various areas: the Bishop of Hereford's visitation returns of 1788 suggest this had happened in his diocese, and in Lincolnshire in 1800 it was estimated that only a third of the population attended parish churches. Neglected parishes, the lack of church building and falling attendance at religious services point to a static religious establishment that failed to adjust positively to rapid social change. One historian has referred to the Church of England as experiencing 'an age of negligence' from 1700 to 1840 because of the clergy's relative lack of attention to pastoral matters (Virgin, 1989).

All these points, however, can be challenged by evidence about the positive features of the Church of England. Bishops' diocesan visitations appear to have been conducted conscientiously for the most part during the eighteenth century. One example for Chesterfield, Derbyshire, for 1751 displays Anglican practice in a positive way **(Doc. 10, p. 126)**. Many other parishes also received favourable reports. For every clergyman singled out as neglecting his duties, there was another one who ministered to his flock faithfully, even where non-residence occurred: good pastoral care could still be carried out by help from resident stipendiary curates or neighbouring clergy. There appears to be no correlation between non-residence and pluralism and lack of services: figures for communion and other Sunday services in the later eighteenth century are satisfactory in a number of dioceses. The seating capacity of many churches was increased by installing galleries. At the end of the eighteenth century in Lancashire, for example, almost three-quarters of the churches were new or larger than a century before. In 1818 the Incorporated Church Building Society came into existence and persuaded

Parliament to pass an act offering £1 million to the church commissioners to build churches in populous areas. Moreover, few examples have surfaced of clergymen who fitted the satirists' focus on clerical greed, apart from parson James Woodforde of Norfolk who left a famous diary detailing his lavish meals and material concerns.

In its pastoral functions, the Church of England appears to have performed soundly in early industrial Britain, though the emphasis lay on sermons and prayer book services in parish churches rather than on choral singing. Communicants were catechised, whereby they responded to questions and answers designed to disseminate the basic principles of Christianity. Much effort was put into Christianising the people through charity, Sunday schools and regular preaching. Services were usually conducted dutifully. The overall tone of services was moderate, operating somewhere midway between the extremes of latitudinarianism and enthusiasm. Vicars still had much influence over ordinary people's lives through the vestry and in administering the rites of baptism, marriage and burial. The Anglican church was not divorced from popular culture. There were church choirs, bell ringers, rush bearers, even amateur orchestras. In many parts of Britain popular Anglicanism remained a focal point for communities, especially those that 'valued tradition, community rituals, and religious harmony' (Hempton, 2002: 84). In 1843 the Prime Minister, Sir Robert Peel, made the creation of ecclesiastical districts possible, so that clergymen could be appointed and endowed before a parish church had been built. This measure aided the spiritual welfare of working-class communities that had expanded in the early nineteenth century without the benefit of a parish church.

THE RISE OF EVANGELICALISM

The impact of evangelical Christianity on the middle and lower classes reached its height between 1782, when Charles Simeon began the Evangelical Movement in Cambridge, and the mid-Victorian period. It found adherents both within the Church of England and among nonconformist sects, but more among the upper and middle classes than among the working classes. Evangelical Christians in the Church of England tended to work through the parochial clergy, whereas Dissenters favoured itinerant missionaries who circulated beyond parish boundaries. Such was the impact of evangelicals as reformers in those decades that one historian has referred to the period as 'the age of atonement' (Hilton, 1988). This phrase draws attention to the central evangelical belief that Christ's death on the cross was the means whereby mankind could be forgiven, experience redemption, and achieve salvation.

Evangelical Christians believed in salvation by faith and proselytising by means of the Scriptures. They were morally earnest men and women who sought to eradicate sinfulness by social reform. They made the pulpit rather than the altar the centre of their worship and concentrated on the work of redeeming individuals. They set exacting standards for the parish clergy. They centred their religious and social activities on chapels, providing a sense of belonging for many ordinary people in the community. Though they espoused an **Arminian theology**, like the Church of England and most Methodists, their rising influence from the 1780s onwards implied that something lacked vitality in the contemporary Anglican church. Evangelical groups were predominantly male-dominated. Though they often regarded women as religiously pure, these groups maintained a grip on the organisation of church and chapel activities. There were relatively few evangelical women preachers, but in the first half of the nineteenth century women participated in many philanthropic activities inspired by evangelical concern, such as setting up rescue houses and visiting institutions.

Evangelical Christians affected society in early industrial Britain in various ways. Imbued with a sense of Christian benevolence, religious zeal and a belief in God's providence, they concerned themselves with issues connected with social improvement. Thus Christian evangelicals, along with Quakers, were at the forefront of the anti-slavery movement: they campaigned vigorously against the British slave trade and slavery in the British Empire on moral and humanitarian grounds, and eventually had considerable success. They gave speeches, lectures and addresses on these topics; published many broadsides, tracts and pamphlets; brought evidence before parliamentary committees; and, in particular, conducted successful petitioning campaigns. By 1792, for example, five years after a **Society for Effecting the Abolition of the Slave Trade** had been formed, anti-slavery campaigners attracted 1.5 million signatures out of a total British population of 12 million on petitions presented to Parliament to abolish the British slave trade. Such campaigners achieved a comparable success in the late 1820s and early 1830s; in 1833 alone, the year of the Emancipation Bill, freeing slaves in the British Empire, they secured the signatures on their petitions of over 20 per cent of all British males aged over 15.

Other social institutions in which evangelical Christians made their impact on early industrial society were Sunday schools and prison reform; these are discussed below in Chapters 5 and 8. But this was not all. Evangelicals were prominent in campaigns to build new churches, in Bible teaching, in the suppression of unruly and lewd entertainments, in the prevention of cruelty to animals, in the improvement of factory working conditions, and in various charitable works. Middle-class women often took a

Arminian theology: Named after the Dutch religious reformer Jacob Arminius (1560–1609). Arminianism embraced the notion of free will and the belief that all people could be saved. It therefore opposed the Calvinist notion of predestination and only the elect being saved. Arminianism was the dominant theology of the Church of England and of the Wesleyan Methodists.

Society for Effecting the Abolition of the Slave Trade: Founded in 1787 as the first national society devoted to the abolition of the British slave trade. Ten of the original 13 members were Quakers. The Society immediately embarked on a public campaign against the slave trade.

prominent role in these activities. The evangelical **Clapham Sect**, formed in 1795, assumed the lead in philanthropic causes linked to the spread of Christian moral principles. Among its members were William Wilberforce, Granville Sharp and James Stephen, all renowned for their abolitionist beliefs. Evangelical Christians also played a leading role in missionary and benevolent societies, such as the undenominational London Missionary Society (LMS), founded in 1795; the British and Foreign Bible Society, founded in 1804; and the National Society to open Christian schools, begun in 1811. The LMS spread Christianity to the Empire. The British and Foreign Bible Society distributed the Bible among the poor and ignorant. The National Society to open Christian schools promoted elementary education for the poor on sound religious principles.

Clapham Sect: An Anglican evangelical group that met regularly at Holy Trinity Church, Clapham, London, in the 1790s. Members engaged in philanthropic, missionary and other collective religious activities, and were known as the 'Saints'. Among their members were William Wilberforce, Zachary Macaulay and James Stephen.

METHODISM AND SOCIETY

Methodism was one of the main fruits of evangelical revivalism. The origins of Methodism lay in the early 1730s when John Wesley, George Whitefield and a small circle of friends met regularly at Oxford University for worship. Known as the Oxford Holy Club, they soon became dubbed 'Methodists' because of the methodicalness of their religious observation. Wesley himself, the son of an Anglican priest, underwent a conversion experience at Aldersgate Street, London, in 1738, where he felt called by God to preach the gospel and to save souls. Wesley, Whitefield, Howell Harris and other early Methodist preachers were offering open-air services by 1739. Wesley communicated the faith he had discovered in his own conversion: he preached about the need for conversion, repentance, and the forgiveness of sins. He also began a mission to spread the gospel to the poor, whom he considered spiritually equal to their social betters. 'We regard no man according to his country, riches, power or wisdom', he wrote. 'We consider all men only in their spiritual state, and as they stand related to a better world' (quoted in Gilbert, 1976: 84).

Methodism: A Protestant denomination that began in the 1730s as an adjunct to the Church of England. Among its founders were John Wesley and George Whitefield. Most Methodists followed an Arminian theology, but there were also Calvinist Methodists. The Methodist movement separated from the Church of England in 1795.

The organisation of 'the People called Methodists' (as they styled themselves) soon took shape. Besides preaching in the fields, which was uncommon though not without precedent, the early Methodists raised subscriptions to build meeting rooms for worship. Members formed societies (i.e. congregations) as part of a circuit, catered to by an itinerant preacher but not by a permanent minister. The societies were divided into bands and classes, where members strengthened their Christian commitment by exchanging their religious experiences and by reading the Bible **(Doc. 11, p. 127)**. The classes were part of a strong networking system that tapped into larger regional circuits of Methodist preachers. An annual Methodist conference was established in 1744 as a focal point to discuss the organisation of these various groups and the religious issues they dealt with. In these ways, Methodism proved an effective movement for spreading the Word of God.

Originally Methodism was a complementary movement to the Church of England; it did not become a dissenting sect until 1795, four years after John Wesley's death, when a schism in the movement led it to separate from the Church of England. Methodism was important in the century after 1740 because it was the fastest-growing Christian denomination in Britain and the main new form of worship that took root among masses of ordinary people. The greatest period of Methodist growth was in the first half of the nineteenth century, when membership figures rose markedly, especially in industrialising areas. Official Wesleyan membership figures for England were 22,410 in 1767, 87,010 in 1801, 188,668 in 1821 and 285,000 in 1851 (when total Methodist memberships comprised 490,000). Methodism had much larger growth rates in this period than the old dissenting denominations, even though they also increased their adherents. In 1851 Methodist attendance at services totalled 1,385,382 compared with 793,142 for the Presbyterians and Congregationalists and 589,978 for the Baptists.

Most Methodists were Wesleyans who followed the doctrine of free will, though a smaller number were Calvinists, especially in Wales. There were various splinter groups of Methodists, such as the Independent Methodists, formed in 1806, the **Primitive Methodist Connexion**, formed in 1812, and the **Bible Christians**, who separated from the Methodists in 1818. These offshoots of Methodism followed less formal ministries than the Wesleyans. There were also differences in religious observance. Thus the Primitive Methodists favoured 'camp meetings', first popularised in England at Mow Cop, Staffordshire, in 1807; these involved convulsions and evangelical hysteria. The Wesleyan Methodists, however, found this anathema to their belief in order and decorum at Christian services. As well as formal members in bands and classes, larger numbers of 'hearers' attended Methodist open-air services. The influence of Methodism spread through factory owners employing Methodist preachers in the mills and advocating the spread of evangelical principles among their workforce.

John Wesley and other early Methodists were successful preachers of the gospel for various reasons. They spread the Scriptures effectively by hiring itinerants who preached wherever they could find an audience, whether in the open air, barns, village halls or yards. Such men had no need to observe the practice of the Anglican church, which confined preaching within parish boundaries. Wesley stated that the whole world was his parish, and he and his preachers followed this dictum. Itinerancy

Primitive Methodist Connexion: Established in 1812 by Hugh Bourne and William Clowes and based on revivalist meetings using dramatic missionary methods. Attracted mainly humble followers.

Bible Christians: A group, also known as the Bryanites, that separated from the Methodists in 1818. They were formed by William O'Bryan as the Bible Christian Society in 1815, and were based particularly in Devon and Cornwall.

meant mobility and a simple means by which Christianity could be spread to outlying parts of the country, including many areas where the Anglican church had no presence. Lay preachers became an essential part of early Methodism, enabling the movement to tap the abilities of those who had not been ordained. Such voluntarism was very much part of the older dissenting tradition. Women led class and band meetings but were allowed to preach only after John Wesley sanctioned this in 1761. Thereafter women preachers played an active role in travelling to more rugged parts of the country to spread the Scriptures, but they 'never gained official status or respect equal to that of the male itinerants' (Valenze, 1985: 51). Women also played no official role within the structure of the Methodist sects. However, humble men and women with sufficient talent for preaching in public or leading classes were encouraged to show leadership. Hymn singing flourished among the Methodist communities, providing a means of communal solidarity and a way of spreading literacy among working people, as the words on hymn sheets were written out line by line. Charles Wesley, the brother of John, was one of the leading contributors to Methodist hymn writing: he wrote over 5,000 hymns, mostly based on biblical themes. All these means of promoting Methodism enabled it to become a movement where social barriers were cut through by a general message of redemption for all.

The style of Methodist preaching tended to be emotional and spontaneous. There was none of the stuffiness or formality associated with some Anglican sermons. Extemporaneous exposition of the Bible was the order of the day. Crowds that assembled for Methodist services were swayed by the preachers' commitment and projection of the need to seek salvation by faith in order to redeem souls. Charismatic preachers such as John Wesley and Whitefield stirred the religious passions of crowds. Though both men were educated and trained in the practices of the Church of England, they could touch the hearts and minds of simpler folk. Wesley also tapped into the world of popular superstition and magical beliefs still found in many parts of provincial Britain. He himself believed in witches and possession by the Devil, in dreams and other forms of foreknowledge, in faith healing and exorcisms, and sometimes highlighted these fears, thereby forging a bond with 'hearers' who had similar beliefs. There was criticism of the emotional scenes associated with early Methodist preaching: swooning, wailing 'hearers' and new converts shouting out their sense of forgiveness could give the impression that gullible people were being manipulated in their feelings, and John Wesley had to defend the reaction of his open-air audiences against charges of cheapening religion. The evangelical zeal of Methodist services was something vital, however, that contributed a new and lasting dimension to worship in Britain.

Methodism was particularly successful among the labouring poor in early industrial Britain, and notably so in areas where the Church of England had left a religious vacuum waiting to be filled. Methodism had its greatest impact in industrial and urban districts. It flourished throughout South Wales among coalmining communities and took firm root in the tin and copper areas of Cornwall. It gained a strong following in the industrial Black Country and the West Riding of Yorkshire. It became popular in cities such as Bristol and Newcastle upon Tyne and attracted followers in the East End of London. Methodist membership figures show that most adherents were skilled artisans rather than the dregs of the working class. The largest occupational group among Wesleyan Methodists between 1800 and 1837 comprised artisans (skilled workers and independent craftsmen) who formed 63 per cent of the total; the equivalent proportion of artisans among all nonconformist groups in the same period was 59 per cent. That Methodism was strong in many industrial communities of Georgian England and Wales is unsurprising, for Methodist values were in close accord with the drive by skilled workers to better their lot in life. Methodist preaching emphasised sobriety, orderliness, punctuality, obedience to authority and the fear of divine retribution. It was a movement that called upon people to prepare themselves for the afterlife and, in so doing, to ensure that quotidian lives were followed in a devout, respectable manner, according to an unflinching faith and with the need to carry out good Christian works.

Many Methodist attributes have been regarded as vices rather than as virtues by those historians who emphasise Methodism's narrowness and repressive side. Generations of readers have alighted upon a chapter in J. H. Plumb's *England in the Eighteenth Century* that includes a one-sided polemic against Methodism as bigoted and warped. Plumb highlighted Methodism's intolerance, its hatred of Papists, its anti-intellectual and philistine elements. He summed it up as 'not a religion *of* the poor but *for* the poor' (Plumb, 1950: 94). E. P. Thompson was the most prominent recent historian to criticise the negative attributes of Methodist preaching. He regarded Methodism as inculcating a sense of sin and shame among working-class followers. He thought it was all too appropriate an adjunct of the dark, Satanic mills – a movement that stifled many working-class communities with its repressive creed of 'Thou shalt not!' and one that was highly suitable for the new time discipline many factory owners wished to foster in their workforce. For Thompson, Methodist principles were inculcated into working communities by those who wished to instil bourgeois values into a potentially unruly workforce. He argued that the Methodists 'weakened the poor from within by adding . . . the active ingredient of submission; and they fostered within the Methodist Church those elements most suited to make up the psychic component of the work-discipline of which the manufacturers stood most in need' (Thompson, 1963: 390).

This emphasis on the negative impact of Methodist preaching on early industrial Britain derives partly from the famous thesis propounded by the French historian Elie Halévy as long ago as 1913. Looking across the English Channel and intrigued by the contrast between the revolutionary tradition in France and the lack of radical success in Britain, Halévy argued that the different trajectories of revolution in both countries could be attributed to the spread of Methodist values among working-class communities in Britain. This, in his view, stifled the potential for protest and revolutionary ideas: Methodists concentrated upon good works and attaining the Kingdom of Christ, and, in so doing, channelled their energies into spiritual concerns and social good. Thus Methodism took the sting out of revolution in Britain and served as an antidote to **Jacobinism**. This broad interpretation became known as the Halévy thesis, and it continues to exert an influence over modern discussions of Methodism's social impact (Halévy, 1913).

Jacobinism: Derived from the followers of the Jacobin Club (1790–94), who were radical followers of Robespierre in the French Revolution. Jacobinism was a term used in the French Revolutionary Wars to refer to British radicals whose political ideology was similar to their French counterparts.

How far should one take on board the negative assessment of the social impact of Methodism, and how far is the Halévy thesis valid? The negative features of Methodism should not be overplayed because communities where Methodism flourished, as in the South Wales valleys, were often based around communal solidarity and mutual fellowship, with the chapel standing as the symbol that drew people together in a supportive, caring way. Methodist meetings helped many ordinary workers to become acquainted with music, literature and simple philosophy and thereby served as a powerful instrument for informal popular education. For each person acquiring some of the supposedly negative values associated with Methodism, there was another nourished and nurtured by it in a positive way. Nor was Methodism necessarily a vehicle for political conservatism, for Methodist converts became notable in the nineteenth century for their connections with Chartism, trade unionism and working-class politics.

As for the Halévy thesis, it is difficult to prove that Methodist numbers were sufficiently numerous to have had the widespread impact claimed: there were not enough Methodists for them to have staved off revolution. Even if we accept a figure of 210,000–300,000 Methodist hearers and adherents by 1800, the total number of people influenced by Methodism was not enough to justify the claims made about its extensive social and political impact. The same is true for the mid-nineteenth century when people attending Methodist services comprised around one-tenth of the population. Most Methodists were then Wesleyans, who had the lowest proportion of working-class members. By contrast, the Primitive Methodists, whose members reached further down the social scale, were relatively small in numbers.

If one is searching for explanations about why Britain avoided a revolution along French lines in the late eighteenth century, one could just as readily lay emphasis on the safety-valve offered by a humane system of poor relief catering for distress in working-class communities, and widespread charitable giving by the middling classes in times of dearth. The weaknesses of those disposed towards revolution, considerable pockets of anti-French feeling, the continuance of protests based upon a 'moral economy', the wide range of styles within the Methodist movement, the disproportionate representation of Methodists in regions where early industrialisation had its greatest impact, the flexibility displayed by parliamentary politicians in offering concessions, and the work of the Utilitarians in social improvement could be added as other plausible explanations for why Britain avoided revolution in the era from the French Revolution to Chartism.

5

Popular Education

In the century after 1750 Britain had a number of fee-paying schools for the wealthy, such as Eton and Harrow, plus the ancient universities of Oxford and Cambridge to cater for the sons of the clergy and the upper classes. The middling orders in society could send their children to grammar schools and, in the case of nonconformists, to dissenting academies such as the school at Warrington made famous by the presence of the chemist and nonconformist minister Joseph Priestley in the 1770s. But these types of schools necessarily catered for only a minority of people. The most important form of education for the mass of the population in early industrial Britain comprised instruction in elementary schools. These establishments catered for children up to the age of 14, when boys commonly started apprenticeships. Such schools were scattered about the country in no discernible pattern and catered for a relatively small proportion of children in 1750, when there was no state provision for education. A century later, however, the situation had changed considerably. State-supported elementary education had been introduced in the 1830s, a wider range of schools for children existed, and a far higher proportion of boys and girls experienced some form of formal education. This is not to argue that educational provision for children was entirely satisfactory in early Victorian Britain; there was much left to be desired in terms of teacher training, pupil attendance and methods of instruction. But the provision available had advanced beyond what was conceivable in the mid-eighteenth century.

Various reasons account for the growth of elementary education in early industrial Britain. Before the age of the factory, schools were set up by private initiative or charitable endowments. Eighteenth-century governments afforded social policy a low priority; they saw their role as providing sound government, conducting foreign policy and safeguarding the nation's finances. Educational schemes promoted by the government were nonexistent. The propertied classes, for the most part, did not see a real need to educate the labouring poor; it was commonly thought that such education would erode deference from the lower orders to their social betters and would promote social instability through the working classes seeking to improve their circumstances. Increased literacy would also mean that ordinary workers would be able to read radical literature. Parents of working-class children were ambivalent about elementary education because it required attendance at school on weekdays when boys and girls could be earning money to supplement family incomes.

The situation changed significantly, however, with extensive population growth, industrialisation and urbanisation between c. 1780 and 1850. The changes filtered through gradually as governments and the educated public came around to the view that a minimum level of literacy and numeracy, along with moral education, would help to channel the energies of the working classes into acceptable outlets. Faced with increasing costs for prisons and poor law provision, both central and local authorities began to appreciate that increasing educational provision and literacy would help urban and industrial society to function more effectively. Another strand of middle-class thought emphasised schooling as the antidote to the idleness of young teenagers unable to find agricultural work in southern England. Religious leaders also became increasingly convinced of the Christian duty to provide schooling for the poor. Thus the Bishop of Chichester in 1812 commended the 'spirit of zeal for the education of the Poor' that had emerged as a means of producing 'a fruitful harvest of soul-saving knowledge to future generations' (Digby and Searby, 1981: 14).

Governments were nevertheless slow to adopt plans to promote elementary education. The Whig reformer Henry Brougham and a House of Commons select committee looked into educational provision for the lower orders in 1816, but plans to introduce a system of popular education through day schools foundered because of the economic troubles encountered in Britain after the end of the Napoleonic Wars, working-class unrest, and the presence of a reactionary Tory government. State-supported elementary education was introduced only in 1833 under a Whig government. By then, the educated classes had long changed their views on the need for popular education. Only by instructing children in reading, writing and arithmetic, buttressed by a sound Christian education, could the working classes be contained and their abilities channelled into skilled work and respectable behaviour. For many working-class parents, nevertheless, the tension between sending their children to school and expecting them to earn their keep from an early age was not resolved by 1850.

ELEMENTARY SCHOOLS

A wide range of elementary schools existed in 1750, and most still existed a century later. Dame schools catered for infants and common day schools for primary-age children. These voluntary institutions both charged modest fees. Dame schools were little more than homely establishments operating from modest premises; the teachers were usually single or elderly women or middle-aged men who had retired from a trade. Childminding was one of the functions of dame schools. Common day schools were run by masters who were often emperors without clothes so far as their educational background was concerned. Some children attended trade schools where, as the name implies, they were trained specifically in simple trades. Often their work was sold in order to support the running of the school.

These institutions were exceeded in importance, however, by charity schools. Many of these were founded in the seventeenth and eighteenth centuries. They catered for children of the labouring classes. Usually they were day schools, though they included some boarding establishments. By 1800 around 179 charity schools existed in the London area, funded by voluntary benefactions. They catered for the children of poor but honest parents, though they did not take children from families receiving poor relief and excluded boys and girls suffering from contagious diseases, lameness or bodily sores. Children usually entered charity schools between the ages of 7 and 11. They could stay until age 14, when boys were apprenticed. Many of these establishments were 'blue coat' schools where children wore the traditional blue coat of apprentices. One of the best known was Christ's Hospital, originally in London but now in Horsham, Sussex.

In Scotland, educational provision was better for children than in England. Although charity schools were more uncommon there than in England, hospitals (i.e. schools) founded for orphans in the Scottish Highlands and bequests for educating the poor in elementary schools catered for working-class children and those living in remote rural areas. More important than either of these establishments were statutory parish schools. The Scottish Parliament of 1696 had passed legislation creating parochial schools on a compulsory basis in each parish. Salaried dominies (i.e. teachers) were employed in these schools. But it proved difficult to maintain the provision of such schools in the urban-industrial lowland belt of Scotland as the population increased there rapidly in the nineteenth century.

None of the above schools catered for the whole range of working-class children and all were voluntary. Before c. 1780 this meant that many children in England and Wales probably had little experience of schooling at all. The situation was better in Scotland, for the reasons just given. Change occurred in elementary education, however, around the beginning of the nineteenth century. The spread of monitorial education from the first decade of that century saw the building of schools promoted by the **British and Foreign School Society (BFSS)**, a non-denominational body that leaned towards nonconformist precepts, and the **National Society for the Education of the Poor in the Principles of the Established Church** (see below). Yet as the

British and Foreign School Society (BFSS): Established in 1804 as a society that embraced the monitorial system and non-denominational elementary schools that were established in south London in 1798 by Joseph Lancaster (1778–1838).

National Society for the Education of the Poor in the Principles of the Established Church: Founded in 1811 as an Anglican society to promote monitorial teaching in elementary schools. Its first superintendent was Andrew Bell, who had devised the 'Madras' system of education, in which much teaching was done by older, able pupils.

population expanded, school provision was hard put to keep pace, despite the emergence of societies promoting education and government aid for school building after 1830. As a partial remedy, the 'ragged' school emerged in the 1840s to provide basic elementary education to the urban poor plus some food and clothing. 'Ragged' schools provided religious instruction and laid emphasis on discipline and duty. Unlike the National and BFSS schools, they did not charge fees. There were 202 ragged schools in Britain by 1852. Despite these developments, by 1870 1.5 million children aged between 3 and 12 (39 per cent of that cohort) did not attend school and no places were available for over a million of them. Compulsory schooling began in Scotland in 1872 and in England and Wales in 1880.

SUNDAY SCHOOLS

The Sunday school movement had its origins in early industrial Britain. It catered for a much larger number of children than any school mentioned so far. Publicised in 1783 by Robert Raikes, the proprietor of the *Gloucester Journal*, Sunday schools spread rapidly throughout England, Scotland and Wales to offer Sunday school instruction to many children and adolescents. Half a million children attended Sunday schools in England and Wales by 1818. By 1851 attendance at Sunday schools covered 2.4 million pupils in England and Wales (13.4 per cent of the total population) and a further 300,000 in Scotland (10.1 per cent). Many Sunday schools were found in urban and industrial areas; they were operated both by evangelicals within the Church of England (whence the movement arose) and by nonconformists. Methodists, in particular, were associated with the growth of Sunday schools, using the gatherings to teach children orderliness, literacy and obedience to God (**Doc. 12, p. 129**). Sunday schools were often attached to particular congregations, though more frequently in England and Wales than in Scotland, where Sabbath schools were established by magistrates and town councils acting together with the Church of Scotland.

Sunday school meetings were often lengthy affairs – it was not uncommon for them to continue all day. Children were divided into classes and taught reading through stories, poems and songs; they partook in prayer and Bible study; and sometimes they were instructed in writing and secular subjects. The Sunday school movement therefore helped, in a rudimentary way, to instil literacy in children in working-class districts and to teach Christian moral behaviour. Sunday school teachers were usually middle-class church and chapel-goers. For the educated middle classes, such schools served as civilising influences on the lower classes: they helped to spread orderly behaviour, rudimentary educational instruction and social cohesion. Raikes himself noted that his Sunday schools in Gloucester were intended to combat misery and idleness among the poor and to inculcate kindliness, duty, decency and discipline, as well as literacy and knowledge of the Scriptures. Many working parents were willing to have their sons and daughters attend Sunday schools because they did not interfere with the earning potential of child labour in factories, mines and workshops.

VOLUNTARY SCHOOLS AND MONITORIAL EDUCATION

The teaching of children in the nineteenth century was dominated by the monitorial system. There are two claimants for the origins of this method of instruction in the first decade of the nineteenth century. One was the Reverend Andrew Bell, an Anglican chaplain in India and subsequently in England; the other was the Quaker schoolmaster Joseph Lancaster, based in Southwark, London. Both devised a simple, cost-effective system of instructing large numbers of pupils with monitors. Older, able pupils (aged from 11 upwards) served as monitors. They were gathered together at the start of the school day by the master, given instructions about what to teach, and distributed around a large classroom to teach basic reading, writing and arithmetic to groups. They used cards, slates, sponges and chalk rather than more expensive books and paper. Lancaster viewed monitorialism as a powerful means of educating the ragged street children he had encountered in south London at a time when there was no state support for elementary education. As he put it,

> every lesson placed on a card, will serve for twelve or twenty boys at once: and, when that twelve or twenty have repeated the whole lesson, as many times over as there are boys in the circle, they are dismissed to their spelling on the slate, and another like number of boys may study the same lesson, in succession: indeed, *two hundred boys* may repeat all their lessons from *one* card, in the space of *three hours*.
>
> (Goldstrom, 1972: 39)

Drill and discipline were central features of monitorialism. Strict regulations governed the conduct of lessons: orders and commands were issued, obedience to instructions was emphasised, children filed in and out of rooms in an orderly way, and the class teacher superintended the monitors (**Doc. 13, p. 130**).

Monitorial education spread rapidly throughout Britain. In 1804 Lancaster opened his Borough Road School in Southwark, where he had 500 pupils. He soon attracted many influential visitors, including British and foreign royalty. In 1808 his school was sponsored by the Royal Lancasterian Institution, which two years later became the BFSS. The Quaker brewer Samuel Whitbread and the anti-slavery campaigner William Wilberforce were members of its organising committee. Lancaster embarrassed himself personally and financially and was ousted from his position at Borough Road in 1810. Bell's parallel advocacy of monitorialism led to his schools being embraced by the Anglican church, which in 1811 established the National Society, referred to above. Among its supporters were the literary writers Robert Southey and Samuel Taylor Coleridge. The monitorial system spread throughout most elementary schools for the rest of the nineteenth century. It was accompanied by much bitterness and competition between the BFSS and the National Society over whether nonconformity or Anglicanism should dominate the moral aspects of teaching children.

The monitorial system had obvious defects. Monitors were not paid or properly trained; they simply progressed to such positions as they grew older and moved up through the school years. Much of what they conveyed to children was learning by rote. The monitorial system was therefore open to the criticism that it was unimaginative and mechanical. Most boys who served as monitors could write from dictation but had little knowledge of punctuation and grammar. They were too young to impart Christian principles meaningfully to younger children, and were not called upon to demonstrate any command of geography, history or general knowledge. They had too many children to supervise. Yet they performed an invaluable function in disseminating a limited form of education to those who might otherwise have received no such instruction.

STATE PROVISION FOR SCHOOLS

State provision for elementary education began with initiatives developed by the Whig government in the 1830s. The Whigs made a modest start to financing schools by providing the first government grant to aid the voluntary societies to construct school buildings. The amount was fixed at £20,000 per year. It was distributed to the National Society and the BFSS and targeted at poorer areas. This was a cautious entry into the funding of state education. The Whigs hedged the grant – a modest annual sum, even by the standards of the time – by stipulating that the money could only be disbursed after voluntary societies had first raised half the subscription money for new school buildings. This favoured the richer or middle-class areas where, naturally, it proved easier to accumulate funds than in poorer districts. When discussions were held over the introduction of the educational grant, a scheme to provide national compulsory schooling in parochial schools for infants aged 6 to 12 was defeated. The Whigs wanted to begin state support of elementary education but they did it cheaply: supporting the voluntary societies was much less expensive than trying to implement a parochial school system.

By the late 1830s it was clear to the Whigs that the educational grant was insufficient for school building and that it had not been deployed effectively in working-class areas. Schools continued to be run by untrained teachers relying on a cadre of monitors who struggled to provide anything more than a rudimentary introduction to the three Rs. In 1839 Lord John Russell, the Home Secretary, took the lead in trying to alter this state of affairs by increasing the annual government grant for elementary education and by introducing inspection and a plan to establish teaching training colleges (referred to at the time as **normal schools**). Russell oversaw the increase of the annual grant to £30,000. It was now stipulated that funds should be given particularly to working-class districts. Russell instigated the appointment of Her Majesty's Inspectors (HMIs). He set up a Committee of the **Privy Council** on Education to administer the grant and the first two inspectors were appointed to oversee its distribution. There were also plans to establish a state normal school on non-sectarian lines.

A ferocious propaganda battle broke out over the status of school inspectors. This brought sectarianism to the surface. Different types of churches felt they could regenerate the moral character of the working population, whereas their opponents should not be allowed to establish their influence. This power struggle permeated much of early Victorian educational provision. But it was not simply a struggle between Anglicans and nonconformists, because the latter had schools built for their own denominations only; it was more often conflict between different wings of the Church of England. On the matter of inspection, a compromise was reached in 1840 between the Committee of the Privy Council on Education and the Archbishop of Canterbury, whereby the Church of England gained the right to appoint inspectors of Anglican schools. In effect, this meant that such inspectors were clergymen. Non-denominational and nonconformist schools were inspected by laymen.

Proposals for teacher training were not implemented until 1846, when the Whig government adopted the Committee of the Privy Council on Education's recommendations for the replacement of monitors by pupil-teachers. These were adolescents apprenticed to the master for five years from the age of 13 and above; they were annually inspected, and grants were

Normal schools: A name given to early Victorian teacher training colleges.

Privy Council: A body that emerged from Henry VIII's royal council. It was a leading executive body until Charles I's reign. It still exists and advises the sovereign on the approval of orders-in-council and the issue of royal proclamations.

paid both to the apprentices and their masters. The best pupil-teachers sat national examinations with the possibility of gaining scholarships to training colleges. If they succeeded in their studies, they could become trained teachers. This was a positive move towards creating a new professional career status for deserving pupils, including those from modest backgrounds. It took some time to gather pace: there were only 681 certificated teachers in 1849. But the pupil-teacher scheme then spread rapidly, along with teacher training: by 1859 there were 34 training colleges and 6,878 qualified teachers. Thirteen of the colleges were open to women. State funding for education increased during the 1840s; it reached £189,000 by 1850 and quadrupled over the next decade.

FACTORY SCHOOLS

Legislation connected with factories and the poor law came to provide the only form of compulsory elementary education in early industrial Britain. In textile areas of the country, factory schooling was offered by some employers from the 1780s onwards to supplement the moral instruction of Sunday schools. The Health and Morals of Apprentices Act (1802) was the first law to lay down a minimum amount of daily schooling for children working in factories who were not under parental supervision. The Act required factory owners to provide a schoolroom and to ensure that apprentices received educational instruction for part of each working day during their first four years in a mill. It was not until the Factory Act of 1833 that a law specified a minimum period of factory schooling per day for all children employed in textile mills. That Act was primarily concerned with restricting the hours of work for women and children in factories, but its educational clauses required mill owners for the first time to demonstrate that children up to age 11 (to rise to 13 after two-and-a-half years) were receiving two hours of schooling a day for six days a week. Employing children in the mills was now predicated on making arrangements for schooling: a certificate of attendance for children in schools had to be kept and shown, if required, to factory inspectors, who were appointed under the 1833 Act to oversee this and other aspects of the legislation.

Factory schooling, however, was only a limited success. Mill owners disliked this form of state intervention in their private businesses. They found it difficult to provide sufficient schoolrooms. It was time-consuming for owners to control when the children left the mill for local day schools and when they arrived back at the factory. Owners were also responsible for truancy. The children themselves were often poorly dressed, dirty and tired from their work when they attended such schools. For these reasons, factory owners became less willing to make voluntary contributions towards schooling working-class child operatives after the 1833 Act, but this did not deter would-be reformers from campaigning to improve the situation. In 1843 Sir James Graham introduced a Factory Bill in Parliament that included a clause specifying that children should receive three hours' schooling in the mills. The Bill included religious clauses, with proposals to make pupils take daily Bible lessons and undergo catechism. Graham's Bill reawakened sectarian religious rivalries. Nonconformists bitterly complained that teachers under this scheme would be exclusively Anglican: it was envisaged that parish clergymen and churchwardens would become *ex officio* members of the schools' administering bodies. After much opposition from factory owners, the Factory Act of 1844, passed by Sir Robert Peel's government, was passed without educational clauses. It shortened hours of work for factory children under 15. This meant that those already attending schools were less tired from their daily work and presumably able to benefit more from the instruction. Legislation passed in 1845, however, gave children in textile factories three hours schooling per day for five days a week. This was later extended to workshops and mines and marked the beginning of a half-time system of education, whereby children in employment devoted equal time to work and education. The system lasted until the end of the First World War.

POOR LAW SCHOOLS

The New Poor Law, ushered in after 1834, had arrangements for the provision of schools for pauper children in workhouses. Often a schoolroom adjoined workhouses. Children were kept separate from adult paupers. These schools catered for 40 to 50 pupils, but they lacked proper teachers and conditions were poor. James Phillips Kay, son of a Rochdale cotton manufacturer, became a poor law assistant commissioner in East Anglia in 1835 and saw for himself the inadequacy of these arrangements. After he was appointed to the Committee of the Privy Council on Education he tried to rectify the situation by setting up larger poor law schools attached to workhouses, which catered for 400 or 500 children. These were established in three metropolitan school districts and six small rural districts. Norwood, in South London, was the best known of these establishments because it was set up as a poor law model school. Together with smaller poor law schools that already existed, these schools catered for 38,000 children by 1855 (out of a total workhouse child population of 51,000). Children from pauper families receiving outdoor relief did not come under the auspices of workhouse schools.

The Poor Law Commission's *Report on the Training of Pauper Children* (1841) endorsed Kay's hope that workhouse education would rear 'hardy and intelligent working men, whose character and habits shall afford the largest amount of security to the property and order of the community' **(Doc. 14, p. 132)**. Kay (later Sir James Kay-Shuttleworth) also hoped that workhouse education would form a model for a nationwide establishment of elementary schools. But this was not to be. For several more decades, the provision of elementary schooling remained varied, stronger in some parts of the country than others, and based upon voluntary provision. The government provided a grant of £30,000 per year from 1846 onwards to improve teachers' conditions in workhouse schools. Kay-Shuttleworth, though not achieving all his aims in workhouse education, was stimulated to promote the pupil-teacher system (described above) as a direct consequence of his visits, which found poor law schools lacking properly trained teachers.

LITERACY AND THE CURRICULUM

Historians have disputed trends in literacy in early industrial Britain: surviving evidence is based on local records that point to considerable regional variations. Between 1750 and *c*.1830, however, it appears that the lack of growth in endowed schools, the employment of children in industrial work, and the lack of necessity for literacy in many routine manual occupations all combined to reduce literacy levels among the labouring population. By the 1830s barely a third of the workers in southeast Lancashire could write their own names on a document (which is the usual measure of literacy by historians). Presumably, however, a higher proportion of these people could read simple passages of print because reading always precedes writing when acquiring literacy. Matters improved somewhat as a result of the expansion of educational provision described above. The Registrar General reported in the census of 1841 that 67 per cent of males and 51 per cent of females were literate; in the 1851 census the figures were 69 per cent for males and 55 per cent for females.

The curriculum in monitorial schools was based on the three Rs, religious instruction and the inculcation of duty and respect for one's social superiors. Arithmetic included addition, subtraction and multiplication tables; reading and writing comprised spelling, grammar, punctuation, dictation and composition. The reading and writing tasks often had a strong moralistic content. The religious instruction involved reading from the Bible, hymn singing and catechisms. In many establishments a gender division existed whereby boys studied additional arithmetic and some history or geography while girls were

Plate 1 A. W. Bayes, A Chartist meeting, Basin Stones, Todmorden, Yorkshire, 1842

Source: Courtesy of Calderdale MBC Museums.

Plate 2 Arkwright's cotton mill at night, Cromford, Derbyshire

Source: Photo © Philip Mould Ltd, London / The Bridgeman Art Library.

Plate 3 The Iron bridge at Coalbrookdale, Shropshire

Source: Courtesy of Ironbridge Gorge Museum, Telford, Shropshire, UK / The Bridgeman Art Library.

Plate 4 Stephenson's Rocket
Source: © Bettmann / Corbis.

Plate 5 An Image of Ned Ludd
Source: Courtesy of the Mary Evans Picture Library.

Plate 6 The 'Peterloo' Massacre, Manchester, 16 August 1819

Source: Courtesy of Manchester Art Gallery, UK / The Bridgeman Art Library.

Plate 7 A Poor Law workhouse, St James' parish, London

Source: Courtesy of the Mary Evans Picture Library.

Plate 8 A Victorian monitorial schoolroom

Source: Private Collection / The Bridgeman Art Library.

confined to reading, writing, arithmetic, religious study and sewing. This distinction reflected middle-class views about the suitability of a wider range of subjects for boys, to prepare them for the world of work, and the more restricted curriculum offered to girls, recognising that most were likely to be confined to the domestic sphere as adults.

Much of the learning was carried out by rote, with chanting of numerical tables, copying lines from books and repeating simple moral homilies. The equipment used, as previously mentioned, was very restricted; teaching was carried out in large schoolrooms; and unruly children could be corrected by corporal punishment or confinement in cages. All these factors contributed to the monotonous but disciplined atmosphere of the monitorial schoolroom. Teaching improved in elementary schools in the late 1840s with the introduction of pupil-teachers (though not every school had them). Able to call upon the help of assistants who were older and better educated than monitors, they developed whole class teaching to specific age groups in lessons devoted to particular topics.

SOCIAL CONTROL AND ELEMENTARY EDUCATION

Kay-Shuttleworth, on account of his work in workhouse education, his position on the Committee of the Privy Council on Education, his control over the early school inspectorate and his drafting of various reports on elementary education, has been seen as the single most important spokesman on elementary education in the 1830s and 1840s. He thought popular education was necessary because many working-class parents were ducking their responsibility of bringing up children in a decent, disciplined way. Kay-Shuttleworth, like many middle-class Victorians, frowned upon idleness and dissipation. He saw the movement towards a wider provision of elementary education and teacher training as a way of instilling bourgeois values into young people, thereby preparing them for an adult life of useful work and an acceptance of their position in society. Thus his plans and writings on education have been seen as an attempt at social control of the working classes (Johnson, 1970).

The degree to which intentions of **social control** were reflected in practice has been questioned by some historians. Certainly, inspectors carried Kay-Shuttleworth's views on rearing cheerful, industrious, peaceful, God-fearing working people into the provinces. But that does not necessarily mean that the intentions prevailed. The main problem in accepting that working-class children were imbued with such values lies in patterns of

Social control: A term used usually with regard to bourgeois reformers in the period c.1830–60 who tried to instil the virtues of sobriety, orderliness, punctuality, thriftiness, godliness, and obedience to authority among the lower orders. Historians have found more examples of the intentions of social control than they have of social control in practice.

attendance. Children were simply not exposed to schooling for sufficient hours for moral views to influence their actions and behaviour. By 1850 most working-class children attended school for only between two and four hours a day: they spent much more time working. Very few children from the lower classes were still at school beyond the age of 10 or 11. The time spent in school was probably only enough for them to learn the basic three Rs and some rudimentary moral and religious instruction. Moreover, in 1851 there were twice as many private as public day schools for working-class children, even though only a third of lower-class pupils were educated in these schools. Sheffield, for example, had about 180 private schools at that time. Working-class parents, it is argued, sometimes preferred these establishments because they lacked the atmosphere of social control and were not dominated by religious groups. Children who attended them could bypass the ethos of those who tried to hand down a particular type of education.

The Sunday school movement has also been seen as an agency for social control through the work of Methodist and other nonconformist preachers and factory owners disseminating the virtues of hard work, temperance, thriftiness, punctuality and godliness among the early industrial workforce and their children. It is doubtful, however, whether social control played a significant part in Sunday schools by 1850. One reason is that many Sunday school teachers were by then from the working classes and not necessarily beholden to bourgeois values. Another explanation is that Sunday schools, though operating in a punctual, disciplined way, were not usually located near factories. Therefore it is difficult to see how the children attending them could have been influenced primarily by the middle-class values of the mill owners.

ADULT EDUCATION

Though formal adult education catered for only a small proportion of workers in early industrial Britain, literacy and technical instruction were spread to workers in various ways. Sunday schools attracted adolescents and adults. Evening classes were organised in many towns, often by religious groups, and reading, writing and arithmetic, along with Bible study, were taught to the working classes, especially those with artisan skills. Self-education should also not be underestimated. From the mid-eighteenth century onwards there was a steady publication of self-help manuals that could be read either individually or in lower-class clubs where people met for improvement and sociability. The most important of these institutions were mechanics' institutes, which arose out of local initiatives. They spread rapidly in the 1820s and 1830s and taught science and elementary subjects to artisans and the lower middle classes. The Glasgow Mechanics' Institute, a pioneer establishment, opened in 1823 and offered courses in chemistry, natural philosophy, mechanics and mathematics; it also had a museum and library. Dr George Birkbeck, a pioneer of the adult education movement, opened the London Mechanics' Institution on 10 February 1824 with an address that discussed the 'growing appetite for knowledge' of the artisanal class. He also outlined the benefits for the nation that would follow from promoting scientific instruction in such institutions **(Doc. 15, p. 134)**. Mechanics' institutes soon began to flourish; there were over 300 by 1841.

Teaching in the mechanics' institutes took place in the evenings, after the work day had ended, and modest fees were charged for attendance. There were lectures on natural history, teaching of the three Rs, and sometimes the provision of reading rooms and libraries. The emphasis on science stemmed from a perception that practical learning-by-doing was beneficial to the economy and workers' aspirations. Middle-class supporters sometimes had motives of control in their patronage of these institutes, but greater stimuli for their educational activity came through local civic pride and a desire to demonstrate progress in the education of working men. Some mechanics' institutes attracted political radicals to their membership, but usually religious or political dogma were avoided. Unskilled manual workers were outnumbered in attendance at these institutes, as one might expect, by skilled artisans and the lower middle classes.

6

The Old and New Poor Laws

The extent of poverty in early industrial Britain is difficult to determine, partly through lack of statistics on unemployment but partly because the condition of poverty depended upon the material expectations of different people, changing levels of productivity in the economy, and the degree of rapaciousness among landowners. Because these matters altered over time, it is difficult to pin down a specific 'poverty line'. Nevertheless, most families in early industrial Britain had some contact with poverty, especially at particular stages of the life-cycle such as when raising children, when ill or when elderly. By 1800, around 28 per cent of the English and Welsh population were in receipt of **poor relief**. Agricultural labourers were subject to seasonal underemployment and slumps in available work as a result of parliamentary enclosure, shifts in food prices and the outcome of yearly harvests. For those working in towns, the demand for unskilled labour was usually swamped by the supply; industrial slumps occurred; wage rates were reduced in difficult times; and workers could be summarily dismissed. No central government support for widows with dependent children or the elderly existed. The state provided no cushion for families facing hardship because of the premature death of the breadwinner. And yet there was a system of relief available to alleviate poverty that was the envy of the rest of Europe. This consisted of the **Old Poor Law**, originating in statutes passed in 1597 and 1601, which became transmuted into the New Poor Law after 1834.

Poor relief: A parish-based system of relief payments for various categories of paupers, given formal establishment under two Acts passed in 1597 and 1601. Poverty was widespread and poor relief continued to be significant until the early twentieth century.

Old Poor Law: Refers to the poor relief system in operation until the Poor Law Amendment Act (1834), established under Elizabethan statutes dated 1597 and 1601, though an earlier Act dated 1552 contained elements of the system. Justices of the Peace had overall responsibility for maintaining poor relief locally. Individual parishes had their poor rate administered by overseers of the poor, who were appointed annually.

THE OPERATION OF THE OLD POOR LAW

Poor relief up to 1834 was based around the principles laid down in the parliamentary statutes on poor relief passed at the end of Elizabeth I's reign. These acts codified and extended existing poor relief measures and divided the poor into three categories: able-bodied paupers who could not find employment; rogues, vagabonds and sturdy beggars who were disinclined to work; and the 'impotent' or deserving poor – the young, the old, the sick, the blind and the handicapped. The statutes targeted different means of alleviating poverty for each group. Under the legislation, the able-bodied poor were provided with outdoor relief, which consisted primarily of dole payments but could also take the form of assistance with rent, housing, clothes or food. Rogues, vagabonds and sturdy beggars, perceived by both central government and local authorities as a threat to the social fabric, were to be whipped or otherwise punished in workhouses or 'houses of correction'. The deserving poor were looked after in almshouses, hospitals, orphanages or poor houses. These differentiated ways of treating poverty were made mandatory for each parish.

Along with this categorisation of the labouring poor, and suggestions for treating them, came further administrative arrangements. The allocation of poor relief lay in the hands of individual parishes; that is, at the lowest level of local government, something appropriate for pre-industrial communities. Poor relief was funded from compulsory ratepayers' contributions into a poor fund. It was thus a form of local taxation. The administrators of the funds were amateur, unpaid officials, usually churchwardens or parish constables appointed by Justices of the Peace; they were known as overseers of the poor. The distribution and collection of the poor rate varied a great deal in individual locations. But supporting paupers at a localised level meant that overseers of the poor could deal with people according to their knowledge of personal histories and circumstances. This often occurred once a week as overseers stood behind trestle tables and paupers queued up to have their circumstances reviewed and their doles paid out. Sometimes overseers' duties made their presence intrusive in communities, but generally their knowledge of individuals enabled them to assess people's needs sensibly **(Doc. 16, p. 135)**.

A major change to the Old Poor Law came in 1662 with the enactment of the Laws of Settlement and Removal (commonly referred to as the Settlement Acts). These tightened up the regulations for claiming poor relief. They specified that relief could now be granted only if one could demonstrate a definite link with a particular parish, and ownership of property worth at least £10 per annum. The nature of the connection varied from one parish to another, but it usually included evidence of being either born, apprenticed, married or resident in a particular locality, or having acquired an inheritance there. If evidence to support these connections could not be produced, two JPs signed removal orders so that those ineligible for relief could be cast out, forcibly if necessary, to the parish where they had a settlement **(Doc. 17, p. 136)**. A stranger could be removed within 40 days of his or her arrival unless he or she owned freehold land. Such expulsions occurred particularly with pregnant women or single mothers with dependent children: under the bastardy laws, they could be dumped over parish borders.

The amount raised by the poor rate in England and Wales increased from about £400,000 in 1696 to £1.5 million in 1776 and to £2 million on average in 1783–85. Thus poor relief more than doubled in the last generations of the pre-industrial economy, outstripping the rate of population growth. This disbursal of monies provided outdoor relief and aided two main categories of paupers: children aged under 15 and the old and infirm. It is viewed by most historians as a humane system that provided relief at a level sufficient to make up income to the position of an agricultural labourer without a family. Property owners had tactics, however, for keeping down the poor rate. Some large landowners deliberately failed to renovate workers' cottages so that farm labourers would have to seek accommodation across parish boundaries and become chargeable to ratepayers of another parish. Local ratepayers closely watched the apprenticeship of pauper children by overseers of the poor, attempting to ensure they were apprenticed to masters outside the parish so that their own parishes would not have to provide relief.

To what extent the Settlement Laws inhibited the mobility of paupers is difficult to say. In some places, where applied rigidly, they definitely deterred labour mobility. This made it difficult for labouring people with families but without work to take the risk of moving lock, stock and barrel to another parish; if no employment was available to welcome the newcomers, the move could be disastrous socially and economically. Yet enough evidence exists to suggest that the Settlement Laws were relaxed in industrial and urban districts in particular, where employment prospects were good, provided that the immigrants produced their certificates authorising removal from their home parish. Moving from one parish to another certainly occurred: by the late eighteenth century, up to a third of the population in some large towns did not have a settlement there.

Outdoor relief dominated the Old Poor Law because it was cheaper and more easily administered than the construction and operation of workhouses. Knatchbull's General Workhouse Act (1723) enabled single parishes to erect a workhouse, if they so wished, to impel the able-bodied poor to work in return for relief. But official returns from 1776 indicate that most of the 2,000 or so workhouses in England held only between 20 and 50 inmates. Often these establishments were poorly run and not cost-effective; the work they gave to paupers consisted of menial tasks such as pinmaking or picking oakum. They lumped all categories of paupers together, which meant that fit adults were housed with orphans, widows, the sick and the destitute. When investigated by Sir Frederick Eden in the 1790s, widely varying conditions were found in these establishments; some were clean and run in a decent way, others were hives of disease, overcrowding and indifferent management. Often they were beset by high costs. Thomas

Gilbert's Act (1782) had attempted to remedy these problems. This legislation encouraged parishes to combine into unions for the purposes of building extra workhouses for the aged, sick and infirm, and to offer outdoor relief and then employment to the able-bodied poor. These provisions were not taken up immediately in many areas, but over 900 parishes had joined to form 67 unions under Gilbert's Act by 1834.

THE OLD POOR LAW UNDER PRESSURE, 1793–1832

The poor law came under considerable pressure during the decades between the outbreak of war with revolutionary France and the coming of the Great Reform Act. Rapid population growth caused employment problems, particularly in the transition from a pre-industrial to an industrialised economy. The estimated population of England and Wales in 1781 was 7.9 million people and 10.2 million thirty years later. It grew further to 12.1 million in 1821 and then increased by 16 per cent – the largest decadal increase in modern English and Welsh history – to reach 14.0 million in 1831. The half-century up to that date witnessed the largest rate of population growth in modern Britain over a comparable time period. It placed significant pressures on the living standards of the labouring population, as Chapter 3 has shown.

Population growth was accompanied by many changes in employment patterns, with a significant shift of workers from the land into urban occupations, the growth of mechanisation and factory-based labour, and the exodus of workers from agricultural work through enclosure. The enclosing of fields in arable counties increased the amount of part-time work available but failed to provide long-term opportunities on the land. Enclosure often meant the erosion of common rights. Deindustrialisation in counties such as Gloucestershire and Devon, where the woollen industries declined from the early nineteenth century, meant that rural dwellers had either to find more agricultural work when cottage industries and enclosed farms were shedding labourers or they had to migrate. Southern agricultural counties were particularly prone to problems associated with labour mobility. People moving from countryside to town faced a potentially precarious existence because they would not always be covered by the settlement requirements of the places to which they migrated. To some extent, this problem was mitigated by a statute passed by the Younger Pitt in 1795, which prohibited the removal of labourers when they became a burden to parish funds. In addition to these problems, the period c. 1790–1832 saw several harvest failures, bread subsistence crises and occasional grain riots, and during the long years of war with France (1793–1815) food imports were often in short supply.

Expenditure on poor relief in England and Wales increased to meet these challenges. Between 1792 and 1812 the rate almost trebled, rising from £2.6 million per annum to £6.5 million. It reached an annual peak of £8 million in 1818. Up to that point per capita expenditure was becoming more generous. In 1783–85 poor relief in England and Wales came to 5s. 2d. per head of population per year. By 1803, the figure had increased to 9s. 2d. A decade later it jumped to 12s. 5d. before declining slightly for several years and then falling to 9s. 8d. per year in 1829–33 (Evans, 1983: 402). Most support was outdoor relief. The amount expended indicates that a generous system of poor relief was in operation to meet the changing needs of the early industrial labouring population.

Experimentation occurred in the payment of outdoor relief in the four decades after 1790. Several new schemes were tried in various parts of the country to cope with increased demands for poor relief at a time when family sizes grew rapidly. In some rural parishes the 'roundsman' system was used, whereby unemployed workers were sent on the rounds in search of work. It required employers to offer work to those seeking labour; if they could not do so, they paid a sum into the parish chest to support relief payments. Elsewhere a system known as the 'labour rate' was followed, under which paupers had a price set for their daily work and occupiers were assessed at a specified rate. The occupiers could either offer work and pay the rate to the individual or, failing that, contribute the equivalent sum to the parish funds. If a wage was offered to a labourer below that specified, the rest of the money had to be donated to the parish. This scheme for subsidising labourers' wages ran into problems, however, after 1815 when farmers found their profits squeezed and their ability to pay wages reduced.

The best-known scheme that modified the granting of outdoor relief in the later Georgian period was the so-called Speenhamland system, created in 1795 at a time of harvest failure and high bread prices. This was originally devised at the village of Speenhamland, just outside Newbury, Berkshire, at which County Quarter Sessions magistrates granted allowances to paupers on a sliding scale based on the price of bread and the number of children (up to a maximum of seven) in a family. The higher the price of bread and the greater the number of children in a labourer's family, the more generous the poor relief granted (**Doc. 18, p. 137**). This humane way of providing for large families in hard times offered a living wage through relief payments, making no distinction between the employed and the unemployed. It became a widespread means of outdoor relief down to the end of the Old Poor Law, though it was not introduced universally throughout the country. Paupers who did not receive such allowances sometimes wrote to overseers of the poor to emphasise their need for relief (**Doc. 19, p. 138**).

CHANGING VIEWS ON THE OLD POOR LAW

Differing attitudes about the poor existed in the second half of the eighteenth century. Some observers thought poor relief claimants were largely idle and irresponsible. Farmers, in particular, often argued that poverty resulted from the fecklessness of workers rather than from inadequate wages. But there was no consensus on whether the problem could be overcome by compulsion to work or by educating the poor to more useful employment. Property owners frequently linked paupers with crime. Certain types of paupers, such as vagrants, found attitudes hardening towards them: the Vagrancy Act of 1744 brought in stiffer penalties for what it termed idle and disorderly persons, rogues and vagabonds, and incorrigible rogues.

The growth of poor law expenditure in the four decades after 1790 stimulated plenty of contemporary commentary on the provision of relief payments. A wide spectrum of views was put forward, ranging from liberal supporters of a generous allowance system to critics of the bills that ratepayers had to foot to support the poor. Evangelicals and humanitarians from the late eighteenth century onwards argued that the poor should be treated generously. Many among the educated classes considered it was the duty of the privileged to support the under-privileged through a spirit of benevolent paternalism. Equally vocal were the views of **political economists**, whose perception of poor relief was much harsher: they considered allowances for able-bodied paupers inadvisable, and worried not just about parish ratepayers' bills but about the moral degradation that could affect the character of poor people who became inured to handouts. The political economist David Ricardo criticised the poor laws for being opposed to the exercise of the free principles of the market. He would have liked to have seen the poor laws abolished, but this was politically unacceptable to Whigs and Tories alike.

The pioneer demographer the Reverend Thomas Malthus was a distinctive and influential critic of the Old Poor Law, especially of the allowance system. He thought the poor would remain poor whatever support was provided and whatever the nature of the social and political system. In his *Essay on the Principle of Population* (1798) Malthus argued that generous provision of outdoor relief to able-bodied paupers encouraged early marriages, large families and reliance on the poor rate for sustaining households. By providing support for large pauper families, Malthus believed the poor law subsidised the work-shy and sanctioned a passive reliance on the parish; it therefore added to the problem of poverty and failed to alleviate the causes of indigence. To Malthus, providing extra bread allowances, such as under the Speenhamland system, was an artificial aid: it militated against workers acting in a self-reliant way according to their circumstances.

Political economists: Practitioners of the theoretical science of the laws of production and distribution. Political economists examined the processes whereby finite resources were allocated among various social classes and the operation of various factors that constrained wealth and productivity.

THE ROYAL COMMISSION ON THE POOR LAW, 1832

Between 1817 and 1832 various parliamentary select committees investigated the problem of poor relief and its connection with labourers' wages. The issues were sufficiently important to lead to the establishment of a nine-man Royal Commission in 1832 to investigate the operation of the poor law. The central figures on the Commission were Edwin Chadwick and Nassau Senior, respectively a civil servant and a political economist, both of whom were strongly influenced by the ideas of Jeremy Bentham, the political and social thinker. Bentham believed in **utilitarianism** and advocated policies that reflected a belief in the 'greatest happiness of the greatest number'. He argued that poor relief should be maintained so that the happiness principle was not eroded by people being subject to starvation or the fear of starvation. But he wanted poor relief to operate differently than it currently did. He considered that accountability was important in social institutions. This could be guaranteed only by installing appropriate administrative personnel and procedures to cut costs and to inspect the system. To monitor such a sprawling system as parish-based poor relief, greater inputs from central government were needed, and the formation of larger units of local government. Bentham thought the Old Poor Law should cut expenditure, and in the 1790s he advocated the establishment of a National Charity Company based on contract management. The scheme proved abortive, but its emphasis on efficiency and accountability was passed on to his followers.

Utilitarians: Followers of Jeremy Bentham who believed that political and reform activity should be devoted to the greatest happiness of the greatest number of people. Often referred to as Philosophical Radicalism, it was a branch of moral philosophy that exerted great influence on British political, economic, social and legal thought during the nineteenth century.

Influenced by these ideas, Chadwick, Senior and their colleagues on the Commission produced a report that highlighted a particular view of the operation of the Old Poor Law. Their findings stressed the economic costs and moral failure that they found in the provision of poor relief. The Royal Commission's report concluded that expenditure on poor relief was too generous; the existing provisions pointed, as Malthus had argued, to the moral failure of permitting large numbers of able-bodied men to claim relief. The report criticised wealthy tenant farmers for manipulating poor relief in rural vestries, deliberately creating a pool of cheap labour and burdening poorer parishes. The potential corruption inherent in operating a system with unelected overseers of the poor in charge of parish funds was highlighted. Underpinning the report were views, congenial to political economists, that the current operation of the poor law created poverty by its generosity and by reducing incentives to seek paid employment; there was little understanding of the fact that the dislocation and underemployment of the early industrial economy was the root cause of poverty. Nassau Senior, who compiled most of the report, had written its main conclusions before all the evidence was gathered: small wonder, therefore, that it argued for the Old Poor Law creating the conditions of poverty.

The report's recommendations attempted to remedy these perceived defects of poor relief. The Commission supported the Benthamite notion of greater administrative efficiency in poor law provision and the introduction of central government intervention in a local-based system through inspection. It argued that individual parishes should be combined into larger units known as unions. It recommended a division between the provision of relief for the deserving and undeserving poor on the basis that the disabled and elderly poor were morally entitled to support, whereas able-bodied paupers should be encouraged to seek work. To ensure that such a division was reflected in the distribution of poor relief, the Commission put forward the test of 'less eligibility', which meant that the able-bodied poor were less eligible for relief (**Doc. 20, p. 139**). It was recommended that outdoor relief should be abolished; that workhouses for separate categories of paupers be built; and that such institutions should support those who could not fend for themselves and serve as a deterrent to fit adults. The erection of new workhouses would be encouraged and the combination of parishes into unions would make this more feasible.

THE POOR LAW AMENDMENT ACT, 1834

The Poor Law Amendment Act of 1834 was the most important legislation associated with the operation of the poor law since its Elizabethan origins. It provided the constitutional framework for the Victorian **'New' Poor Law**, and its central propositions remained in effect until poor relief was dismantled between the First and Second World Wars. Brought in by a moderate Whig government, the Poor Law Amendment Act, as its title suggests, was an adjustment to the status quo rather than a wholehearted change in poor relief provision. It was enacted with cross-party support in Parliament. In the House of Commons the vote was overwhelmingly in favour of the Bill becoming law (319 votes to 20), but in the Lords the Bill encountered stiff opposition and was passed only after the Marquis of Salisbury, acting as spokesman for the Tory peers, convinced Chadwick and Senior that they should drop the clause ending outdoor relief. The ideas of the Royal Commission on the Poor Laws were taken into account by the government but were not implemented in their entirety. In particular, outdoor relief, much criticised in the report, continued as the main type of relief after 1834, and the Benthamite principle of 'less eligibility' as a workhouse test was not implemented.

New Poor Law: Refers to the poor relief system in operation after the passing of the Poor Law Amendment Act (1834). It was characterised by greater centralisation in the organisation of poor relief, by the principle of 'less eligibility' applied to able-bodied paupers, and by attempts to erect more workhouses. The system was not dismantled until the arrival of old age pensions marked a shift in policy under the Liberal government of 1906–14.

The provisions of the Poor Law Amendment Act were fourfold. First, central government became involved in the operation of poor relief for the first time, with the establishment of a Poor Law Commission based in London. Three men were to be appointed to this body, which operated under Chadwick's secretarial guidance. These arrangements continued until 1847 when a Poor Law Act replaced the Commission with a Poor Law Board overseen by a president, who was a crown minister, and two secretaries. Second, Poor Law Guardians were now to be elected by local ratepayers and property owners; they replaced the previously unelected overseers of the poor. However, local JPs could sit on the boards *ex officio* because of their position as magistrates. The distribution of poor relief no longer lay exclusively in their hands but was administered by the guardians. Third, parishes were grouped into unions and the Act stipulated that workhouses could be built if the unions wanted them. It was thought that combining parishes in this way would spread the costs of building new workhouses. Nevertheless, individual parishes were expected to remain responsible for their own paupers. Fourth, the link between central government and the provinces was provided by appointing assistant commissioners to check the operation of the new system. Under the legislation, it was left to the commissioners to propose general policy with regard to the New Poor Law. These inspectors could compare its implementation in different localities and suggest ways of improving its finance or administration; they could issue orders and regulations to put their recommendations into practice. Little was said in the Poor Law Amendment Act about the administration of workhouses, the education of pauper children or the Settlement Laws. But despite these omissions, the new legislation was the first attempt to create a national system of poor relief and to instil uniformity into local practice.

THE IMPLEMENTATION OF THE NEW POOR LAW

One objective of the New Poor Law was to cut the number of pauper recipients and, hence, the expenditure on poor relief. This aim was realised after 1834. In that year the number of paupers on relief in England and Wales totalled 1.3 million (8.8 per cent of the population). In 1850 1 million paupers (5.7 per cent of the population) were granted relief. Annual average expenditure on paupers dropped from £6.7 million in the last years of the Old Poor Law (1829–33) to £4.9 million in 1834–38. It declined further to £4.7 million on average between 1839 and 1843. By 1844–48 poor relief increased modestly to £5.2 million per year, but this amounted to only 6s.

2*d*. per head, just over half the rate given in the second decade of the nineteenth century (Evans, 1983: 402–3). Since many northern industrial areas were slow to implement the Poor Law Amendment Act, this drop in relief meant that southern rural counties were disproportionately hit by falling relief scales.

Cutting relief payments fitted the thinking of the Royal Commission on the Poor Laws, but parsimony also resulted from the failure in 1834 to alter rateable values in parishes. Under the New Poor Law, parishes were required to fund the poor in the new unions; the per capita rate paid by ratepayers, however, remained unchanged in many cases. Moreover, manufacturing and mercantile property were relatively lightly assessed for rateable purposes, which meant that many occupiers of moderate income and modest properties paid more than their fair share to the poor rates. In practice, the lack of a revised, uniform system of rating householders, and the relatively light burden on industrial magnates, meant that impoverished parishes with large numbers of paupers could not provide sufficient funds for their contribution to poor relief, a problem exacerbated during many difficult years of industrial slump and high incidence of unemployment during the '**hungry forties**'.

The poor law unions were established swiftly after 1834. The nine assistant commissioners appointed, increased to 16 in 1835, set about combining parishes into unions without delay. By the end of 1835 they had already combined 2,066 parishes into 112 unions; this covered about one-tenth of the total population of England and Wales. By the end of 1839 13,691 parishes out of 15,000 had been grouped into 583 unions. The principles for forming unions varied. In some cases, the commissioners attempted to group unions around an existing market town. Another practice was to defer to local gentry influence, where a local magnate wished to keep parishes over which he had influence within one union: such was the case with the Duke of Richmond's patrimony in Sussex and Earl Spencer's Northamptonshire estates. In most parts of the country the creation of the new unions proceeded in a peaceful manner. The commissioners lacked the statutory power to act in parishes that came under Gilbert's Act, and so those parishes remained outside the framework of the New Poor Law.

The workhouse system was intended to symbolise the New Poor Law and after 1834 the unions began to make greater use of such institutions. Older, existing buildings were adapted for this purpose in some localities, but large, central workhouses were erected elsewhere. The Royal Commission of 1832 had recommended that all paupers should be subject to a workhouse test, and Chadwick, among others, had envisaged that the new unions would build different types of separate, specialist workhouses for the aged, for the sick, for children and for the mentally ill. The Poor Law Amendment Act had fought shy, however, of granting statutory authority to remove all paupers to

Hungry forties: A phrase that evokes the deep depression, widespread unemployment and popular discontent of the 1840s, a decade that witnessed Chartist protests, the Irish potato famine, the campaign against the Corn Laws and mass emigration from Ireland.

workhouses. In practice it was cheaper for parishes to continue paying outdoor doles rather than provide indoor relief. Many local ratepayers, feeling already burdened in their support for poverty, refused to pay for specialist workhouses; and so the less expensive option of providing new central workhouses was pursued – if it was followed at all.

These new workhouses were intended to act as a deterrent to the ablebodied poor. Accordingly, they were designed and run as forbidding institutions. Many were large stone structures with the outward appearance of a prison; not surprisingly, their opponents referred to them as 'bastilles', a symbol of oppression etched into popular consciousness from the time of the French Revolution. They were divided into separate wards for adult men, adult women, children, the sick and the mentally incapacitated. Inmates wore uniforms. The daily regimen was a relentless routine of work – hence the name 'workhouse' – and strict meal times and curfews. Adult men worked on manual tasks such as breaking stones or picking oakum; adult women undertook laundry work, stitching and seaming of garments and cleaning. The food provided was monotonous and stodgy. Inmates were subject to the discipline overseen by the master of the workhouse. Since many of these men were recruited from a military background, the regimen tended to be spartan and strict. In effect, workhouses catered not for the majority of paupers, who continued to claim outdoor relief, but for the ill, the simple, the orphans and the aged.

Some workhouses were run humanely: the inmates were treated kindly, reading rooms might be provided, and sympathy for the plight of older married paupers could be expected. But, equally, other workhouses were unpleasant, severe institutions: children could be punished for bedwetting, food could be adulterated, dormitories made uncomfortable. Charles Dickens memorably portrayed the misery associated with workhouses in *Oliver Twist*, in which Oliver's request for more food before a shocked workhouse master and a silent dining hall full of hungry pauper children became an iconic vignette of the miserable plight of orphans in the workhouse. Workhouses such as Andover, Hampshire, became notorious when it was discovered, in 1845, that able-bodied inmates ate marrow from bones supplied for crushing as a result of hunger stemming from the workhouse governor's fraudulent reduction in their diet.

Overpopulation and seasonal underemployment among the labour force meant that the workhouse test of 'less eligibility' was never introduced comprehensively. Initially, the introduction of the New Poor Law led to attempts in many areas to shift paupers into workhouses. But this was an expensive option compared with the continued provision of allowances. By the late 1830s outdoor relief still predominated in industrial centres and urban areas and remnants of the Speenhamland system were still found. Married men with families appear to have been given priority in many localities, for some workhouses reported that during winter only single men and orphans were among their inmates. In rural districts, farmers on the Board of Guardians preferred to pay allowances in order to keep a reserve workforce at their beck and call. There was the realisation that the free market could not provide the employment or sufficient wages for a large proportion of a growing national population. In 1850 the mean number of indoor paupers in England and Wales receiving relief came to 123,004 (0.77 per cent of the population). They were outnumbered by outdoor paupers, totalling 1,008,700 people in 1850 (5.7 per cent of the population). It became increasingly difficult for able-bodied adult men to claim outdoor relief, although destitute women and children could usually claim such support up to the 1870s.

The Poor Law Amendment Act, despite its framers' intentions, left the Settlement Laws unscathed. In 1840, for example, an estimated 40,000 paupers were removed from their parish of residence to their place of settlement. It became more difficult for paupers to claim settlement after 1834 in parishes to which they had migrated, for several reasons. First, the receiving parishes, which tended to be more urban than rural, pressurised those seeking work not to claim poor relief, and settlement removal orders were used as a threat. Second, the basis upon which paupers could claim settlement no longer included apprenticeship or hiring. In fact, the qualifications for settlement were tightened up by insistence that only birth or marriage counted as legitimate criteria for claimants. Third, employers often favoured paupers whose settlement lay in another parish, thinking that these were probably hard-working individuals. But although claiming settlement was difficult after 1834, the system was mitigated in several ways. One lay in the common practice of agricultural parishes agreeing to relieve workers who had migrated to towns: this encouraged urban employers to offer work to those willing to be mobile. Another lay in the statutory decision in 1846 to secure people from removal who were resident in a new parish for five years. The extent to which the Settlement Laws deterred labour mobility is difficult to determine. In theory, they should have done so because some people would be unwilling to uproot themselves to a parish where they could not claim poor relief in hard times. In practice, however, the lure of better wages, especially in industrial centres, and the arrangement described above for liaison between urban and rural parishes over claims, meant that many workers moved in search of pastures new.

The Poor Law Amendment Act sidestepped the problem of educating pauper children, but a number of assistant commissioners after 1834 were concerned about the demoralising effect of workhouses on the young. James Phillips Kay, later an important figure in elementary educational provision, was one such commissioner. He favoured the building of poor law district schools, large enough to accommodate hundreds of children, which would be situated away from workhouses and financed by the combined resources of several unions. Liverpool and Manchester were two major provincial cities where poor law schools were established. But the provision of poor law schools remained patchy throughout Britain by 1850, as Chapter 5 has shown.

Medical services under the New Poor Law experienced difficulties. Though many contemporaries welcomed the improvements in medical assistance under the new system, many medical attendants provided in some workhouses in the period 1834–42 were untrained. In 1842 a General Medical Order was issued whereby unions were divided into medical districts not exceeding 15,000 people and relieving officers were instructed to provide medical care for both indoor and outdoor paupers. This was a notable improvement, but it was beset by practical problems, including unions that underfunded the medical services, poorly trained nurses, inadequate facilities and grimy conditions.

The New Poor Law was not greeted everywhere with compliance. Poor law riots occurred between 1834 and 1837 in several counties. At the Milton union, near Rochester in Kent, an announcement that relief would henceforth be paid in kind rather than cash was greeted by angry crowds seizing the relieving officers' papers and pelting them with stones. Elsewhere, workers' demonstrations, jostling of officials and angry meetings took place. The winter of 1837–8 saw an upsurge of anti-poor law demonstrations in the industrial north. Oldham in Lancashire, a cotton mill town, was at the heart of these disturbances, but poor law guardian meetings were disrupted in other Yorkshire and Lancashire towns. In Wales opposition to the New Poor Law was common, notably in the **'Rebecca' riots** of 1843–4, during which many workhouses were attacked. In the industrial north and Wales, such opposition was fuelled by working-class radicalism, which spilled over into Chartism and complaints about factory conditions; but Tory opponents of political economy also expressed their dissatisfaction with the New Poor Law. Though some outbreaks led to disruption of public order, poor law commissioners and magistrates drew upon police detachments and military units to restore order.

Rebecca riots: A crusade against toll gates, and to a lesser extent against workhouses, that occurred in Wales in 1843–44. The protests were organised by the Children of Rebecca, named after the biblical precedent of Rebecca, daughter of Isaac.

THE POOR LAW IN SCOTLAND

Poor relief in Scotland was organised differently from in England and Wales. There was no statutory poor law north of the border until 1845, but provision for poor relief existed under the legal and administrative systems retained by Scotland after the Act of Union with England in 1707. Scottish poor relief was a voluntary system that relied on contributions from Presbyterian kirk parishioners, coordinated by the minister and his elders who discussed the granting of relief in a church court that included members of their congregation. It was supplemented from the late seventeenth century onwards by parish-based assessments that increased contributions to the poor rate. A Scottish Poor Law Act of 1579 specified that relief should be given to the 'poor, aged and impotent'. From 1752 onwards, legal decisions granted large landowners the control of the poor rate and its collection and distribution. This brought the Scottish relief system nearer to the parish-based provision common in England and Wales. The able-bodied poor did not receive relief in Scotland to the same extent as in England; nor was the Speenhamland system imitated. But unemployment for able-bodied workers was a less pressing problem in Scotland than in England: the largely rural population was much less numerous than its English counterpart; there was more subsistence agriculture in Scotland than south of the border; and the Scottish tradition of married men being hired for employment by the year kept the pool of underemployed labourers at an acceptably low level.

By the early Victorian era, pauperism was increasing in Scotland, not least because of employment difficulties that accompanied industrialisation in the Scottish lowlands. In addition, the breaking up of the Scottish kirk in 1843 and the creation of the Scottish Free Church meant that voluntary provision of poor relief under kirk control was no longer viable. In 1843 a Royal Commission investigated the problem of poverty in Scotland. Its recommendations were incorporated in a Poor Law Amendment Act of 1845, which ushered in a Scottish New Poor Law. This differed from its English counterpart of 1834 in that it did not centralise the administration of poor relief and avoided reorganising the 880 Scottish parishes into unions. It was a considerably more laissez-faire measure than Westminster had introduced for England and Wales 11 years earlier. Parochial boards were now appointed annually in each parish to raise and allocate poor relief. They were guided by a Board of Supervision based in Edinburgh. There was still no legal right to outdoor relief in Scotland, but in practice this proved the easiest and most economical way of relieving paupers. Workhouses, which had existed in Scotland before 1845, were maintained as institutions for the infirm and elderly. There was no deterrent principle hanging over the implementation of the New Poor Law in Scotland. Funds for the poor were increasingly collected as part of local taxes, but it was left to the discretion of the parochial boards whether to raise such monies on an individual's income or rateable property value. For these reasons, the introduction of the Scottish New Poor Law proved less contentious that its English counterpart.

7

Popular Protest

Riots, protests and popular demonstrations were regular occurrences in England, but early industrial Britain witnessed important changes in the organisation, scale and impact of disruption and violence on the streets. Thus, as Roy Porter commented succinctly, 'Georgian England was pockmarked with disorder' (Porter, 1982: 118). The truth of this statement is borne out by the fact that over 400 separate riots took place during the eighteenth century. The regularity of disturbances to peace and order is not surprising given that most of the population was unrepresented in Parliament and could not therefore register dissatisfaction with the existing political order at general elections. Moreover the economic changes that transformed early industrial Britain, along with their social consequences, caused many dislocations in people's lives that could lead to protest. This is true of the commercialisation of agriculture and the effects of parliamentary **enclosure**, and of the transition of labour into urban and factory locations, for in these spheres of activity legislation to protect workers' rights and employment was virtually non-existent before the early nineteenth century.

Enclosure: The privatisation of land by parliamentary statute, though sometimes private enclosure awards occurred. Usually the land concerned was previously subject to communal rights. Many schemes for parliamentary enclosure were passed from 1604 onwards. Parliamentary enclosure was particularly prominent during the reign of George III (1760–1820).

The variety of popular protest was fully evident in the century after 1750. The most common form of crowd action consisted of grain or bread riots. These accounted for over half the recorded crowd disturbances of the eighteenth century, and continued into the early decades of the nineteenth century. They were essentially protests against the hoarding of grain by dealers in times of bread shortages and high prices. They occurred throughout provincial Britain, mainly in small market towns. Turnpike riots began in the 1720s and continued through to the 1760s. These were demonstrations mainly by colliers protesting about the imposition of tolls on improved roads. They have been documented particularly for the coalmining areas on the east side of Bristol and in north-east Somerset. Toll gate riots also occurred in Wales in 1841. Anti-enclosure riots broke out during the eighteenth century in counties such as Northamptonshire, Leicestershire and Wiltshire, where much common land was privatised during the reigns of the first three Georges.

All the crowd demonstrations referred to so far directly stemmed from changing socio-economic conditions. Other riots had specific, individual causes. Frequent riots occurred at Tyburn, near Marble Arch, London, where public hangings were held regularly until the gallows there were pulled down in 1783. These disturbances arose because of the tussle over dead bodies by the families of the deceased, who wished to give their loved ones a decent, Christian burial, and apprentice barber-surgeons, who needed the bodies for anatomical dissection. Politics and religion, sometimes in combination, also triggered disturbances. Early Methodist preachers sometimes found their open-air meetings broken up by crowds opposed to their evangelical zeal. In 1753 the introduction of a parliamentary Bill to naturalise Jews in England led to some ugly anti-Semitic riots. The opposition to this measure helped to secure the repeal of the Jewish Naturalisation Act in December 1754. More common were protests against local militia. Widespread riots against the **Militia Act** occurred in numerous English counties in 1757, 1759, 1761, 1778 and 1796. The most serious of these riots was at Hexham, Northumberland, on 9 March 1761. A crowd of 5,000 people gathered to protest against the Militia Act under which poor people could be conscripted for three years whereas, owing to a balloting system, the rich could buy their way out of this fate. The crowd targeted the Moot Hall, where the ballot papers were kept. The North Yorkshire militia infiltrated the crowd and mowed down 52 people.

Roman Catholics were sometimes the targets of eighteenth-century crowds. Popular celebrations of Guy Fawkes day, representing the symbolic burning of Catholics, sometimes aroused violence. The introduction of a Catholic Relief Bill in Parliament in 1778 triggered serious outbreaks of public disorder. Violence against the measure occurred in Scotland in 1779. More important were the Gordon riots of 1780, in which the Protestant leader Lord George Gordon led an attack on the proposals to extend toleration to Papists. London was taken over by the mob. Newgate gaol was burned and the inmates set free. After five days of rioting, the King called in the troops. They were ordered to shoot by magistrates before the Riot Act was read. Hundreds of people were hurt, 285 died, and 25 were hanged for their role in the riots. The Gordon riots led to greater carnage than any other popular disturbance in eighteenth-century Britain.

If the Gordon riots were a mixture of religious and political protest, other demonstrations were more purely political. Prominent among such protests in the eighteenth century were demonstrations during the 1760s in London that accompanied the travails of the would-be reformer John Wilkes over the legal issues of his various arrests, the legitimacy of disallowing him from taking up his parliamentary seat and the reporting of parliamentary debates in the newspaper press. In the early nineteenth century crowd demonstrations with

Militia Act: Three Militia Acts were passed in the early years of Charles II's reign (1661–63). These statutes established the legality of the militia under the ultimate authority of the monarch. Militia service was carried out on a voluntary basis, except in times of threatened invasion when a ballot might be called, as happened with the highly unpopular Militia Act of 1757.

some political content (how much will be discussed below) included the Luddite attacks on machinery in the industrial north and Midlands in 1811 and 1812; the 'Peterloo' massacre of 1819 in Manchester; the agricultural 'Swing' riots throughout much of southern and eastern England in the early 1830s; the demonstrations over the Great Reform Bill in Nottingham, Bristol and other towns in late 1831; and various Chartist demonstrations throughout the country in the decade 1838–48.

The means available to tackle outbreaks of popular protest were relatively limited before c.1800 but they became more formidable in the first half of the nineteenth century. Most eighteenth-century disturbances were quashed by posses rounded up by local magistrates, sometimes with assistance from the local militia. There was no police force until the 'Peelers' (paid, uniformed police) were established in 1829, though they operated only within seven miles' radius of central London. Troops were sometimes called out to quell protests, occasionally en masse. Thus the Luddite disturbances were sufficiently disturbing to public order that over 11,000 troops were dispatched by the government to Yorkshire in the summer of 1812. But such a resort to the regular army to put down protests was uncommon.

Jacobite: A name given to supporters of the exiled James II, his son and grandson, based on their hereditary claim and divine right to the dual throne of England and Scotland and (after 1707) of Britain. The Jacobite movement existed mainly from the Glorious Revolution (1688) until the Battle of Culloden (1746).

A political machinery existed to deter crowd protesters. The passing of the Riot Act in 1714, resulting from **Jacobite** demonstrations against the newly installed Hanoverian monarchy, defined a riot as an outbreak of violence in a public place by three or more people. It was the tenth act passed in England since the fourteenth century for dealing with tumults, disturbances and riotous assemblies. It was the most famous of these statutes, and was not repealed until 1967. Carrying a severe penalty, it was put into action after a riot had begun, by magistrates reading out the proclamation included in the Act to a crowd. Those assembled then had 60 minutes to disperse, otherwise they were technically felons without benefit of clergy; in other words, they were guilty of a crime punishable by death. Some disturbances, such as the breaking of turnpike toll gates, were dealt with by making such offences punishable by seven years' transportation.

GRAIN RIOTS AND THE MORAL ECONOMY OF THE CROWD

Most crowd demonstrations were planned in advance and, contrary to the once prevailing view, few were examples of unthinking mob activity. For many eighteenth-century popular disturbances, the actions of the crowd display a 'moral economy' – an attempt to ensure that fair practices were followed against the encroachments of a market economy. This approach to crowd behaviour underscores the rational selection of targets by crowds, especially concerning food protests, whereby free market principles were stigmatised as illegitimate and opposed to community needs. Turnpike rioters exercised their moral economy by breaking down toll gates in protest at the implementation of what they regarded as a tax on their existing use-rights of the roads. Anti-enclosure demonstrators protested against the erosion of common rights on the land and the cutback in traditional perquisites. In these instances the moral economy of the crowd reflected a desire to maintain existing social practices and to safeguard against the introduction of more exploitative practices in small towns and the countryside. After each type of disturbance it was common for the crowds to disperse: they had achieved their limited objectives, and they had no ulterior programme of social or political reform. This pattern of protest can best be seen in food or grain riots, which were the quintessential example of unrest based upon notions of a moral economy.

Protests against food shortages were the most common type of popular disturbance in England and Wales from the late seventeenth century until the first two decades of the nineteenth century. Wheaten bread – a coarser foodstuff than most bread sold today – was the staple diet of the labouring poor in Georgian England and Wales, and so it is unsurprising to find that demonstrations occurred when grain supplies were low and prices were high. In many parts of the country high prices led to moves to stop the movement of grain in 1766, 1772, 1795–6 and 1800. Such protests happened after poor harvests and/or when dealers in grain hoarded supplies and waited for prices to rise further before selling **(Doc. 21, p. 140)**. Women were as much involved as men in these demonstrations. Grain riots occurred throughout the nation but especially in the Midlands and the West Country. There were waves of food riots in 1756–7, 1766–8, 1772–3, 1783, 1795–6, 1799–1801, 1812 and 1816. Grain riots occurred later, in 1847 and 1867 for example, but generally after the end of the Napoleonic Wars food crises were avoided when prices rose.

Food riots usually involved a cross-section of the populace in ports, market towns and trans-shipment points; they were more common in urban locations, therefore, than in the countryside. In 1795 and 1796, for instance, which were both bad years for harvests, at least 50 food protests occurred at small ports such as Wells-next-the-Sea, Seaford, Boston and Wisbech and at small market towns such as Hitchin and Potters Bar, from which grain was carried on the waterways to London. In these and similar places a non-agricultural population became connected with disturbances over food shortages. Few food riots occurred in London, as the metropolis was usually better able to market foodstuffs to its population because of a well-developed supply system.

The tactics of the protesters varied. In most cases, they gathered as a group to take sacks of grain from greedy market dealers. They then emptied the sacks, sold the grain at fairer prices, and returned the empty sacks to the dealers. Other tactics were to intimidate the hoarders of grain, to prevent the trans-shipment of grain along waterways, and to attack mills and granaries. Once these actions were taken, crowds dispersed: they were attempting to protect communities against exploitation, not protesting against the general inequalities of a society based on hierarchy and vertical divisions. Some protests were prolonged and involved bloodshed. In 1766–7 bitter food riots occurred, for instance in Somerset and Wiltshire, in which people were wounded and 3,000 troops were assembled to quell the protests. The role of deliberate agitation in the food riots is difficult to pinpoint, though individual protests were accompanied by 'levelling' threats and words of resentment against those better off.

These demonstrations were spontaneous protests against unfair practices. They stemmed from material deprivation. The grain riots appear to fit E. P. Thompson's notion of the moral economy of the crowd, for protesters had a collective sense of the injustice of withholding the basic food supply of the nation in difficult times (Thompson, 1991). Nevertheless, one difficulty with this interpretation of bread protests is that they occurred invariably in the Midlands and the West Country, as already mentioned, but high prices and grain shortages were usually a national phenomenon. Why therefore grain riots broke out in some regional areas rather than others is difficult to explain, because presumably a moral economy was characteristic of pre-industrial life throughout the country. Overall, however, food protests, though widespread, were a transient phenomenon, with no political or revolutionary agenda.

WILKES AND LIBERTY

Wilkes and Liberty: The famous chant of the British and American supporters of the would-be political reformer John Wilkes in the decade after 1763. There were 'Wilkes and Liberty' petitions, banners and teacups.

Compared with bread riots, outbreaks of public disorder associated with the maverick politician and journalist John Wilkes had a much more political hue. Between 1763, when Wilkes came to national attention while MP for Aylesbury, and 1772, when the political interest he had aroused had subsided, London and parts of urban provincial England witnessed a number of **'Wilkes and Liberty'** protests. The issues surrounding Wilkes's rise to national political prominence are complex. Briefly, he took it upon himself, on separate occasions, to attack the monarchy over the handling of the peace negotiations at the end of the Seven Years War; to criticise the use of **general warrants** to arrest him on a charge of seditious libel; and to campaign against the banning of the reporting of parliamentary debates in the press. These were all controversial public issues. It was dangerous practice for an MP to criticise the monarchy, albeit under Wilkes's journalistic hat in his paper the *North Briton*. Whether a general warrant was an acceptable method for securing an arrest led to much public debate. The attempt to suppress reporting of Parliament's deliberations, especially at a sensitive time in Anglo-American relations, raised cries against government secrecy and the attempt to suppress the freedom of the press.

Wilkes's supporters organised protests on his behalf when he was imprisoned in the Tower of London in 1763 and when he returned from the continent after five years' exile in 1768 and attempted to re-enter Parliament in several by-elections in the Middlesex constituency while still declared an outlaw. The presence of Wilkes in the metropolis and during the by-elections led to popular disorder, attacks on metropolitan property, and a massacre outside the King's Bench prison, London, on 10 May 1768, in which 10 or 12 rioters were killed by grenadiers firing on them. 'Wilkes and Liberty' crowds were well organised and a threat to public order in London. Wilkes's supporters, including many middling tradesmen and petty artisans, also challenged the government in print and through speeches and petitions. They demonstrated that political life outside the confines of Westminster politics was vigorous and something with which to be reckoned. They displayed an ideological interest in parliamentary reform that some historians have seen as a first step towards the growth of political democracy.

REVOLUTIONARY PROTEST?

The movement for parliamentary reform revived for a few years after 1779, when the **Yorkshire Association** campaigned for more equal electoral representation of the population and for shorter Parliaments. But the momentum of the campaign faded away after a moderate measure for parliamentary reform foundered in April 1785. The impetus for political reform revived considerably, however, in the early 1790s under the influence of French revolutionary notions of liberty, equality and freedom. The formation of various radical groups was a feature of these years. The most prominent such group was the **London Corresponding Society (LCS)**, founded in 1792 and led by the shoemaker Thomas Hardy, but there were various provincial groups such as the Sheffield Society for Constitutional Information that also advocated annual Parliaments and universal manhood suffrage (i.e. the right of

General warrants: Warrants issued for the arrest of unspecified persons under the provisions of the Licensing Act of 1662 for use against the authors, publishers and distributors of seditious publications. They became controversial in the years 1763–65 when they were issued against those responsible for publishing issue no. 45 of Wilkes's weekly paper the *North Briton*, which attacked the King's speech to Parliament.

Yorkshire Association: Formed in 1779 with the aim of shortening Parliaments and campaigning for a more equal representation of the people at general elections. The Association promoted economic reform, the addition of an extra 100 county MPs, and triennial Parliaments. It ceased activity in April 1785 without achieving its objectives.

London Corresponding Society (LCS): Formed in January 1792 to promote the cause of universal manhood suffrage and annual Parliaments and to maintain links with other corresponding societies. Its founder was Thomas Hardy, a shoemaker. Most members were artisans and working men. The Society was suppressed by government statute in July 1799.

every adult male to vote at general elections). Some radicals, albeit a minority, pressed for a more thoroughgoing change in British constitutional affairs by veering towards republicanism. Tom Paine's *The Rights of Man* (1792) was particularly influential in spreading this message. It argued in favour of anticlericalism, egalitarianism and redistributive taxation to promote public education and welfare, and sold a quarter of a million copies within a year of its publication.

The resurgence of political radicalism, inspired by Jacobinism, was countered by loyalist associations and by 'Church and King' riots in Birmingham in 1791 and Manchester in 1792 that supported a monarchical society in which church and state were constitutionally intertwined. The **Habeas Corpus Act** was suspended temporarily in 1794, and then again in 1798. At the end of 1795 the Younger Pitt's government passed the Seditious Meetings Act and the Treasonable and Seditious Practices Act, which respectively restricted public meetings and political lectures and extended the law of treason to spoken and written words. This so-called 'reign of terror' intimidated radicals, but in practice only a handful of people were sentenced under the **'Gagging' Acts**. Most prosecutions were carried out under different legislation relating to sedition and seditious libel. Once again, however, there were few prosecutions; the threat was more significant. Nevertheless, the suppression of potentially radical groups continued. The LCS was banned by law in 1799. The government, worried by workers combining to form trade unions, passed the Combination Acts in 1799 and 1800 to stem the tide of working-class activism (**Doc. 22, p. 141**).

Though political radicalism in Britain was inspired by the French Revolution, it is questionable how far protest in Britain was revolutionary in intent or practice. Elie Halévy argued in *A History of the English People in 1815* (1913) that the spread of nonconformist values among the workforce, and specifically the impact of Methodist preaching and teaching, was sufficient to take the sting out of radical protest in these years. His views have already been discussed and evaluated in Chapter 4. A good many historians in the English empirical tradition have identified numerous riots, disturbances, even threats of revolution, in the half-century after 1789, but have not discerned anything more than a rudimentary revolutionary threat that reared its head on sporadic occasions before fading away or being dealt with effectively by the forces of law and order. One historian has gone so far as to dismiss notions of a possible British revolution in the late eighteenth and early nineteenth centuries as '*la révolution manquée*' – something that did not happen and stood no chance of occurring other than in the minds of left-wing historians (Hartwell, 1984). E. P. Thompson provided the most sustained analysis that opposes this view. He argued that the English working class was 'made' in the period 1790–1832 and that a continuous underground radical

Habeas corpus: A Latin phrase meaning 'you have the body'. This was the common law writ that could obtain the release of those imprisoned without charge or not brought to trial. A Habeas Corpus Act of 1679 defined its use. Parliament temporarily suspended the Act in times of emergency in 1715, 1794 and 1817.

'Gagging' Acts: The six Acts passed in 1819 after the Peterloo Massacre. They allowed magistrates to search premises for arms; permitted seizure of seditious writings; prohibited meetings of more than 50 people; prevented military drilling; increased newspaper duties; and accelerated judicial proceedings.

tradition, often with revolutionary intent, survived throughout a period of largely Tory rule and many attempts to suppress radicalism. For Thompson and his followers, Britain came near to revolution during the Great Reform Bill crisis in 1830–32. This could be attributed to the growth to maturity of a working-class consciousness about the marginal position of most labourers in politics and society under the 'Old Corruption' (the unreformed political and ecclesiastical system) of the late Hanoverian period (Thompson, 1963). The extent to which a radical tradition persisted, and the degree to which working-class protest became politicised, can be traced by considering popular protest from the Luddites through to the Chartists.

THE LUDDITES

Protests against the introduction of machinery into the textile industries occurred from the 1770s onwards in the West Country woollen industry. Riots occurred at Shepton Mallet, Somerset, in July 1776 over the introduction of machinery. Frome, in the same county, experienced machine breaking in December 1797. And between April and August 1802 shearmen's riots occurred in Wiltshire in opposition to the introduction of gig-mills. These protests were all put down. A more widespread movement against new technology occurred with the Luddite movement just after the turn of the nineteenth century. Luddism represented a significant transitional point in the history of popular demonstrations because it combined socio-economic protest with an element of political opposition to the government and was organised on a widespread scale in the East Midlands and north of England. Sustained protest on a regional scale was a relatively new occurrence. Named after the mythical Ned Ludd, celebrated in popular ballads of the time, the Luddite attacks comprised a spate of machine breaking in the textile industries in 1811 and 1812, though similar incidents occurred sporadically down to 1816.

Luddite attacks occurred for the most part in three counties – Lancashire, Yorkshire and Nottinghamshire. They were connected with the installation of machinery into textile production in factories and with the introduction of new work practices. Specifically, the protesters targeted the cotton spinning machines in the south Lancashire cotton mills, the power looms in woollen mills in Yorkshire's West Riding, and the stocking frames in the Nottinghamshire hosiery industry. Groups of textile workers in disguise would meet under cover of darkness, break and enter industrial premises, and sabotage the machinery. In Yorkshire and Lancashire this was sometimes carried out with large sledgehammers. In Nottinghamshire Luddite attacks targeted the jackwires on machines: these were pulled out and all the jacks fell to the floor to make machines inoperable. Such attacks were well co-ordinated and taken as serious industrial disruptions by local manufacturers and magistrates. The best-known single incident was an attack by over 100 Luddites after nightfall on Rawfolds mill near Huddersfield, Yorkshire, in April 1812, after which the mill owner was shot dead. Spies were used by local magistrates to arrest those guilty. Three ringleaders were executed at York Castle in January 1813, by which time the Luddite rising in Yorkshire was over.

The Luddites were protesting partly at new technology in the textile industries and the potential harm to their livelihoods through the installation of labour-saving machinery. But they had more specific concerns about the erosion of their handicraft skills through what they regarded as the poorer quality clothing produced by the new machines. For instance, the Notting-hamshire Luddites protested about the loss of skills and job satisfaction that occurred with the introduction of knitting frame machinery. Whereas previ-ously handicraft framework knitters had made stockings from start to finish themselves, the new techniques required them to make pieces of fabric and then see them taken away to be cut up and fashioned into garments else-where. Yorkshire and Lancashire Luddites had similar reservations about removing their skilled labour from the entire process of making a piece of clothing. Thus Yorkshire croppers were angry that their skill in using heavy shears and weights to press the blade of their handicraft cropping imple-ments – and thereby imparting a close finish to the cloth – was being eroded by mechanical cropping. An anonymous threatening letter from Ned Ludd warned manufacturers of Luddite solidarity in an attempt to redress the situation (**Doc. 23, p. 142**). Luddite protests were thus as much about the cultural changes involved in deskilling and feelings of self-worth in employ-ment as about loss of earnings through being out-competed by machine technology.

The degree to which the Luddites were more than industrial protesters has long been debated. Malcolm Thomis and Peter Holt considered that the movement was 'more a spasm in the death throes of declining trades than a birth pang of revolution' (Thomis and Holt, 1977: 33). At the other extreme lies the verdict of E. P. Thompson: 'Luddism was *a quasi-insurrectionary* movement, which continually trembled on the edge of ulterior revolutionary objectives' (Thompson, 1963: 553). These interpretations come from com-pletely opposite perspectives, but they both can be modified. In Notting-hamshire Luddism largely seems to have been an industrial movement, for there is little evidence of any ulterior political motivation and organisation: machine breakers worried at the erosion of handicraft skills used the means at their disposal to register their dissent. In that sense, Nottinghamshire Luddism could be interpreted as a backward-looking movement, attempting to preserve the traditions of the past. In south Lancashire and the West Riding of Yorkshire evidence has been found of secret oath-taking, arms-holding and rudimentary plans for an uprising against the government. Thus some Luddites in those counties were politically motivated. How far their plans for insurrection were coordinated or realisable is nevertheless doubtful. There is a further problem, concerning the primary evidence on these clandestine activities. Much documentary material on Luddite political motivation is taken from the reports of spies employed by the Home Office. Thompson felt that such evidence could be taken at face value; other historians have regarded it with more circumspection.

For these reasons, Luddism should be regarded as mainly an industrial form of protest that shook the establishment. It was a movement with political concerns, but these were never developed as fully as the machine breakers hoped. Luddite protests involved virtually no attacks on government buildings, courthouses or barracks. Luddism was too geographically isolated from London to offer an effective challenge to the government of the day. Furthermore, there is no evidence of links between Luddite leaders and followers in Nottinghamshire, Lancashire and Yorkshire; protesters stayed within the bounds of their own counties. Yet Luddism was important for showing the depth of contemporary concern about fundamental changes in work practices in a period of great social change, and for demonstrating the fears of the ruling orders in suppressing the movement.

FROM LUDDISM TO THE REFORM BILL RIOTS

Large crowd protests occurred several times in the years of difficult social and economic transition after Waterloo, when unemployment was high, several harvests failed and a reactionary Tory government under Lord Liverpool consolidated protectionism in the form of the **Corn Law** (1815). During the four years after 1815 large open-air crowd gatherings became frequent and the main tenets of parliamentary reform were aired by gifted orators such as Henry Hunt. The disorder that accompanied the Spa Fields riots in London in December 1816, when radicals attempted to seize the Tower of London and the Bank of England, and the mobbing of the Prince Regent's coach as he travelled from the state opening of Parliament in January 1817, increased government uneasiness. The putative revolt staged for Pentrich, Derbyshire, six months later, though it turned out to be a fiasco, with poor leadership, deserting followers and inadequate planning and execution, showed that some working-class men were willing to protest without middle-class support.

Corn Laws: Protective duties on corn were first introduced in 1804. The Corn Laws refer to two protectionist measures: the Corn Law of 1815, which prevented the import of foreign grain until the domestic price reached 80 shillings per quarter, and another Corn Law of 1828, which introduced a sliding scale of tariffs. Both statutes were intended to protect the landed interest, following the collapse of artificially high grain prices after the end of the French Revolutionary and Napoleonic Wars.

Popular protest was becoming more regular and organised on a larger scale. The mêlée at the large open-air meeting at St Peter's Fields, Manchester, on 16 August 1819, remembered as the 'Peterloo' massacre, was a symbolic occasion when demands for parliamentary reform were made and resisted by local authorities. Nearly 60,000 people were present at the rally. The magistrates sought to arrest the leading speaker, 'Orator' Henry Hunt, and those with him on the platform. They ordered the Manchester Yeomanry Cavalry to carry out the arrest. This volunteer regiment was very unpopular because it was largely recruited from the sons of factory owners. The cavalry got stuck and so the magistrates sent in a regular cavalry unit to rescue the volunteer regiment. Objects were thrown and sabres were used. Many were injured and 11 people were hacked or crushed to death. One special constable's eyewitness account dwelt on the presence of armed radicals and the chaos of the occasion (Doc. 24, p. 143). The banning of crowd meetings under the 'Gag' Acts of 1819 temporarily quietened down the political atmosphere by introducing punitive measures against radical meetings, literature and arms. The transition to Liberal-Tory measures after 1822 signalled the abandonment of repressive measures and helped to usher in a few years of quiescence. Public protests dampened down quickly and the government was able to repeal the Combination Acts in 1824 and 1825.

The repeal of the Test and Corporation Acts in 1828 and the arrival of Catholic emancipation the following year eliminated the discrimination that had long existed against nonconformists and Roman Catholics in British public life. Henceforth Dissenters and Catholics could vote at general elections and hold government office; they could also enter Oxford and Cambridge universities. These successful reform campaigns fed into the demands for parliamentary reform. When the Whigs came to power under Earl Grey in 1830 – after decades in the political wilderness – they placed parliamentary reform at the top of their political agenda. The tortuous passage of three Reform Bills through Parliament between late 1830 and the early summer of 1832 led to several sets of riots that were important outbreaks of public disorder. In October 1831 crowds frustrated at the delay in the handling of parliamentary reform in the Lords, where the Reform Bill was thrown out by 41 votes, burned down the council chambers in Bristol and damaged Nottingham Castle, as well as perpetrating outbreaks of violence in other parts of the provinces. In May 1832, when Grey's government resigned while the Lords once again prevaricated over parliamentary reform, anarchy broke out on London's streets for a month and contemporaries feared a revolution was at hand.

We will never know just how near Britain was to revolution during the May days of 1832. E. P. Thompson saw these outbreaks as the culmination of an underground tradition of political radicalism stemming back to the ideals of the French Revolution. He particularly underscored Francis Place's role in these organised protests (Thompson, 1963). This interpretation stretches the potential for revolution too far, though the seriousness of the crowd protests is not in question. Indeed, the period 1830–32 witnessed a number of separate outbreaks of collective disorder in Britain that were unprecedented in scale. Besides the Reform Bill riots there were the **'Swing' riots** that involved rural incendiarism in southern and eastern English counties by agricultural workers protesting against the introduction of machinery into harvesting, seen as a direct threat to their livelihoods **(Doc. 25, p. 145)**. These outbreaks of violence occurred during the late summer and autumn of 1830 and in the summer of 1831. Fears of crowd disturbances by the authorities were exacerbated by the wave of political revolutions that broke out in France, Belgium and other parts of Europe in 1830, which threatened to spread a radical message among the British populace.

Swing riots: Named after the mythical Captain Swing, whose name was often appended to threatening letters, these were riots that occurred throughout much of rural southern and eastern England in 1830–31. The main tactic of the protesters lay in the breaking up of threshing machines.

CHARTISM

The last major crowd demonstrations in the generation before the mid-nineteenth century were associated with the Chartists. These were mainly working-class activists who supported the drive to persuade Parliament to adopt the 'People's Charter'. Stimulated by the radicalism of such groups as the **Birmingham Political Union**, already flourishing in the period of the Reform Bill riots, and the London Working Men's Association, founded in 1836, this Charter was launched at a mass rally held in Birmingham on 6 August 1838. It called for changes that radicals had long proposed – political rights for working men, something that the 1832 Reform Act had failed to deliver. The People's Charter therefore had six main aims: universal manhood suffrage, the payment of MPs, the abolition of property qualifications for voting, the holding of secret ballots at general elections, annual Parliaments and equal electoral districts. The campaigns to secure these rights were prominent over a decade down to 1848, when Chartism peaked and then experienced an anticlimax from which it never recovered.

Birmingham Political Union (BPU): Founded in 1830 by Thomas Attwood, Member of Parliament for Birmingham between 1832 and 1839. The BPU agitated for parliamentary reform. In April 1837 the BPU drew up a National Petition calling for sweeping changes in the economy and system of parliamentary representation.

Chartism was a more sustained protest movement than any previous popular disturbances discussed in this chapter. This reflected the importance of the political aims embodied in the People's Charter and the sense of grievance felt by many working men who were excluded from the political process. Women also participated extensively in Chartist associations, though they sometimes found themselves regarded as subaltern activists in a masculine cause. Chartism found its main roots among urban and industrial communities. South Lancashire, the West Riding of Yorkshire, lowland

Scotland, the mining valleys of South Wales, the Potteries, Tyneside, Leicester, Coventry, Birmingham and the East End of London were all prominent areas of Chartist activity.

There were many regional and local variations in Chartism but also some common characteristics. One binding thread was a common Chartist culture in which political education was spread among working men and women at lectures, evening meetings held in town halls and mechanics' institutes, along with large open-air camp rallies that imitated the gatherings of Primitive Methodists. These open-air gatherings frequently brought together thousands of people; they became the main means through which the oral culture of radical politics spread. Sometimes they were held as torchlight processions after dark. At these venues Chartists shared a secular fellowship, a common purpose, and a commitment to the politicisation of working-class people. In some ways, the cultural characteristics of Chartism were its most lasting legacy.

Chartists devoted much time to petitioning Parliament to secure their Charter. They were involved in three famous national Charter campaigns in which a mass petition was presented at Westminster. On each occasion – in 1839, 1842 and 1848 – their high hopes led to failure: each of the petitions, despite thousands of signatures, was rejected by the Commons overwhelmingly and the People's Charter thereby remained an ideal rather than a reality. Unfavourable reaction to these disappointments was unsurprising given the sheer number of people who signed the petitions: in 1842 the signatories amounted to a third of the adult population (Chase, 2007: 205). Strikes and disturbances after each failure were occasionally serious, as in the fracas between Chartists and the London Metropolitan Police in Birmingham's Bull Ring in July 1839 and in the disturbances in London over the summer of 1848. But all these disorderly events were quashed by the forces of law and order. After the debacle of the third petition, Chartism slumped irreversibly in its support. Though pockets of Chartist activity still existed by the early 1850s, it was a movement that had faded away by the later part of that decade. The Chartists never achieved any of their six points during the period when they were active. Yet their objectives, save for annual Parliaments and equal electoral districts, eventually became accepted as part of modern parliamentary democracy.

The failure of Chartism as a movement of political protest in its own time lay partly in the excessive amount of energy poured into the three petition campaigns and partly in the internal divisions and contradictions among its leaders and members. Each of the three national petitioning campaigns was hampered by the fact that there were no Chartist MPs, and few Chartist sympathisers, in the reformed House of Commons who were prepared to liaise with the leaders over petitioning. Support within Parliament was necessary and was singularly lacking. In addition, spurious signatures were desperately added to the petitions, particularly that of 1848, which included the names of the Duke of Wellington and Queen Victoria. The false names appended to the Chartist petitions undermined their credibility.

The Chartists were effective at carrying out other forms of written propaganda, writing many tracts, pamphlets and broadsides. They secured extensive coverage in the Leeds radical newspaper the *Northern Star*, which became Chartism's main printed form of propaganda in northern industrial communities. This paper sold around 10,000 weekly copies by January 1838 (Chase, 2007: 16–17). But the leadership of the movement became fragmented. Indeed, after the failure of the second national petition in 1842 the main Chartist leaders tended to follow their own hobby horses. William Lovett emphasised the educational aspects of Chartism, thinking that franchise reform was only one aim of Chartism and that of at least equal significance was the creation of self-instruction among the working classes through disseminating political knowledge. Feargus O'Connor, an Irish firebrand of the movement, advocated a Land Plan, whereby funds would be used to buy allotments that could then be rented out to Chartists as individual tenancies at a yearly rate for a certain number of acres. This would produce profits that could be used to buy more land and spread the scheme further. It was implemented for six years from 1845 to 1851 but it faced many difficulties **(Doc. 26, p. 145)**. The Land Plan collapsed after fellow Chartists attacked it as detracting from the battle for political rights. Robert Lowery and Henry Vincent took up the cause of temperance and teetotalism, arguing that working class people who drank excessively did not deserve the right to vote. Bronterre O'Brien became attracted to socialism. Other Chartist leaders, especially in Scotland, became convinced that the movement's focus should be Christianity. This splintering of Chartism diffused the overall impact of the movement politically. Chartism was, in the famous words of Joseph Rayner Stephens, a 'knife and fork question, a bread and cheese question' – a movement that thrived when people were hungry (quoted in Jones, 1975: 121). Thus support for Chartism flourished in urban and industrial areas during hard times, such as in 1842 when there was widespread unemployment and a poor harvest, and correspondingly faded when better economic conditions prevailed.

The majority of Chartists avoided violence but some Chartist protesters resorted to intimidation on the streets to further their cause. Moral-force Chartists were distinct from those prepared to countenance physical force. Birmingham's Bull Ring, in the city centre, experienced riots associated with Chartists on 4 July 1839. The meeting and the disorder were a direct reaction to large outdoor gatherings being banned by the government earlier that year. A posse of police cleared away the protesters. In November 1839 serious rioting broke out in Newport, Monmouthshire, when John Frost led 3,000 colliers on a march to set free local Chartists imprisoned there. The local authorities knew little of the preparations for this rising. Nevertheless, local soldiers were dispatched to disperse the crowd, with the result that 24 people were killed, 125 arrested and 21 charged with high treason. Chartist agitation, using physical force, occurred in Bradford, Yorkshire in early 1840 **(Doc. 27, p. 146)**. Rioting in Lancashire and Cheshire in poor economic times in the autumn of 1842 led to widespread 'plug' riots in which Chartists were involved. These demonstrations were so-called because the protesters removed the boiler plugs from steam machinery, thereby sabotaging its use. The 'plug' riots were followed by a wave of strikes that affected 14 English counties, 8 Scottish counties and 1 Welsh county. Many Chartists were arrested and some of their leaders transported.

The last wave of violence associated with Chartism came in the spring of 1848 when crowds in London ran amok in some streets and public places. This caused serious problems for metropolitan order. It was the first time that Chartist protest had disrupted London's security in a significant way and the protests continued at intervals for several months. But the momentum of the Chartist demonstrations faded after the failure of the third national petition. Police were deployed in sufficient numbers to quell the disturbances. Political agitators among the Chartists, with support from Irish radicals and stimulated by the spread of republicanism throughout many European countries in 1848, gave the protests a potential for revolutionary activity, but this was never broadly based enough or sufficiently well coordinated to cause lasting problems for the government of the day.

8

Crime, Justice and Punishment

rime was a constant concern to the propertied classes and the law-makers of early industrial Britain. Certain parts of the nation, notably mining and forested areas, appeared to operate as lawless areas where crime flourished beyond the reach of effective controls. Such was the case in Wychwood forest, Oxfordshire, and in the coalmines in the Kingswood area, east of Bristol. Over time, apprehensions about the spread of crime increased. The burgeoning British population after *c*.1740 and the gradual redistribution of people from the countryside to towns and from rural employment to urban trades was accompanied by occasional crime waves that struck fear into all of society, notably when men were demobilised after major wars and struggling to find employment. The circulation of republican and libertarian ideas in the French Revolution made many middle-class people fear that criminality was increasing: if it were not contained, it would spread throughout the lower orders to foment antagonism against the status quo. By 1845 Friedrich Engels wrote that 'the incidence of crime has increased with the growth of the working-class population and there is more crime in Britain than in any other country in the world' (quoted in Philips, 1993: 158). This opinion is obviously unverifiable but it is one among many contemporary comments drawing attention to the growth of offences against the law in the first half of the nineteenth century.

There was considerable debate during the long eighteenth century about the nature of certain crimes and whether they deserved the stigma attached to them. These discussions centred on innumerable types of theft, the most common form of serious crime. Social crimes were often seen by the labouring poor as morally acceptable practices, but the propertied classes took a dim view of property appropriation. Some people regarded pilfering from work as a perk of the job; lawmakers, on the other hand, categorised the practice as embezzlement. Poaching was condoned by many rural dwellers as a legitimate way of controlling vermin, but to many farmers it was an illegal encroachment on their property **(Doc. 28, p. 147)**. Smuggling seemed to some a way of bypassing excessive customs duties on foreign wines, brandy and tobacco, but to law enforcers it was an illegal way of evading lawful duties. Despite these differences over the legitimacy of certain crimes, however, there seems to have been a general consensus that most crimes against property were reprehensible and anti-social.

Most prosecuted crime dealt with offences against property. Throughout England and Wales over 80 per cent of indictable committals in the century after 1750 consisted of non-violent offences against property. Serious crimes against the person (rape, murder, manslaughter, infanticide) comprised no more than 15 per cent of committals. The incidence of crime, evidenced by indictments, appears to have risen considerably after the end of most wars: demobilisation usually brought an increase in crime and sentencing in court. The level of capital crimes dropped away significantly when conflicts began and young men were recruited into the armed forces, but during wars women comprised a larger share of those indicted. The absence of national statistics on crime in the eighteenth century makes it impossible to determine whether accusations of rising crime levels were anything more than exaggerated contemporary fears. Where these seemed to grow, in the second half of the century, they probably reflected a general rise in the population plus more prosecutions for theft. An increasing proportion of people brought to court were prosecuted in the early nineteenth century: between 1805 and 1842 figures for committal of indictable offences show a fourfold increase.

The law provided various ways of tackling crime and meting out justice. Since the Glorious Revolution of 1689 English people had firmly believed their freedom was protected under the rule of law. The common law, with its emphasis on the jury system, served as the cornerstone of this belief. But laws were enacted by those in possession of land and money, and it is hardly surprising therefore that the criminal law expanded significantly in early industrial Britain to tackle crimes against property. The most notorious aspect of this expansion came with the rise of capital crimes. Between c.1688 and 1820 more and more offences punishable by death were added to what

Bloody Code: A term applied by historians to the series of criminal statutes enacted by eighteenth-century British Parliaments, many of which prescribed the death penalty. There were over 200 capital statutes by the end of the eighteenth century.

became known as the '**Bloody Code**'. Many such crimes already existed under common law, but they were now explicitly added to the statute books. Over 150 such offences were made capital crimes in that period, including over 50 at one fell swoop with the Waltham Black Act (1723), ostensibly aimed at poaching from the royal forests. It was not until the 1820s that many capital offences were repealed by various statutes dealing with obsolete laws, something that was influenced by the reprieve of so many capital offenders. The Criminal Justice Act of 1827 abolished 'benefit of clergy', a hangover from the ecclesiastical court of the sixteenth century that was extended to people who could demonstrate basic literacy. In so doing, the statute restricted the death penalty to felonies from which benefit of clergy had previously been excluded. The Whig governments of the 1830s continued to reduce the number of capital crimes, taking account of the findings of a Royal Commission on the Criminal Law. By 1841 this resulted in the death penalty being used almost solely for those convicted of murder.

There was a general expansion in the inclusion of non-capital crimes on the statute book in early industrial Britain, especially those dealing with summary jurisdiction. Most non-capital crimes consisted of grand larceny (defined as theft of goods worth more than 39 shillings) and petty larceny (stealing goods worth less than that amount). The distinction between the two types of larceny was abolished in 1827 and replaced with a new offence called simple larceny. Larcenists could be pickpockets, livestock stealers, game poachers, thieves taking clothes, food, coal and industrial goods, and perpetrators of other crimes against property. A summary of one trial involving a pickpocket at the Old Bailey illustrates how courts handled such cases (**Doc. 29, p. 148**).

Along with the changes in statute law concerning crimes came new ideas about punishment and increased means of law enforcement. By 1850 there were more laws against property crimes, a wider range of criminal punishments, and more direct and effective policing of communities compared with a century before. This chapter considers the changes occurring in crime, justice and punishment in early industrial Britain.

THE OPERATION OF THE LAW

The operation of the law was channelled through the work of barristers, attorneys (i.e. solicitors), magistrates and judges, as well as a host of litigants, plaintiffs, defendants, clerks and witnesses operating via various courts. Three common law courts regularly met at Westminster Hall, London; these were the courts of **Common Pleas**, King's Bench and **Exchequer of Pleas**. The Court of Chancery exercised a supervisory function over these courts. There were other courts such as Courts of Requests, which mainly dealt with widows seeking pensions, and various ecclesiastical courts, which frequently heard matrimonial disputes. Throughout Britain quarter sessions and assizes were the focal point of most legal sittings. Quarter sessions, held four times a year and presided over by **Justices of the Peace (JPs)**, dealt with most functions of local government. Assize courts, held twice a year in most county towns, were the main link between central and local government. Judges dispatched to the provinces from Westminster issued sentences at the assizes, which were divided into regional districts. They dealt with more serious crimes than quarter sessions. It was therefore at assizes that

Common Pleas: The Court of Common Pleas was a common law court that generally met at Westminster. Its business came to centre on disputes between private individuals and on the registration of land transactions.

Exchequer of Pleas: The oldest of the common law courts. Originally intended to adjudicate matters pertaining to the royal revenue, its case load increased in the seventeenth and eighteenth centuries in common law and equity by accepting fictitious pleas of suitors that they were debtors of the crown.

Justices of the Peace (JPs): The most important officers in local government from the fourteenth to the nineteenth centuries. They presided at quarter sessions and dealt with minor charges before the law. They were also involved with the poor relief system.

consideration of murder, rape, burglary, counterfeiting and grand larceny took place.

The ideological purposes of the law in eighteenth-century England have been seen as displaying majesty, highlighting terror and granting mercy. Administering criminal justice thereby had a class dimension, for it involved the imposition of a code worked out by lawyers and property owners that was deemed appropriate for legal dealings with the unpropertied. Majesty operated through the status and elevation of the legal profession, meeting in the ancient law courts, using a technical language, dressed in an intimidating garb. The emphasis on terror lay in capital punishment and the use of the gallows for serious crime. Mercy, however, was equally in evidence through the discretionary power of judges and magistrates to offer lesser sentences by commuting crimes or offering pardons. The interaction of the three elements of majesty, terror and mercy gave the law a legitimating power. People accepted the law as the arbiter of justice in the state; terror through the death penalty symbolised the ultimate deterrent to wrongdoing; mercy showed the human side of decision making in dealing with individual cases (Hay, 1975). The strong discretionary element in the operation of justice placed much emphasis on the legal profession's assessment of the character and previous criminal record of those brought before the courts. Only with changes to the criminal law and police reform from the 1820s onwards was judicial discretion curtailed.

Before 1750 capital crimes were dealt with either by public hangings or, after the introduction of the Transportation Act (1718), by banishment from Britain. Whether those found guilty of capital offences were strung up at the gallows or sentenced to exile as convicts lay at the discretion of judges. Some judges meted out punishments with deterrence in mind; others preferred more reformative measures. Royal pardons or commutations to lesser sentences, however, were common: in 24 years between 1749 and 1799 over half of those convicted of capital crimes in London and Middlesex were reprieved. For non-capital crimes against property, there were various punishments in the early eighteenth century: some offenders were transported, some received physical punishment and others were placed in different types of gaols. Relatively few convicted felons received sentences of permanent imprisonment before the later eighteenth century: existing gaols were too small to accommodate them and there was no general acceptance that prisons were a solution to crime. Already by c.1775 this distribution of punishments was beginning to change, nonetheless, and a transformation in modes of punishment occurred down to the middle of the nineteenth century. The main changes concerned the erosion, but not the eradication, of physical punishment; the growth of transportation as a secondary form of punishment; and the evolution of prisons as an attempted solution to criminal behaviour.

PROSECUTION

Throughout the century after 1750 prosecution continued to be undertaken largely by victims against the perpetrators of crimes or, less commonly, by individuals selected to act on behalf of victims. Therefore prosecution was essentially a matter of private initiative. Because the process of the law was often long-drawn-out, with decisions reached slowly, and because the costs in detecting offenders and paying lawyers' fees were high, a great many crimes were never brought before the courts: victims sometimes did not have the patience, the time, or the funds to do so. Many people let matters drop or sought private retribution or out-of-court financial settlements. A study of crime in Essex from 1740 to 1820 has concluded that possibly under 10 per cent of identifiable crimes led to prosecution (King, 2000). Parish constables could search for perpetrators of crimes in local communities but they were often reluctant to do so since they received no salary and had to claim back expenses made from their own pocket. Moreover, people in Georgian Britain regarded active prosecutors as a necessary evil; they soon took umbrage against magistrates and constables who intervened too zealously in local, private matters. Unless offences were seriously aimed at the person, it was an unspoken rule that constables and bailiffs did not search for crime or criminal activity unless a citizen asked them to do so. Magistrates played an important intermediary role in prosecutions. They exercised summary jurisdiction, awarding modest penalties; they presided at petty sessions or quarter sessions; and they referred cases to a higher court for trial. Sometimes they settled disputes between criminals and victims by threats, correspondence and bringing parties together to sort out difficulties without charges being pressed.

In early industrial Britain various acts were passed to make prosecution more feasible for victims of crime. An act of 1778 gave an allowance to all prosecutors and witnesses in felony prosecutions, irrespective of whether a conviction resulted. A statute of 1818 extended this allowance in felony cases to prosecutors and witnesses for all expenses involved, including those incurred in bringing the case to court. A law of 1826 extended the allowance further for felony prosecutions. In each case prosecutors had to submit a claim for reimbursement from a court, however, and the full amount requested was not always paid. Besides these statutes, local prosecution associations became widespread from about 1780 onwards, though they originated around a century before. Consisting of between 20 and 50 members, there were over a thousand of these associations by the time of the Younger Pitt. They clubbed together to pursue and prosecute anyone offending against one of their members. Such associations dealt with all sorts of propertied crime, including petty larceny, highway robbery, sheep rustling, industrial embezzlement, poaching and housebreaking. Increased means for securing prosecutions brought more people into court, as mentioned earlier.

ENFORCING THE LAW

Law enforcement underwent considerable change in early industrial Britain. Until the end of the American Revolution, enforcing the law was left to individual parishes, villages and towns, to implement mainly through parish constables and nightwatchmen. These unpaid officials, usually chosen by the local parish vestry, were probably reasonably effective at 'policing' small communities where they knew many people on a face-to-face basis. In larger urban areas, they had a more difficult task because of the anonymity associated with conglomerations of people. Maintaining the law was also the traditional preserve of an unpaid magistracy. At petty sessions JPs entered into committal proceedings and decided whether people should be forwarded for trial at quarter sessions or assizes; they licensed alehouses and specified rates; and they considered offenders such as rioters and poachers. At quarter sessions JPs heard non-capital cases and handled many aspects of local services; they tried private individuals for breaches of the law; they heard presentments against parishes that neglected their duties; and they listened to appeals against decisions by local justices. From the early 1790s, particularly in London, stipendiary magistrates were appointed to deal with the increased legal work incurred at a time of burgeoning population growth.

There was no police force in existence in eighteenth-century Britain. The only group approximating the police consisted of pursuers and thief-takers in London. These were established by the novelist and London magistrate Henry Fielding in 1753 and continued the next year by his blind half-brother Sir John. Both of the Fieldings served in succession as chief magistrates of Bow Street. The Bow Street Patrol, an armed group, was called upon to detect crimes and arrest culprits in the metropolitan area, mainly operating in the evening up until midnight. By 1800, however, it only totalled 68 men. Sir John Fielding drafted plans for a more systematic centralised police in the metropolis but his proposals were not followed up during his lifetime. Weak civil police forces were not very often supplemented by the use of the armed forces, though as a last resort the army and navy could be called upon to support the establishment.

Installing more systematic policing was something discussed by social commentators in the period between the French Revolution and Catholic emancipation: the growing population in an urban and industrial setting, and the potential problem of working-class unruliness, provided an impetus for the dissemination of ideas about regular law enforcement. Patrick Colquhoun, the reformer and stipendiary magistrate for Westminster, advocated in 1796 that a uniform and centralised system of 'criminal police' should be established in London to take over many functions of parish constables, nightwatchmen and magistrates. Changes in the provision of policing were delayed, however, until the late 1820s. Several reasons account for this hiatus. Some Tory gentry in Parliament regarded the notion of a centralised police force as an attack on an Englishman's liberties, and many liberals and radicals shared this concern. To many property owners, the notion of a central police force cut across the long-established system of parish-based law enforcement. Financial considerations played their part, too, in making ratepayers reluctant to support ideas for a professional police force. There were also radical critics of police reform who thought that involving central government in policing was all too redolent of tyranny. On a number of occasions police reform was raised in Parliament in the period c.1785–1825, but for these reasons the issue was quashed.

Nevertheless, in a single decade three statutes ushered in the new police, who were paid, uniformed and controlled by a bureaucracy that represented the ruling elite. In 1829 the Metropolitan Police Act established a constabulary for London, excluding the City of London, that came under the direction of the Home Office. Most superintendents, inspectors and sergeants appointed were recruited from army regiments. The Act was the brainchild of Robert Peel, then Home Secretary, who produced criminal statistics plus speeches on the unruliness of a growing metropolis to convince his Tory colleagues of the need for such legislation. In 1835 the **Municipal Corporations Act** required boroughs to establish a borough police force under the control of a watch committee. The police clause of this statute was influenced by the widespread urban protests and riots that had alarmed propertied men throughout the nation during the Reform Bill crisis of 1830–32. But the Whig government also hoped to rationalise the existing confused system of watchmen and constables and bring them under the aegis of elected councils. In 1839 a Rural Constabulary Act was passed that allowed counties in England and Wales to develop a county police force. The passing of this law was again partly stimulated by fears of working-class protesters causing public disorder, as occurred in some Chartist and anti-poor law demonstrations of the late 1830s. All three statutes were preceded by much discussion by the educated classes about the need for better policing. To take one example, the 1839 Act was preceded in some areas, such as Kent, by the application of the 1833 Lighting and Watching Act, which permitted vestries to appoint an inspector who then hired paid watchmen to police rural parishes.

How effective were these new constabularies? All took time to settle down. The first two Metropolitan police commissioners wanted to recruit a

Municipal Corporations Act (1835): Provided for the creation of town councils to be elected on a wide franchise. Many new industrial towns, formerly without self-government apart from vestries or improvement commissions, took advantage of the Act to secure incorporation (grant of powers of local self-government by an elected corporation).

disciplined and efficient police force. But this was not easy to establish quickly. The initial recruits for constables, for example, included many men who drifted by the wayside as a result of drunkenness, insubordination, dishonesty or slackness. A fair number had to be dismissed. A high proportion of unskilled rural recruits, who received little formal training, proved unsuitable for the job. The effectiveness of the new police was hampered by the patchy implementation of the policing statutes enacted after 1829. Many growing towns lay outside the scope of the Municipal Corporations Act and were therefore not obliged to provide a borough police force. Many counties failed to respond to the 1839 Act by installing new police because existing interests thought the current system was mainly satisfactory; if a crisis of public order occurred, then the army could be called upon to intervene. It was not until the County and Borough Police Act of 1856 came into effect that every county had to establish a police force. By mid-century many areas of England and Wales had still not seen the changes in the practice of policing put into practice. In terms of police surveillance, working-class communities and undesirable groups, such as vagrants and poor Irish migrants, took up much police time; whether one regards this as effective depends upon the degree to which monitoring of orderliness and decency among certain working-class groups is seen as a salutary objective or not.

The introduction of new police services was not welcomed everywhere. Hostility to the 'Peelers' was common in London in the 1830s: they were regarded as costly, badly disciplined and sometimes brutal. The commissioners of police were burned in effigy during Guy Fawkes' Night celebrations in London during the 1830s. Anti-police rioting occurred at Colne, Lancashire, in April and August 1840. Police attempts to control space by curtailing annual fairs or interfering with the practices of local street traders created animosity among some sections of the working classes. But both respectable workers and the bourgeoisie welcomed the work of the new police in improving public security. Whether the new police were effective in preventing crime is difficult to evaluate, given the need to compare evidence on the situation with or without policing. Statistics on arrests, however, suggest that by the mid-nineteenth century the new police were reasonably successful at apprehending those guilty of street offences such as drunkenness, disorderliness, soliciting for money or sex, and illegal street trading.

PHYSICAL PUNISHMENTS

Physical punishments commonly in use in the early eighteenth century included public whipping, branding on the thumb or the cheek, the pillory, the stocks and, less frequently, the ducking stool. These punishments originated in the Middle Ages; all were administered for offences in local communities; all were intended to identify, shame and ridicule offenders in public. Whipping and branding were often used for punishing rogues, vagabonds and petty thieves. The pillory, where people stood upright with their head fixed through a board and their feet fastened to holes in wooden planks, was the fate of those convicted of sedition, cheating, perjury, sodomitical offences and keeping a brothel. The stocks, where people sat and had their feet and sometimes their wrists fastened in holes in wooden boards, were used for similar crimes. The ducking stool was commonly used for those (nearly all women) accused of witchcraft. Gibbeting occurred occasionally. The ultimate form of physical punishment was the hangman's noose on the gallows. The most famous location for public hanging was Tyburn, near Marble Arch, London, where on eight days of the year those sentenced to death were strung up before large crowds assembled to witness the event. William Hogarth indelibly portrayed the scene in his famous print depicting the bustle of the fair at Tyburn.

Gradually these various forms of bodily punishment came under attack. The emergence of Enlightenment thought, emphasising mankind's ability to progress from a less civilised state to a higher plane, meant that physical punishments came to be regarded as barbaric survivals of a bygone era. Moreover, exhibiting culprits in public came to be viewed as an ineffective way of dealing with crime: as people became more mobile during industrialisation, it was no longer appropriate to single them out in a community where they might be anonymous rather than recognisable. Branding was abolished in 1779 and whipping declined in the 1780s. Flogging continued in the armed forces, but even that was subject to a reform campaign in the early nineteenth century. The famous Tyburn hanging days came to an end in 1783, owing to concerns about the outbreaks of public disorder that accompanied them. Public hangings in London were removed to Newgate gaol. Gibbeting was abolished in 1834. Public executions were curtailed in 1868 but hanging behind prison walls continued as the means of capital punishment up to 1967, when execution was abolished in Britain.

CONVICT TRANSPORTATION

Convict transportation operated on a voluntary basis from the Restoration period onwards, but it became a part of state policy after Parliament passed a Transportation Act in 1718. This secondary punishment catered for felons convicted of capital crimes, who received sentences of either banishment for life or 14 years' exile, and, on a larger scale, for felons found guilty of non-capital crimes against property, who received seven-year sentences. The Transportation Act was originally passed because the new Hanoverian regime wanted to buttress its authority after a crime wave hit London in the aftermath of the War of the Spanish Succession (1702–13). Convict transportation thereafter became part of British penal policy for a century and a half. From 1718 to 1775 some 50,000 convicts were dispatched to the North American colonies, principally Virginia and Maryland, where their labour was sold for their term of service to buyers who set them to work in local industry and agriculture. Transportation was halted during the War of American Independence. During that period many convicted felons were confined on hulks on the Thames and at ports such as Portsmouth. The convicts were put to hard labour on these old warships. But the hulks suffered from overcrowding and unsanitary conditions, which meant they could be only a temporary expedient.

After the end of the War of American Independence, transportation was revived but the destinations were remote Australian ones – New South Wales to begin with and, later, Van Diemen's Land and Western Australia. Exile to these destinations appeared to offer a lower-cost alternative to providing extra prisons at home. Between 1788, when the First Fleet reached Botany Bay, and 1868, when convict transportation ended, some 162,000 felons were dispatched 'down under' by government vessels to endure exile as their punishment. State involvement in convict transportation and the types of societies that accommodated British convicts changed over time. Whereas the convicts sent to North America before the American Revolution had entered free colonies to join other types of labourers, the convicts sent to Australia initially lived in a penal colony. Only gradually, with the growth of free white settlement, did Australian convicts find themselves living in a more open society. When felons were transported to North America, there was a lack of government involvement with the deterrent or rehabilitative possibilities for convict labour. After felons were shipped to New South Wales, however, the state assumed a more active role in the administration of the system via the Home Office (created in 1782) and through colonial governors and a government-run penal colony.

Transportation became the most important secondary punishment meted out in English and Welsh courts. It was less commonly sanctioned by Scottish judges, who used it as a resort for those convicted on capital charges. Transportation was a halfway house between sentencing to hanging and recommendations for whipping and branding. It was an intermediate punishment for large numbers of felons brought before the courts who might otherwise be sentenced to hanging if found guilty of capital offences or subjected to physical chastisement if sentenced on non-capital charges. The value of transportation for Hanoverian and early Victorian statesmen resided in the fact that it permitted exile of criminal offenders without local or national officials having to define its purposes beyond the fact of banishment. It was not that the state did not know what to do with convicted felons. Rather, it suited the state's maintenance of power (based on protecting property rights of the landed classes) to avoid interference in who was transported and who was not: that was left to the discretion of judges and magistrates.

PRISONS

Various types of prisons existed in Georgian Britain, but before the American Revolution most of them were small institutions that did not cater for permanent incarceration of criminals; they tended to be used as places for holding people awaiting trial. Gaols were not regarded as severe enough institutions to cause serious offenders to feel retribution for their wrong deeds. Debtors' prisons were a specialised institution in which inmates were kept at their creditors' expense until they could pay their debts or were declared insolvent by parliamentary act. The best-known debtors' prisons were in London; they included **King's Bench**, the Fleet, Marshalsea and Ludgate. Throughout provincial England and Wales county or borough gaols could be found. These were more often than not buildings converted inadequately from other purposes: they could be parts of castles or structures adjoining town halls. They usually catered for around 50 inmates, though larger ones, notably London's Newgate, could hold 200 prisoners. There were also houses of correction or bridewells, which were institutions where the poor were put to work and profits made from their outwork (which included ropemaking and handling garments). None of these institutions were envisaged as a permanent solution to crime before 1775. And all were in need of an overhaul. The prison reformer John Howard visited most county and borough gaols in 1775 and found conclusive evidence of the poor and sometimes cruel way in which they were run, the stodgy diets of the inmates, the overcrowding of cramped premises, and the prevalence of infectious diseases, notably 'gaol fever', which was spread by rats. He published his findings in a comprehensive survey titled *The State of the Prisons in England and Wales* (1777), which was widely read and influential **(Doc. 30, p. 150)**.

Many changes occurred in the prison system between the War of American Independence and the early Victorian era. Howard recommended various improvements: better regulations to combat verbal abuse and trafficking in money by staff; more regular inspection; solitary confinement in cells to benefit prisoners' consciences; performance of worthwhile labour by inmates;

King's Bench prison: A high court prison that catered for those imprisoned for debt. Inmates were held on civil rather than criminal charges and were allowed considerable autonomy in their living conditions. Debtors were often kept in the King's Bench prison at their creditors' expense.

more hygienic conditions; the observation of fixed hours of rising, work, prayer, and reading the Bible; and provision of prison uniforms. These recommendations were largely embodied in the Penitentiary Act (1779), the first major statute passed by central government that aimed to transform the prison system. The Act provided for two new penitentiaries to be built in London, one to hold males, the other for females. But this proved a controversial proposal: much educated opinion considered that gaols should remain the responsibility of boroughs and counties rather than planned by the state.

Though the Penitentiary Act was never implemented as intended, about a dozen gaols along the lines envisaged by Howard and by the framers of the Act were constructed in the last two decades of the eighteenth century. The best known, a new penitentiary in Gloucester, was the work of a local county justice with the grand name of Sir George Onesiphorus Paul. He introduced a system of night cells and day cells for inmates, encouraged hygienic conditions and instituted a system of solitary confinement. But despite isolating prisoners in cells, he found it difficult to prevent them from communicating with each other. His gaol also experienced a number of disturbances, including a large uprising in 1815 quelled only by corporal punishment. New gaols, along the lines envisaged by the Penitentiary Act, were also opened at the end of the eighteenth century in Oxfordshire, Lancashire and Dorset.

New penitentiaries were intended to inflict mental pain on prisoners and make them search their conscience to repent of their misdeeds. Such an emphasis on cleansing the mind and redeeming one's soul through solitary, silent discipline was in keeping with the movement against physical punishment in the second half of the eighteenth century. An addition to the penitentiary, again with an emphasis on reforming the minds and characters of inmates, came with Jeremy Bentham's plan for a national penitentiary, which he called a Panopticon. This scheme, published in 1791, had inspection, surveillance and private prison labour as its hallmarks. The Panopticon was intended to be a honeycomb structure with open-topped cells arranged in a circle around a central watchtower from which guards could oversee prisoners at any time of the day or night. The prison officers were to be inspected to ensure their impartiality in treating inmates. Prisoners were to undertake work for private contractors that could make the institution profitable. Bentham regarded his plan as a rational, cost-effective way of administering punishment. He spent 20 years trying to persuade governments to adopt the panopticon and eventually succeeded in having his plan accepted, but it never came into being because of uneasiness about a profit-making private enterprise becoming the model for English prisons and because an appropriate site could not be found.

The penitentiary movement came under pressure in the period of the French Revolutionary and Napoleonic Wars. The emphasis on solitude was criticised as an inhumane way of treating prisoners, as bad in its way as physical punishment. Penitentiaries seemed to liberal critics to be too similar in structure and operation to factories, and were opposed on the grounds of being geared to the profit motive. The installation of Jacobin prisoners in penitentiaries in the 1790s aroused fears that gaols would become hotbeds of republican sedition. A number of protests by prisoners, including a major revolt at Coldbath Field prison, Clerkenwell, London, in August 1800, also led to a reaction against the new prisons. The failure of a large new metropolitan penitentiary, Millbank, to operate successfully after its opening in 1816 led to criticism of the new prisons being built.

The prison reform movement revived in the period 1817–20 largely through the work of the Quaker philanthropist Elizabeth Fry. She was a reformer who arrived in the right place at the right time. The number of accused people brought to trial increased threefold between 1805 and 1820. British prisons were overcrowded in the hard times that followed the end of the Napoleonic Wars. Therefore solitary confinement soon became impractical. Recognising the pressures on the prison system, Fry visited London's Newgate and bridewells in Edinburgh and Glasgow to try out humane ways of treating and reforming prisoners. She was inspired in this work by her religious zeal and an evangelical belief in benevolence and carrying out good deeds that might lead to a moral reformation in people's behaviour. At Newgate, Fry was influential in the setting up of separate wards for men, women and children. She installed a monitorial school. She insisted on decent clothing and restrained behaviour and eradicated gambling, debauchery and foul language. She instituted a daily regimen of prayer and useful work. This humane system of operating prisons was widely copied throughout Britain in the 1820s. It was assisted by the passage of the Gaols Act in 1823, which set standards for humane incarceration of criminal offenders on a national basis.

Unfortunately, Fry's methods did not make a significant impact on the number of felons receiving prison sentences. Her principles on prison organisation were challenged in the late 1820s by harsher approaches to punishment. Treadwheels, invented by Samuel Cubitt, were installed in many prisons in the 1820s, forcing recalcitrant inmates to suffer repetitive, dangerous physical action by grinding the air on the wooden slats that revolved around a cylindrical drum. Prisoners were made to observe rules of silence, their diets were reduced and the monitorial education introduced by Fry was abandoned. New penitentiaries were built that were intended to strike terror into the populace. The starkest symbol of the early Victorian prison at its most imposing was Pentonville prison, opened in north London in the early 1840s. Prisoners incarcerated there were largely kept in their cells in solitude apart from when they were allowed exercise or attended chapel. Their heads were shaven and they were given a gaolbird uniform with an identifying number. Strict rules governed the entire daily round. Repression and severity had become the distinguishing features of penitentiaries by the mid-Victorian era (Ignatieff, 1978).

Part 3

ASSESSMENT

9

Conclusion

British society experienced extensive social change in the century after 1750, at a time of increasing population growth, greater urbanisation and the consolidation of a capitalist economy. Patterns of work and leisure were transformed for most people in early industrial Britain. The most obvious change in work patterns came with the rise of factories, associated with labour mobility, the installation of new machinery and the division of workers into specialised tasks. Factories were prominent in the Midlands, north of England and lowland Scotland by the early nineteenth century. They did not feature prominently in other industrialising areas of the nation even as late as 1850, so that Birmingham and the Black Country and Sheffield and its hinterland, to select examples, were not characterised by factory employment by that date. In those areas, and in other parts of the country, cottage industry was still a significant employer of labour. Yet it would be wrong to assume that domestic industry was unchanging. In cities like London, handicraft industry became transformed into sweated labour by the early Victorian period. Groups such as handloom weavers found their work opportunities eroded and their wages plummeting after the weaving of textiles entered factories in the 1820s. And even in places where cottage industry seemed to follow a course established for generations, changes occurred, with some regions, such as East Anglia and the West Country, experiencing deindustrialisation.

Significant changes occurred in the gender division of labour in early industrial Britain: women were increasingly employed in more menial industrial tasks in factories, assigned to jobs where skilled work on new machines was not required. In agriculture, too, women's work changed during the century after 1750: women were increasingly sidelined from their traditional role in dairying; they found it more difficult to secure well-paid harvest work; and they were often seen as suitable for little more than weeding and stone-picking. Though women contributed importantly through their supplementary earnings to family incomes, most adult females had few opportunities for advances in employment and by 1850 found themselves coping with male attitudes that prized the role of the male breadwinner and regarded the domestic hearth as a woman's proper sphere. In the cotton textile mills, adolescent girls could find plenty of independently waged work, but married women tended to drop out of that particular workforce. Faced with the demands of running a home at a time of high average family size, most adult women found that their employment was casual, part-time or attached to the home.

Space and time constraints, as well as changing middle-class attitudes, altered the leisure activities of working people in Britain during the early industrial revolution. Those who migrated from countryside to town found the congestion of urban centres unconducive for the open-air recreations found in rural Britain. Increased working hours in industry and the decline of Saint Monday in many areas eroded the amount of time available for leisure. The gentry gradually withdrew its support for coarser working-class entertainments; legislation was enacted in the 1820s and 1830s to curb some blood sports; and the middle classes, including most evangelicals, sought to promote more orderly, rational leisure pursuits for working people in order to combat the boisterous and unruly nature of many traditional amusements. The one main area of the working man's recreation that proved difficult to control was the public house.

Living and health standards underwent changes as Britain industrialised. The growth of large industrial towns such as Leeds, Bradford and Sheffield increased environmental pollution, while adequate sewerage and drainage was poor in many areas until the first national Public Health Act was passed in 1848. Killer diseases were rife, contributing to high levels of infant mortality. Sudden epidemic outbreaks of contagious diseases, notably cholera, proved difficult to control. A strong case could be made for deterioration in the environmental and epidemiological context of most people's lives during early industrialisation. The century after 1750 witnessed significant changes in the diet, nutrition, life expectancy and wages of the working classes, though there is no consensus about the benefits achieved. Thus, for example, historians still dispute the degree to which workers' real incomes increased in the period c.1790–1850: some emphasise gains in real wages, particularly in the 1840s, while others find only a modest overall increase in real wages over those decades. But there is no evidence of wholesale deterioration in wages for the entire working population in the first half of the nineteenth century, nor is there dispute that, over the long term up to the present day, workers' living standards improved.

Religious and educational provision for the lower classes both experienced considerable change in early industrial Britain. Protestant nonconformity, especially Methodism, gained adherents and provided a wider range of

Christian worship than the Church of England could offer. The Methodists were particularly successful in spreading the gospel to the labouring poor through itinerancy, charismatic preaching, the organisation of bands and classes, hymn singing, the deployment of lay men and women, and the growth of Sunday schools and chapel communities. Though numerically too small to take the sting out of working-class radicalism, the Methodists, and nonconformists generally, played a significant role in spreading orderliness, punctuality, thriftiness and obedience throughout the lower orders. Even the Church of England, once seen as a moribund institution in Georgian Britain, is now usually accorded a more positive role in catering for the pastoral needs of ordinary people in the period of early industrialisation.

Popular education was heavily influenced by Christian morality and played a larger role in the lives of working communities after 1800 compared with the situation before that date, largely because of the rise of monitorial schools. Though limited in their educational aims and methods, these establishments at least enabled the three Rs to be spread among many more children in 1850 than in 1750. The state was slow to provide support for education, but it entered into provision for schooling after the Great Reform Act and introduced training colleges and a pupil-teacher system by the 1840s, which were important for the future development of elementary education. The emergence of mechanics' institutes in the 1820s also provided an educational outlet for the aspirations of skilled working men.

Increased population, social and geographical mobility and periodic agricultural and industrial slumps all brought uncertainty to workers' lives in early industrial Britain, but the parish system of poor relief adapted to meet changing circumstances. The payment of outdoor relief became more generous in many parishes in the later phase of the Old Poor Law (*c.*1790–1832), notably under the allowances created by the Speenhamland system. Per capita expenditure on poor relief rose significantly between the end of the American Revolution and the aftermath of the Napoleonic Wars. Thereafter a backlash occurred as poor relief came under attack from those who felt it was morally and economically disastrous. After the implementation of the New Poor Law in 1834, relief was more difficult to obtain, workhouses were given a higher priority, and expenditure on the poor laws was cut back. Though parish poor relief was admired throughout continental Europe, where there was no equivalent system of catering for paupers, the poor laws in England and Wales were applied in an increasingly harsh fashion by the early Victorian period.

Early industrial Britain witnessed various changes in crime and the law. Statutes against crimes concerning attacks on property became increasingly characteristic of Georgian Britain, and the death penalty was enshrined under the various statutes that comprised the 'Bloody Code'. It was not until the

1820s that many of these laws were revised and repealed. Changing attitudes towards punishment meant that physical chastisement was reduced during the eighteenth century, whereas secondary punishments, especially convict transportation, increased and prisons assumed a higher priority in dealing with criminals. Changes in the operation of prisons were complex during the period of early industrialisation, oscillating between enlightened attempts to reform prisoners and harsher attempts to stigmatise them. But there is little doubt that, after Elizabeth Fry's prison reforms were attacked, penitentiaries became a more severe form of incarceration for offenders. Policing, which was in its infancy in Britain in the mid-eighteenth century, emerged rapidly in London, and later in boroughs and counties, from the late 1820s onwards.

Many changes in the law, poor relief, religion and working patterns were influenced by parliamentary legislation – and yet Britain was not a parliamentary democracy until the later nineteenth century. Thus the social changes accompanying British industrialisation occurred well before the working man received the vote at general elections. Unable to influence the course of social change directly through voting, it is unsurprising that many people protested on the streets against grievances in early industrial Britain. Some outbreaks of collective disturbance focused on socio-economic conditions, such as grain riots; some had a mixture of political and religious motives, such as the Gordon riots of 1780. Other demonstrations mixed economic with political protest, such as the Luddite machine breaking and the Chartist crowd actions. Throughout the century after 1750, popular protest became more organised, more political and more of a threat to the status quo. But though some of the disturbances were serious and many resulted from legitimate grievances, local and central authorities contained the outbreaks. More articulate and effective political radicalism was one of the consequences of social change in early industrial Britain, but critiques of the existing establishment were only infrequently revolutionary in potential.

Part 4

DOCUMENTS

Document 1   NEW LANARK, A MODEL FACTORY, 1784–91

A description of the work, health, diet and morals of a well-known cotton mill in Scotland.

New Lanark, where the cotton mills are situated, is about a short mile from Lanark. It is entirely the creation of the enterprising and well known Mr. David Dale.

In 1784 Mr Dale feued [leased] the site of the mills and village, with some few acres of ground adjoining. This spot of ground was at that period almost a mere morass, situated in a hollow den, and of difficult access. Its only recommendation was the very powerful current of water that the Clyde could be made to afford it; in other respects, the distance from Glasgow and the badness of the roads were rather unfavourable.

The first mill was begun in April 1785, and a subterraneous passage of near 100 yards in length was also formed through a rocky hill for the purpose of an aqueduct to it. In summer 1788 a second one was built . . . and the proprietor has since erected other two, all of which are meant to be driven by one and the same aqueduct. In March 1786 the spinning commenced, and the manufactory has been in a constant progressive state of advancement.

In March 1791, from an accurate account then taken, it appears that there were 981 persons employed at the mills, whereas there are now (November 1793) 1,334 (men 145; women 217; boys 376; girls 419; masons, carpenters, labourers, employed in erecting buildings, and mechanics 177).

With regard to the health of the workpeople, it is sufficient to say that of all the children provided with meat and clothing by the proprietor amounting this and last year to 275, and for seven years back never fewer than 80, only five have died during the period of 7 years. In mentioning so extraordinary a fact, it may be expected that something should be said of their diet and treatment.

The diet consists of oatmeal porridge, with milk in summer or sowens, i.e. oat-meal flummery, with milk in winter twice a day, as much as they can take, barley broth for dinner made with good fresh beef every day; and as much beef is boiled as will allow 7 oz English a-piece each day to one half of the children, the other half get cheese and bread after their broth, so that they dine alternatively upon cheese and butchermeat, with barley bread or potatoes; and now and then in the proper season they have a dinner of herrings and potatoes.

They, as well as the others, begin work at six in the morning, are allowed half an hour for breakfast, an hour for dinner, and quit work at 7 at night; after which they attend the school at the expense of the proprietor till 9. They sleep in well-aired rooms, three in a bed; and proper care is taken to remove those under any disease to separate apartments . . .

Great attention is paid to the morals of the children and others at these mills. Large manufactories have sometimes been considered in another light, but Mr Dale and all concerned must have the voice of the public of the contrary. Marriages have greatly increased in the parish since their erection, as the benefits arising from a family are obvious. Indeed the anxiety of the proprietor to have proper teachers and instructors for children will even redound to his honour . . . Families from any quarter possessed of a good moral character, and having children fit for work, above nine years of age, are received – supplied with a house at a moderate rent, and the woman and children provided with work. The children, both those fit for work and those who are too young for it, have the privilege of attending the school gratis, the former in the evening, the latter during the day. Three professed teachers are paid by Mr Dale for this purpose, and also seven assistants who attend in the evenings, one of whom teaches writing. There is also a Sunday school at which all the masters and assistants attend.

Before leaving this article of cotton mills I cannot help noticing a circumstance peculiar to such manufactures, which may afford a useful hint to poor widows with families. In most other manufactures, a woman who has a family, and becomes a widow, is generally in a most helpless situation. Here the case is very different, for the greater number of children a woman has, she lives so much the more comfortably; and upon such account alone, she is often a tempting object for a second husband. Indeed, at cotton mills, it often happens, that young children support their aged parents by their industry.

The people [of Lanark] are, in general, industrious though not remarkably so. They are naturally generous, hospitable, and fond of strangers, which induces them sometimes to make free with the bottle, but drunkenness, among the better class of inhabitants, is of late rather unusual. Upon the whole, they are a decent, orderly people, and crimes are seldomer committed here than in any other parish of equal population. In short, they are generally honest, decent, religious, and strict in their attendance at divine worship.

Source: William Lockhart of Baronald, *A Statistical Account of Scotland*, 1795, vol. 15, reprinted in Roy Porter and Edward Royle (eds), *Documents of the Early Industrial Revolution* (Cambridge: University of Cambridge Local Examinations Syndicate, 1983), pp. 99–101.

OCCUPATIONS IN 1851 **Document 2**

An extract from the census of Great Britain for 1851, showing the number of persons engaged in different occupations. The sheer number of agricultural jobs indicates that industrialisation was incomplete by the mid-nineteenth century.

	Male	Female
Total population	10,224,000	10,736,000
Population of ten years old and upwards	7,616,000	8,155,000
Agriculture: farmer, grazier, labourer, servant	1,563,000	227,000
Domestic service (excluding farm service)	134,000	905,000
Cotton worker, every kind, with printer, dyer	255,000	272,000
Building craftsman: carpenter, bricklayer, mason, plasterer, plumber, etc.	442,000	1,000
Labourer (unspecified)	367,000	9,000
Milliner, dress-maker, seamstress (seamster)	494	340,000
Wool worker, every kind, with carpet-weaver	171,000	113,000
Shoe-maker	243,000	31,000
Coal-miner	216,000	3,000
Tailor	135,000	18,000
Washerwoman		145,000
Seaman (merchant), pilot	144,000	
Silk worker	53,000	80,000
Blacksmith	112,000	592
Linen, flax worker	47,000	56,000
Carter, carman, coachman, postboy, cabman, busman, etc.	83,000	1,000
Iron worker, founder, moulder (excluding iron-mining, nails, hardware, cutlery, files, tools, machines)	79,000	590
Railway driver, etc., porter, etc., labourer, platelayer	65,000	54
Hosiery worker	35,000	30,000
Lace worker	10,000	54,000
Machine, boiler maker	63,000	647
Baker	56,000	7,000
Copper, tin, lead-miner	53,000	7,000
Charwoman		55,000
Commercial clerk	44,000	19
Fisherman	37,000	1,000
Miller	37,000	562
Earthenware worker	25,000	11,000
Sawyer	35,000	23
Shipwright, boat-builder, block and mast maker	32,000	28
Straw-plait worker	4,000	28,000
Wheelwright	30,000	106
Glover	4,500	25,000
Nailer	19,000	10,000
Iron-miner	27,000	910
Tanner, currier, fellmonger	25,000	276
Printer	22,000	222

Source: Parliamentary Papers, 1852–3, vol. LXXXVIII, Part 1.

RICHARD OASTLER ON CHILD LABOUR IN YORKSHIRE MILLS **Document 3**

In the early 1830s Oastler led the agitation against the exploitation of children in the textile districts of northern England. In this evidence given before a parliamentary committee, he compares child labour in the factories to West Indian slavery and accuses the mill owners of breaking up family life by exploiting child labour for long hours.

Richard Oastler, appearing before the Committee, when asked, 'Has your mind been latterly directed to the consideration of the condition of children and young persons engaged in the mills and factories', made answer:

The immediate circumstance which led my attention to the facts was a communication made to me by a very opulent spinner [Mr John Wood, of Horton Hall, Bradford], that it was the regular custom to work children in factories 13 hours a day, and only allow them half an hour for dinner, and that in many factories they were worked considerably more . . . From that moment, which was the 29th of September 1830, I have never ceased to use every legal means, which I had it in my power to use, for the purpose of emancipating these innocent slaves. The very day on which the fact was communicated to me, I addressed a letter to the public, in the *Leeds Mercury*, upon the subject. I have since that had many opponents to contend against; but not one single fact which I have communicated has ever been contradicted, or ever can be . . .

The demoralizing effects of the system are as bad, I know it, as the demoralizing effects of slavery in the West Indies. I know that there are instances and scenes of the grossest prostitution amongst the poor creatures who are the victims of the system, and in some cases are the objects of the cruelty and rapacity and sensuality of their masters. These things I never dared to publish, but the cruelties which are inflicted personally upon the little children, not to mention the immensely long hours which they are subject to work, are such as I am very sure would disgrace a West Indian plantation.

On one occasion . . . I was in the company of a West India slave master and three Bradford spinners; they brought the two systems into fair comparison, and the spinners were obliged to be silent when the slave-owner said, 'Well, I have always thought myself disgraced by being the owner of black slaves, but we never, in the West Indies, thought it was possible for any human being to be so cruel as to require a child of nine years old to work twelve and a half hours a day; and that, you acknowledge, is your regular practice . . .'

In the West Riding of Yorkshire when I was a boy it was the custom for the children to mix learning their trades with other instruction and with amusement, and they learned their trades or their occupations, not by being put into places, to stop there from morning to night, but by having a little work to do, and then some time for instruction, and they were generally under the immediate care of their parents; the villages about Leeds and Huddersfield were occupied by respectable little clothiers, who could manufacture a piece of cloth or two in the week, or three or four or five pieces, and always had their family at home: and they could at that time make a good profit by what they sold; there were filial affection and parental feeling, and not over-labour.

But that race of manufacturers has been almost completely destroyed; there are scarcely any of the old-fashioned domestic manufacturers left, and the villages are composed of one or two, or in some cases of three or four, mill-owners, and the rest, poor creatures who are reduced and ground down to want, and in general are compelled to live upon the labour of their little ones. It is almost the general system for the little children in these manufacturing villages to know nothing of their parents at all excepting that in the morning very early, at 5 o'clock, very often before 4, they are awaked by a human being that they are told is their father, and are pulled out of bed (I have heard many a score of them give an account of it) when they are almost asleep, and lesser children are absolutely carried on the backs of the older children asleep to the mill, and they see no more of their parents, generally speaking, till they go home at night, and are sent to bed.

Now that system must necessarily prevent the growth of filial affection. It destroys the happiness in the cottage family, and leads both parents and children not to regard each other in the way that Providence designed they should . . . With regard to the fathers, I have heard many of them declare that it is such a pain to them to think that they are kept by their little children, and that their little children are subjected to so many inconveniences, that they scarcely know how to bear their lives; and I have heard many of them declare that they would much rather be transported than be compelled to submit to it. I have heard mothers, more than on ten or eleven occasions, absolutely say that they would rather that their lives were ended than that they should live to be subjected to such misery. The general effect of the system is this, and they know it, to place a bonus upon crimes; because their little children, and their parents too, know that if they only commit theft and break the laws, they will be taken up and put into the House of Correction, and there they will not have to work more than 6 or 7 hours a day.

Source: Parliamentary Papers, 1831–2, vol. XV, pp. 445–55.

FESTIVALS, HOLIDAYS AND LOCAL COMMUNITIES   **Document 4**

Notes the controversy over the place of festivals and holidays in social life but argues that they are important for the recreation of the labouring population.

The utility of festivals to nations and society in general is a question of considerable controversy: the opposing arguments are founded chiefly on the interruptions they occasion in public business, the facilities they afford to improvidence and idleness, and the abuses by which they have been too frequently disgraced among the working-classes, to the injury of both their means and morals. There is a sad truth in this last objection; but, on the other hand, it is contended that the institution of festivals is natural to humanity, and one of the distinguishing traits of our species; that they serve great moral purposes, in reviving the pious or elevating recollections connected with those events which they generally commemorate, and apt to be forgotten in the dusty bustle of business, or the dull routine of mechanical employment. It is also maintained that they contribute to the cultivation of social virtues, and refresh, with needful relaxations and amusement, the toil-worn lives of the labouring population, which without them would be 'all work and no play,' with the proverbial consequence – that all human privileges and arrangements are liable to abuses, and those to which they have been subjected, are no arguments against festivals.

Source: Article titled 'Festivals and Holidays' in *Chambers's Edinburgh Journal*, January–June 1849, p. 222, quoted in Bob Bushaway, *By Rite: Custom, Ceremony and Community in England 1700–1880* (London: Junction Books, 1982), p. 13.

TWO FAMILY BUDGETS, 1794   **Document 5**

Taken from a major inquiry into the condition of the poor by Sir Frederick Eden. The estimates show that even families in employment could find it difficult to balance their budgets.

A Banbury labourer

The family consists of a widower between 50 and 60 with two daughters aged 21 and 13 and a son, 7 years old. The elder daughter was sick and looked after the house. The younger daughter went to school and the boy earned nothing.

	[£]	[s]	[d]
Earnings (weekly)		8	0 for 48 weeks
		9	0 for 4 weeks
Weekly Parish allowance for children		2	0
Expenses (yearly)			
Bread	13	13	0
Tea and sugar	2	10	0
Butter and lard	1	10	0
Beer and milk	1	0	0
Bacon and other meat	1	10	0
Soap, candles etc.		15	0
House rent	3	0	0
Coal	2	10	0
Shoes and shirts	3	0	0
Other clothes	2	10	0

A Wolverhampton spectacle frame maker

The family consists of a man (40 years old) his wife and four children; viz. boys of ten and seven, girls of two and six months.

	[£]	[s]	[d]
Earnings (yearly)	49	9	4
Expenses (yearly)			
84 stones of flour	10	4	9
12 lbs meat per week	10	8	0
Butter, cheese	4	11	0
Milk	1	6	6
Small beer	1	6	6
Strong beer	2	13	0
Vegetables	4	0	0
Tea, sugar, soap, candles	5	0	0
Rent	6	0	0
Taxes		10	0
Shoes and clothing	4	10	0

Source: F. M. Eden, *The State of the Poor*, 3 vols (1798), vol. 2, pp. 585, 661.

PAUPERISM AND PUBLIC HEALTH, 1842   **Document 6**

*Outlines the results of an inquiry into the sanitary conditions of the working
classes and highlights the impact of epidemics and disease on life expectancy.*

That the various forms of epidemic, and other disease caused, or aggravated,
or propagated chiefly amongst the labouring classes by atmospheric impurities
produced by decomposing animal and vegetable substances, by damp and
filth, and close and overcrowded dwellings prevail amongst the population
in every part of the kingdom, whether dwelling in separate houses, in rural
villages, in small towns, in the larger towns – as they have been found to prevail in the lowest districts of the metropolis.

That such disease, wherever its attacks are frequent, is always found in
connexion with the physical circumstances above specified, and that where
those circumstances are removed by drainage, proper cleansing, better ventilation, and other means of diminishing atmospheric impurity, the frequency
and intensity of such disease is abated; and where the removal of the noxious
agencies appears to be complete, such disease almost entirely disappears.

That high prosperity in respect to employment and wages, and various
and abundant food, have afforded to the labouring classes no exemptions
from attacks of epidemic disease, which have been as frequent and as fatal in
periods of commercial and manufacturing prosperity as in any others.

That the formation of all habits of cleanliness is obstructed by defective
supplies of water.

That the annual loss of life from filth and bad ventilation are greater than
the loss from death or wounds in any wars in which the country has been
engaged in modern times.

That of the 43,000 cases of widowhood, and 112,000 cases of destitute
orphanage relieved from the poor's rates in England and Wales alone, it
appears that the greatest proportion of deaths of the heads of families
occurred from the above specified and other removable causes; that their
ages were under 45 years; that is to say, 13 years below the natural prob-
abilities of life as shown by the experience of the whole population of
Sweden.

That the public loss from the premature deaths of the heads of families is
greater than can be represented by any enumeration of the pecuniary bur-
dens consequent upon their sickness and death.

That, measuring the loss of working ability amongst large classes by the
instances of gain, even from incomplete arrangements for the removal of
noxious influences from places of work or from abodes, that this loss cannot
be less than eight or ten years.

That the ravages of epidemics and other diseases do not diminish but tend
to increase the pressure of population.

That in the districts where the mortality is the greatest the births are not only sufficient to replace the numbers removed by death, but to add to the population.

That the younger population, bred up under noxious physical agencies, is inferior in physical organization and general health to a population preserved from the presence of such agencies.

That the population so exposed is less susceptible of moral influences, and the effects of education are more transient than with a healthy population.

That these adverse circumstances tend to produce an adult population short-lived, improvident, reckless, and intemperate, and with habitual avidity for sensual gratifications.

That these habits lead to the abandonment of all the conveniences and decencies of life, and especially lead to the overcrowding of their homes, which is destructive to the morality as well as the health of large classes of both sexes.

That defective town cleansing fosters habits of the most abject degradation and tends to the demoralization of large numbers of human beings, who subsist by means of what they find amidst the noxious filth accumulated in neglected streets and bye-places.

That the expenses of local public works are in general unequally and unfairly assessed, oppressively and uneconomically collected, by separate collections, wastefully expended in separate and inefficient operations by unskilled and practically irresponsible officers.

That the existing law for the protection of the public health and the constitutional machinery for reclaiming its execution, such as the Courts Leet, have fallen into desuetude, and are in the state indicated by the prevalence of the evils they were intended to prevent.

Source: Poor Law Commissioners, 'Report on the sanitary conditions of the labouring population of Great Britain', *Parliamentary Papers*, House of Lords, 1842, vol. XXVI, pp. 369–70, quoted in B. W. Clapp (ed.), *Documents in English Economic History: England since 1760* (London: Bell, 1976), pp. 419–21.

Document 7   ANNUAL AVERAGE PRICE OF BRITISH WHEAT PER QUARTER, 1801–51

Shows the annual fluctuations in the price of the main staple item in the labouring population's diet.

	s	d		s	d		s	d
1801	119	6	1818	86	3	1835	39	4
1802	69	10	1819	74	6	1836	48	6
1803	58	10	1820	67	10	1837	55	10
1804	62	3	1821	56	1	1838	64	7
1805	89	9	1822	44	7	1839	70	8
1806	79	1	1823	53	4	1840	66	4
1807	75	4	1824	63	11	1841	64	4
1808	81	4	1825	68	6	1842	57	3
1809	97	4	1826	58	8	1843	50	1
1810	106	5	1827	58	6	1844	51	3
1811	95	3	1828	60	5	1845	50	10
1812	126	6	1829	66	3	1846	54	8
1813	109	9	1830	64	3	1847	69	9
1814	74	4	1831	66	4	1848	50	6
1815	65	7	1832	58	8	1849	44	3
1816	78	6	1833	52	11	1850	40	3
1817	96	11	1834	46	1	1851	38	6

Source: W. T. Layton and Geoffrey Crowther, *An Introduction to the Study of Prices*, 2nd edn (London: Macmillan & Co., 1935), p. 234.

AVERAGE WEEKLY WAGES IN SOME INDUSTRIAL OCCUPATIONS, 1849–51   **Document 8**

Location and Trade	Sex	Wage	Job description	Additional
Yorkshire (woollen and worsteds)	male	25/– to 27/–	wool sorters	for fine cloths 15/– to 20/– for less fine
	female	6/– to 7/–	picking and boiling	
	female and male	12/–	power loom weavers	
	Male	18/– to 20/–	finishers	
	Male	30/–	hot pressers	
	Female	7/– to 8/–	burling	for domestic work

Location and Trade	Sex	Wage	Job description	Additional
Leicester (hosiery)	Male	20/–	fancy trade	children 5/–
	Female	10/–	fancy trade	
Birmingham (brass)	Male	35/– to 40/–	brass metal maker	
	Male	35/– to 50/–	brass modeller	
	Male	30/–	brass moulder	
	Female	10/–	lacquerer	girls 4/– to 7/–
	Female	7/– to 8/–	brass nails, stamper, burnisher, weigher,	packer
	Male	15/– to 21/–	brass thimble maker	
	Female	7/– to 9/–	brass thimble maker	
Potteries	Male	42/– max	dipper	but pays boy asst. 4/–
	Male	30/– to 40/–	thrower	
	Male	30/– to 35/–	dishmaker	
	Male	20/– to 50/–	painter	varies according to skill
	Female	9/– to 12/–	painter	
South Staffs. (coal)	Male	4/4^{1}/2d per day	colliers	
	Female	10d to 1/– per day	bankswomen	
(iron works)	Male	18/– to 25/–	blast furnacemen	wages fluctuate with state of trade
	Male	25/– to 30/–	forgemen	
	Male	7/6d to 10/–	underhands	
	Female	4/– to 6/–	about blast furnaces and coke ovens	
Derbyshire (lace)	Male	21/– to 30/–	tenters of machines	
	Female	5/6d to 9/–	wooden bobbin winders	
Lancashire Manchester (spinning)	Male	40/– to 50/–	spinner	
	Male	13/– to 15/–	card room hands	
	Female	7/– to 11/–	drawing room tenters	depends on type of frame (less than figs. quoted if coarse yarn)

Source: Based on information in the *Morning Chronicle* collated in Angela V. John, *Unequal Opportunities: Women's Employment in England 1800–1918* (Oxford: Blackwell, 1986), pp. 39–40.

RELIGION AND CLASS, 1849   **Document 9**

Extract from a survey of British Christianity in 1849 that highlights the class dimension in religious life.

In Great Britain, we carry our class distinctions into the house of God, whether the edifice be a splendid monument of art, or whether it be nothing superior to a barn. The poor man is made to feel that he is a poor man, the rich is reminded that he is rich, in the great majority of our churches and chapels. The square pew, carpeted, perhaps and curtained, the graduated scale of other pews, the free-sittings, if there are any, keep up the separation between class and class; and even where the meanly-clad are not conscious of intrusion, as is sometimes painfully the case, the arrangements are generally such as to preclude in their bosoms any momentary feeling of essential equality. We have no negro pews, for we have no prejudice against colour – but we have distinct places for the pennyless, for we have a morbid horror of poverty. Into a temple of worship thus mapped out for varying grades of worshippers, in which the lowly and the unfortunate are forbidden to lose sight of their worldly circumstances, some such, spite of all discouragements, find their way. In the singing, it may be, they can join, and mingle their voices and their sympathies with those around them – unless, indeed, the more respectable tenants of the pews, deeming it ill-bred to let themselves be heard, leave the psalmody to the Sunday-school children, and the vulgar. Possibly, their emotions may be elicited by prayer – seldom, we should think, by the discourse. It may be excellent, persuasive, pungent – but, in multitudes of cases, it will also be cast in a mould which none but the educated can appreciate. Let it not be said that this is owing exclusively to their ignorance. 'The common people heard' our Lord 'gladly' – the early reformers won their way to the inmost hearts of the lowliest of men – and even those who in our day are judged to be too uncultured to profit by the ministry of God's word from the pulpit, are sufficiently intelligent to derive interest from a public political meeting, to appreciate the points of a speech from the hustings, and to feel the force of an argument when put to them in private . . . It is the entire absence of colloquialism from the discourse – an absence imposed upon the speaker by that sense of propriety which the aristocratic sentiment engenders. The etiquette of preaching prescribes an exclusively didactic style – and an address, the aim of which is to save souls, is supposed to approximate towards perfection, in proportion as it is free from conversational blemishes and inaccuracies, satisfies a fastidious and classical taste, and flows on in one unbroken stream from its commencement to its close. The consequence is, that whilst some few are pleased, and perhaps, profited, the mass remain utterly untouched. Oh! for some revolution to break down for ever, and scatter to the four winds of heaven, our pulpit formulas and proprieties, and leave men at liberty to discourse on the sublime verities of the Christian faith, with the same freedom, variety, and naturalness, with which they would treat other subjects in other places! The service concludes, and the worshippers retire. Communion with God has not disposed them to communion with each other, beyond the well-defined boundaries of class. The banker or the merchant pays no more attention to the small tradesman, or the tradesman to the labourer, in the sanctuary than out of it. All is artificial and conventional there as elsewhere. The distinctions which obtain in the world, and which do little to improve it, obtain likewise in the Church, and are preserved with the same unyielding tenacity.

Source: E. Miall, *The British Churches in Relation to the British People* (London: 1849), pp. 210–13, 222–23.

Document 10   THE VISITATION OF CHESTERFIELD, DERBYSHIRE, 1751

An example of an Anglican visitation return, showing that public worship in this parish was performed according to the requirements of the Church of England.

I. The number of families in this Parish is about twelve hundred, amongst which many are Dissenters, Presbyterians, Independents and Quakers but know not the particular number, and two or three Papists. II. There is a Presbyterian and Quaker meeting house in this parish but know not if licenced. They assemble on the Sunday twice, morning and afternoon, and the Quakers on Thursdays. The Presbyterian Teacher's name is Haywood. III. There is a publick free school endow'd with £50 pr an. in this Town in which the youths are fitted for the University; and there are many smaller schools to teach children to write and read and in which they are instructed in the doctrine of the Church of England by their Masters and Mistresses. It is to be wished they were brought more duly to the church. IV. There are two Almshouses in this Town for poor widows and women and many other charitable endowments. Lands to the value of ten pounds or twelve pounds pr. ann. are left for repair of the church and an impropriation at Attenborow in Nottinghamshire is given in part to the poor here, and there are 20 Gentn Trustees. The other endowments are entrusted with the Corporation or in ye Corporation and Vicar. They are properly managed and I hope no frauds or abuses are or will be committed in the management of ym. V. I do reside personally and constantly in the Parish in my vicarage house, unless when I go to another Rectory to reside there which is 12 miles distant. I have another small cure at Wingerworth, a curacy one mile distant from hence which I serve once every Sunday in the morning or afternoon alternately. VI. I have no curate in this parish but serve it myself. VII. I do not know of any who come to Church, who are not baptiz'd and have given due notice for all of competent age who are not already confirmed to offer themselves to the Bishop for Confirmation. VIII. Publick Service is read in this church on the Lord's Day at ten in the morning and two in the afternoon. Prayers are read at eleven in the morning every Wednesday, Friday and Holyday throughout the year and at morning and evening in the Passion Week. IX. The children are catechized here during Lent and many come to the Church to repeat their Catechism and be instructed in it. X. The Holy Communion is administered in this Church the first Sunday in the month, on Christmas Day, Good Friday, Easter Day, Low Sunday, Whit Sunday and Trinity Sunday. There are three or fourscore usually receive but many more at the Solemn Festivals and I believe there were 150 or thereabouts at Easter and Whitsuntide last. XI. The name of the Patron of the Living is Dr George Dean of Lincoln. The Great Tythes are impropriate to the Deanery of Lincoln. Its reputed value is about £500 p. an. and the Lessee is George Smyth Esq of the city of Gloucester. Wm Wheeler. Vicar of Chesterfield.

Source: John Beckett, Margery Tranter and Wendy Bateman (eds), *Visitation Returns from the Archdeaconry of Derby 1718–1824*, Derbyshire Record Society, vol. XXIX (2003), pp. 26–27.

A METHODIST CLASS MEETING, *c.*1822   **Document 11**

Joseph Barker was raised as a Wesleyan and became a travelling preacher for the New Methodist Connexion. He was expelled in 1841 and became a Unitarian before ending up as a Primitive Methodist local preacher. Here he describes the class meetings that lay at the core of Methodist life.

The class-meetings are held weekly. The classes ought, according to rule, to consist of ten or twelve members; but they sometimes contain as many as thirty, forty, or fifty, and at other times not more than three or four. Each member kneels down as soon as he enters, to pray a little by himself. The leader then begins the meeting by giving out a hymn, and the members stand up to sing. Then the leader prays, gives out another hymn, and then tells his experience. Sometimes he tells what trials he has met with, and what deliverances he has experienced through the week, what joys and sorrows he has had, how he felt at the love-feast, the prayer-meeting, or the fellowship-meeting, what liberty he had in secret prayer, how he felt while reading the Scriptures, or hearing sermons, or while busy at his work, what passages have come to his mind, or what promises have been applied to his soul. At other times he simply tells how he feels at that moment; while at other times he says nothing about his experience or feelings, but just gives thanks to God for what He has done for him, in a general way, or offers a few words of exhortation or preaching to the members. He then asks each member in turn the state of his mind. A very common form of the question is, 'Well, brother, or well, sister, how do you feel the state of your mind to-night?' At other times it will be, 'Well, brother, will you tell us what the Lord is doing for you?' Different leaders have different ways of proposing the question, and the same leader varies it at times. When the question is put, the member answers. Some of the members tell a long and flaming story; others say little, or next to nothing. Some speak loud, and even shout; others speak so low that they cannot be heard, either by the leaders or the rest of the members. Some are always happy, according to their story; others are always doubtful and fearful, and can never say much either about their feelings or performances. One tells you he has been on the sunny side of the hill all the week; another says he has been on the mount of transfiguration, and that he could say with one of old, 'Master, it is good to be here.' . . .

It was to one of those classes I went. The leader was a draper of Bramley, called G– B–. He was a ready talker and a zealous Methodist. He was loud in his praying, rather bold in his manner, but very ignorant; and willing, for anything I could ever see, to remain so. He was a great preacher's man, and fond of little honours and would do anything to be well thought of or favoured by the preachers. He knew, too, that to be on good terms with the preachers was the way to get customers to his shop; and he was very fond of gain. He had no scruples against laying up treasure on earth, though he read over Wesley's rules to us every quarter. He was a great respector of persons; and though he seemed to have sense enough to know that it was wrong, he had not virtue or shame enough to keep him from practising it even in the face of the whole class. He had abundance of respect for the richer members of his class, or at least he was abundantly ready to show respect to them; but, with the poorer members he could use as much freedom as you like. He would tell the poorer members to speak up; but he never told the richer ones to do so, though the richer ones were generally most prone to speak low. The rich members used generally to get into one corner by themselves, while the poor ones sat anywhere about the room. When he came to the rich members' corner, and found that scarce one of them could speak loud enough to be heard, either by himself or us, he used to feel rather at a loss sometimes what to do, especially when he had just before been urging some of the poorer members to speak; but he durst not complain, not he. Then how did he do? He did just like himself. When he knew that some would be thinking, Why does he not ask them to speak up? he would exclaim, 'Glory be to God! They are as happy as queens here in the corner.' I wonder how we could bear with such a shallow, worthless person for a leader; but we knew no better, I suppose, then?

Source: *The Life of Joseph Barker Written by Himself* (1880), pp. 44–46, 51–52, quoted in D. M. Thompson (ed.), *Nonconformity in the Nineteenth Century* (London: Routledge & Kegan Paul, 1972), pp. 48–50.

SAMUEL BAMFORD ON SUNDAY SCHOOLS   **Document 12**

Samuel Bamford (1788–1872) was a Lancastrian silk weaver and wrote widely about political, social and economic aspects of south Lancashire in the first half of the nineteenth century. Here he describes a Methodist Sunday school that he attended at Middleton, near Oldham, Lancashire, in the late 1790s.

Every Sunday morning at half-past eight o'clock was this old Methodists school open for the instruction of whatever child crossed its threshold. A hymn was first led out and sung by the scholars and teachers. An extempore prayer followed, all the scholars and teachers kneeling at their places; the classes, ranging from those of the spelling-book to those of the Bible, then commenced their lessons, girls in the gallery above, and boys below. Desks which could either be moved up or down, like the leaf of a table, were arranged all round the school, against the walls of the gallery, as well as against those below, and at measured distances the walls were numbered. Whilst the Bible and Testament classes were reading their first lesson the desks were got ready, inkstands and copy-books numbered, containing copies and pens, were placed opposite corresponding numbers on the wall; and when the lesson was concluded the writers took their places, each at his own number, and so continued their instruction. When the copy was finished, the book was shut and left on the desk, a lesson of spelling was gone through, and at twelve o'clock singing and prayer again took place, and the scholars were dismissed. At one o'clock there was service in the chapel, and soon after two the school reassembled, girls now occupying the writing desks, as boys had done in the forenoon, and at four or half-past the scholars were sent home for the week.

My readers will expect hearing that the school was well attended, and it was so, not only by children and youths of the immediate neighbourhood, but by young men and women from distant localities. Big collier lads and their sisters from Siddal Moor were regular in their attendance. From the borders of Whittle, from Bowlee, from the White Moss, from Jumbo, and Chadderton, and Thornham, came groups of boys and girls with their substantial dinners tied in clean napkins, and the little chapel was so crowded that when the teachers moved they had to wade, as it were, through the close-ranked youngsters.

Source: Samuel Bamford, *Passages in the Life of a Radical*, ed. H. Dunckley (1893), vol. 1, pp. 100–1.

Document 13   WORK AND DISCIPLINE IN THE MONITORIAL SCHOOL, 1810

Describes the principles of Joseph Lancaster's monitorial system.

It is unavoidable, on a large scale of education, to do without giving many commands, and some of a very trivial nature. On my plan, many of the commands, which would be given by the master, are given by the monitors. As it is not proper that commands, without number, and perhaps of a nature opposite to each other, should be given at random by the monitors, it becomes needful to limit the number that are to be given, as much as may be. It is an important object to secure implicit obedience to those commands on the part of the scholars: and, for the monitors to acquire as prompt a manner in giving them, as will secure the attention of the classes, and lead them to a ready compliance. The first of these objects is easily attained. It is only to write down on paper the commands most necessary to be given by the monitor to his whole class; and, it is essentially needful, that he should not vary from the rule once laid down. The general commands common to all schools are detailed in the Appendix.

The practice of giving short commands aloud, and seeing them instantly obeyed by the whole class, will effectually train the monitor in the habit of giving them with propriety. Thus, for instance, 'Front,' 'Right, or Left;' '*Show Slates*, or clean *Slates*,' are all things that must be occasionally done in school. Having a series of commands applicable to the duties of classes and of a school, is only defining what already exists in the nature of things, and which would be done in a vague manner unless so defined and commanded.

The classes should learn to measure their steps when going round the school in close order to prevent what else would often occur from their numbers, treading on each other's heels, or pushing each other down. In this case, measuring their steps commands their attention to one object, and prevents their being unruly or disorderly. It is not required that the measure should be exact, or be a *regular step*; but, that each scholar shall attempt to walk at a regular distance from the one who precedes him. When a new scholar is first admitted, he is pleased with the uniformity, novelty, and simplicity of the motions made by the class he is in. Under the influence of this pleasure he readily obeys, the same as the other boys do. None of these commands are in themselves, an hardship; and they are well supported by the force of habits easily acquired, from the circumstance of being congenial to the activity of the youthful mind. The power of example greatly facilitates the establishment of order. Children are mostly imitative creatures: they enter a new school; they see all in order around them; they see promptness and alacrity in obeying every command that is given; they do as they see others do, by the influence of their example. Before the effect of novelty is worn off, new habits are formed; and the happy children who are trained under the mild and generous influence of the British system of education, learn obedience with pleasure, and practice it with delight, without the influence of the rod or cane to bring them to order . . .

Paper of Commands on Coming Out to Shew Writing

Out. Front. Look – (to the Right or Left, by a motion made with the hand by the commanding monitor.) – Take up Slates. Show Slates. – (Here the monitor inspects.) – Left hand Slates. Right and Slates. Single. – (In a line.) – Double. Step forward. Step Backward. Go. Show Slates, to the Master, or Inspecting Monitor.

On Returning to the Class
Look. Go. Show Slates. Lay down Slates. In.

On Going Home
Out. Unsling Hats. Put on Hats. Go . . .

Rules for Appointing Monitors of Tuition

First, the monitors appointed must understand, and be quite perfect in the lessons they are to teach, as to good reading and spelling.

Secondly, they must understand the mode of teaching.

Thirdly, in the first five classes, monitors may be appointed from the next superior class, to teach the one immediately below it. Thus the second, or two-letter class, will furnish monitors who may teach the first, or alphabet class; the third will supply monitors for the second; the fourth for the third; and the fifth for the fourth; the sixth class will supply a choice of monitors for the fifth, for itself, and for the order of the *school. Under* the seventh class, each class will supply boys to teach the class below it; this will ground the monitors in the lessons they have themselves last learned, by the act of teaching them. From the sixth class upwards, the classes will supply boys to act as monitors, and teach themselves; the teachers of the sixth, seventh and eighth classes, may be chosen out of the said classes, as any boy who can read can teach; the art of tuition, in those classes, depending only on the knowledge of reading and writing. The system of inspection of progress in learning, as it respects the scholar, is *only* on *his* part mental; neither inspection nor the mode of instruction require any other qualification, on the part of the teacher, than the mere art of reading and writing, united with orderly behaviour.

Of Monitor's Tickets, Superintendant's List, and the Office of Monitor-General

Every monitor should wear in school a printed or leather ticket, gilt, and lettered thus: – Monitor of the first class – Reading Monitor of the second class – Monitor of the third class, with variations for Arithmetic, Reading, Spelling, & c.

Each of these tickets to be numbered. A row of nails, with numbers on the wall, marking the place of each ticket, to be placed in every schoolroom; the nail numbered 1, being the place for the ticket No. 1. When school begins, the monitors are to be called to take their tickets; every ticket left on a nail, will shew a regular monitor *absent*, when an occasional monitor must of course be chosen . . .

All the monitors should have a written or printed paper of their 'Duties,' which they should particularly study, and repeat once a week. Those duties, which are the same in all schools, and which apply generally to the mode of teaching, may be had printed, as see the APPENDIX, containing a list of things wanting in the outfit of a new school. These duties each monitor should paste in the books belonging to his class. The larger series of papers on the duties of monitors, should be read for a class lesson by all boys selected as regular, or auxiliary monitors, in order to prepare them, by a knowledge of their duty, for the proper discharge of it.

Source: Epitome of Joseph Lancaster's Inventions and Improvements in Education (1810), pp. 40–45, quoted in Anne Digby and Peter Searby (eds), *Children, School and Society in Nineteenth-Century England* (London: Macmillan, 1981), pp. 153–55.

Document 14   A VIEW OF WORKHOUSE EDUCATION, 1838

Presents the findings of Sir James Kay-Shuttleworth, an assistant poor law commissioner, and later a spokesman for popular education, on the state of education in the New Poor Law schools.

The following Table shews the state of the instruction of the children in the workhouses, even after some improvements had been effected in the schools; and an idea of the state of the children before these improvements were in progress, may possibly be in some degree realised from an attentive consideration of these facts.

	Youths from 9 to 16	Boys from 2 to 9	Girls from 9 to 16	Girls from 2 to 9	Total
Number who can Read well	206	70	173	30	479
Number who can Read imperfectly	217	149	207	186	759
Number who cannot Read	62	267	38	225	592
Number who can Write well	122	6	47	1	176
Number who can Write imperfectly	138	56	97	33	324
Number who cannot Write	211	398	262	407	1278

There are some slight inaccuracies in this Table, which do not, however, impair the general statement.

It is difficult to perceive how the dependence of the orphan, bastard, and deserted children, and the children of idiots, helpless cripples, and of widows relieved in the Union Workhouses, could cease, if no exertion were made to prepare them to earn their livelihood by skilful labour, and to fit them to discharge their social duties by training them in correct moral habits, and giving them knowledge suited to their station in life . . .

The number of children maintained and educated in the workhouses of Norfolk and Suffolk is considerably less than in some other parts of England. Thus I am aware that the workhouse schools in the county of Kent contain a much greater number of children in proportion to the population; but on the other hand, in the north of England a smaller number of children will probably be found to be dependent on the rate-payers.

If the children maintained in the workhouses of the rest of England be admitted to bear the same proportion to the population as in Norfolk and Suffolk, the workhouses of England contain 49,556 children between the ages of 2 and 16, of whom 48,022 are more permanently resident in the workhouses.

If the want of classification and the absence of correct discipline which prevailed in the old workhouses continued in the new, a great number of these latter children would acquire the habits of hereditary paupers, or even of felons, and *if only one-tenth of them (which would by no means be improbable,) became dependent during six months of each year*, with families of the ordinary size, they would occasion a burden of 112,353*l.* per annum . . .

The classification of the children separately from the adults (excepting their parents) is preserved with care in the workhouses of Norfolk and Suffolk, but cannot be rendered perfect in any workhouse as at present regulated. The adult paupers maintained in workhouses are generally persons of confirmed pauper habits, from whose society the children could acquire nothing but evil.

Children should not be taught to consider themselves paupers; and this result can scarcely be avoided if those who have lost their natural guardians are trained in a workhouse, under the same roof, and in unavoidable contact, with paupers. This stigma, and the consequent loss of self-esteem, would be entirely removed if the children were taught at a central school, with other children not received from the workhouses, nor the offspring of pauper parents . . .

The great object to be kept in view in regulating any school for the instruction of the children of the labouring class, is the rearing of hardy and intelligent working men, whose character and habits shall afford the largest amount of security to the property and order of the community. Not only has the training of the children of labourers hitherto been defective, both in the methods of instruction pursued, and because it has been confined within the most meagre limits, but because it has failed to inculcate the great practical lesson for those whose sole dependence for their living is on the labour of their hands, by early habituating them to patient and skilful industry.

Source: Sir J. Kay-Shuttleworth, 'On the establishment of county or district schools, for the training of the pauper children maintained in union workhouses', *Journal of the Royal Statistical Society*, 1 (1838), pp. 16, 20–23.

Document 15   ADDRESS AT THE OPENING OF THE LONDON MECHANICS'
INSTITUTION, 10 FEBRUARY 1824

The address was made by Dr George Birkbeck (1776–1841), the founder of the adult education movement that sought to popularise scientific knowledge through mechanics' institutes.

Gentlemen; – With feelings of exultation, unutterable, I rise to offer my warmest, heartfelt congratulations, on this momentous occasion. This hour is witness to hopes, long, ardently, and anxiously cherished by me, now rapidly realizing in the visible and effective existence of *A Mechanics' Institution* in the emporium of the world.

Had you, Gentlemen, beheld the small number of artizans, who, in a large and flourishing city, were willing to accept the earliest invitation to enter the temple of science, this striking scene would be contemplated with gratitude and delight, still more lively and enthusiastic; with gratitude, arising from the permission to behold the extended impulsive operation of the growing appetite for knowledge, one of the noblest propensities of man; with delight, from perceiving that the mighty spirit of the age, which has been pervading the whole rational creation, has at length fructified the intellectual mass, and roused it from death-like slumber, to animation and activity. The inquiring spirit of the age has loudly demanded that the door of Science should be thrown open, and that its mysteries should be revealed to all mankind . . . 'There is a *time*,' the wisest of mortals has declared, 'for all things;' and the ardour with which the present project has been embraced, proves beyond the possibility of question, that this is the time for the universal diffusion of the blessings of knowledge. 'There is a *tide* in the affairs of men,' one of the most splendid examples of human genius has affirmed, 'which, taken at the flood, leads on to fortune.' The tide of knowledge, within a recent period, has been rapidly rolling on towards this elevation; and if we do not neglect the golden opportunity, we shall achieve that intellectual fortune, in which consists, alike, individually and aggregately, the most substantial riches and the most substantial glory.

It is not my intention to place before you the vast and varied results of this projected union of science and art; or, in other words, of this combination of the discoveries of the philosophic mind, with the inventions of mechanic genius: the objects and the effects of this combination will be far more intelligibly and impressively depicted, by the liberal and enlightened Professor to whom you will soon have the pleasure and advantage of directing your attention. [Professor Millington was to deliver an Introductory Lecture on the Elementary Principles of Mechanical Science.] I shall content myself with advancing and illustrating the position, that knowledge, by whomsoever obtained, like virtue, which it strikingly resembles, is its own reward; that, therefore, the pleasure flowing from mental exercise, and the satisfaction resulting from the attainment of truth, are sufficient compensations for the labour of study, when unattended by pecuniary or commercial advantage.

Source: Mechanics' Magazine, Register, Journal and Gazette, 28 February 1824, pp. 418–21.

THE DUTIES OF AN ASSISTANT OVERSEER OF THE POOR, 1832   **Document 16**

Indicates the intrusiveness of local officials, whose main function was to administer poor relief efficiently.

It is his duty to make himself intimately acquainted with the situation of every family or person who usually claims relief, with the amount of his wages, the person by whom employed, the number in each family, the ages of the children, their health and various wants; and to be prepared at all times to give every information concerning these objects to the Vestry or any of its members, without whose consent and directions (except in case of necessity) no relief can be given. By these means frauds and impositions are detected, and such is the difficulty of practising them, that they are not often attempted. Since this plan has been adopted, the amount of the poor-rates has been gradually abating.

Source: H. Gawler, *Farm Reports, or Accounts of the Management of Select Farms, no. 1. North Hampshire* (*c*. 1832), Cope Pamphlets, vol. 44 (Cope Library, University of Southampton), 1, p. 23.

Document 17   SETTLEMENT EXAMINATION AND REMOVAL ORDER, WILTSHIRE, 1766

Illustrates the social information contained in settlement examinations con-ducted under the Old Poor Law. Details on occupations, marital status and mobility are all taken into account in the justices' decision to issue a removal order.

11 Oct. 1766. Edward Wheeler, broadweaver, now in the tithing of Great Trowle (Troll), parish of Bradford before Joseph Mortimer and John Bythesea.

Born in Market Lavington. 45 years old. When he was 11 he was apprenticed by the parish officers of Market Lavington to Joseph Somner, broadweaver, of the parish of Melksham until he was 24. He lived with and served Somner in Melksham between 10 and 11 years, then his master, not having sufficient work to employ him, gave him leave to go and work anywhere. So he left him and went to Trowbridge where he worked as a journeyman broadweaver to John Vale of Studley (Studly), parish of Trowbridge, for 14 or 15 years. His master never had any profit or advantage out of his work from the time he left him. About eight years ago he had the spotted fever at Trowbridge, which made him incapable of maintaining himself and family, having then a wife and two small children. The parish of Trowbridge then removed him and his family to Melksham, where they were received as parishioners and allowed some maintenance until they were able to support themselves. Then he moved from Melksham to the tithing of Great Trowle where he has lived ever since as a journeyman weaver. He was married at Trowbridge about 14 years ago to Mary his present wife by whom five children now living,

Ann 11 years or more, Betty nine, John seven, Mary four and William one year and a half.

Removal Order. Edward Wheeler, wife and five children to Melksham.

Source: Phyllis Hembry (ed.), *Calendar of Bradford-on-Avon Settlement Examinations and Removal Orders*, Wiltshire Record Society, 46 (1990), p. 27.

THE SPEENHAMLAND DECISION, 6 MAY 1795   **Document 18**

This decision by local Berkshire magistrates introduced an allowance system as part of the Old Poor Law. Recipients could claim outdoor relief for direct supplements to their wages, according to the price of bread and the size of their families.

At a General Meeting of the Justices of this County, together with several discreet persons assembled by public advertisement, on Wednesday the 6th day of May 1795, at the Pelican Inn in Speenhamland (in pursuance of an order of the last Court of General Quarter Sessions) for the purpose of rating Husbandry Wages, by the day or week, if then approved of, Charles Dundas, Esq., in the Chair [nineteen names follow],

Resolved unanimously, That the present state of the Poor does require further assistance than has been generally given them.

Resolved, That it is inexpedient for the Magistrates to grant that assistance by regulating the Wages of Day Labourers, according to the directions of the Statutes of the 5th Eliz. and 1st of James: But the Magistrates very earnestly recommend to the Farmers and others throughout the county, to increase the pay of their Labourers in proportion to the present Price of Provisions; and agreeable thereto, the Magistrates now present have unanimously Resolved, That they will, in their several divisions, make the following calculations and allowances for relief of all poor and industrious Men and their families, who to the satisfaction of the Justices of their Parish, shall endeavour (as far as they can) for their own support and maintenance. That is to say,

When the Gallon Loaf of Second Flour, weighing 8 lb. 11 ozs. shall cost 1s.

Then every poor and industrious Man shall have for his own support 3s. weekly, either produced by his own or his family's labour, or an allowance from the poor rates, and for the support of his Wife and every other of his family, 1s. 6d.

When the Gallon Loaf shall cost 1s. 4d.

Then every poor and industrious Man shall have 4s. weekly for his own, and 1s. 10d. for the support of every other of his family.

And so in proportion, as the price of Bread rises or falls (that is to say) 3*d*. to the Man, and 1*d*. to every other of the family, on every 1*d*. which the loaf rises above 1*s*.

Source: Berkshire Sessions Order Book (1791–95), quoted in Joel H. Wiener (ed.), *Great Britain: The Lion at Home: A Documentary History of Domestic Policy 1689–1973*, 4 vols (New York: Chelsea House, 1974), vol. 1, pp. 804–5.

Document 19   A PAUPER LETTER OF 1826

An example of a letter by a pauper to an overseer of the poor. The letter was written by George Craddock in Westminster, London, to Robert Alden in Colchester, 21 August 1826.

I am Verry sorry to be under the necessity of trobling you again for Relief And I am likewise Verry Sorry the Gentlemen of the parrish are disatisfied at my not being able to work for the Suport of myself and family I was eight weeks with my friends in the Country And during that time I was not able to work one day they where not able to Suport us any longer which Ocasioned me as Summer was aproaching to return to London And try if I could gain alittle Suport by Selling fruit which I did as much as my health would permit me to do – And Contrary to my own wish I aplied to you last time my wife being desirous to try every honest means wee posably could to Keep out of the workhouse only for her perswasions I should have come home then and now I must Inform you as near as posable the State of my Complaint every time I go to a place of easement my fundament Comes down and be it what time of day it will I am forced to go to bed Imeadiately for two or three hours in the most Excruciating pains posable And at all times I wear abandage to that part to Keep it in Its place – And I am So Short Breathed that I can hardly get about at any time the – Gentlemen of the parish will have the goodness to deal with me as they think proper And I shall be perfectly Satisfied with their desicion but if they Should think proper not to Send me any more relief I hope you will have the goodness to Send me apost paid letter as Soon as you posably can – for literrealy Speaking we have lived ahalf Starved life these Sixteen months past – so that it matters not to me where I spend the remainder of my miserable Existance hoping that god will have mercy on my Soul I remain the
    Gentlemens and your Obedient And Verry Humble
      Servant Geo Craddock
      94 Chapter Street Vauxhall
      road Westminster

Source: Thomas Sokoll (ed.), *Essex Pauper Letters, 1731–1837* (Oxford: Oxford University Press, 2001), 523, pp. 468–69.

THE PRINCIPLE OF 'LESS ELIGIBILITY'   **Document 20**

A guiding principle of the New Poor Law was that of 'less eligibility', as laid down by the Royal Commission on the Poor Law in 1832.

(a) The principle of 'Less Eligibility'

The most pressing of the evils which we have described are those connected with the relief of the Able-bodied. They are the evils, therefore, for which we shall first propose remedies.

If we believed the evils stated in the previous part of the Report, or evils resembling or even approaching them, to be necessarily incidental to the compulsory relief of the able-bodied, we should not hesitate in recommending its entire abolition. But we do not believe these evils to be its necessary consequences. We believe that, under strict regulations, adequately enforced, such relief may be afforded safely and even beneficially.

In all extensive communities, circumstances will occur in which an individual, by the failure of his means of subsistence, will be exposed to the danger of perishing. To refuse relief, and at the same time to punish mendicity when it cannot be proved that the offender could have obtained subsistence by labour, is repugnant to the common sentiments of mankind; it is repugnant to them to punish even depredation, apparently committed as the only resource against want.

In all extensive civilized communities, therefore, the occurrence of extreme necessity is prevented by alms-giving, by public institutions supported by endowments or voluntary contributions, or by a provision partly voluntary and partly compulsory, or by a provision entirely compulsory, which may exclude the pretext of mendicancy.

But in no part of Europe except England has it been thought fit that the provision, whether compulsory or voluntary, should be applied to more than the relief of *indigence*, the state of a person unable to labour, or unable to obtain, in return for his labour, the means of subsistence. It has never been deemed expedient that the provision should extend to the relief of *poverty*; that is, the state of one, who, in order to obtain a mere subsistence, is forced to have recourse to labour.

From the evidence collected under this Commission, we are induced to believe that a compulsory provision for the relief of the indigent can be generally administered on a sound and well-defined principle; and that under the operation of this principle, the assurance that no one need perish from want may be rendered more complete than at present, and the mendicant and vagrant repressed by disarming them of their weapon – the plea of impending starvation.

It may be assumed, that in the administration of relief, the public is warranted in imposing such conditions on the individual relieved, as are conducive to the benefit either of the individual himself, or of the country at large, at whose expense he is to be relieved.

The first and most essential of all conditions, a principle which we find universally admitted, even by those whose practice is at variance with it, is, that his situation on the whole shall not be made really or apparently so eligible as the situation of the independent labourer of the lowest class. Throughout the evidence it is shown, that in proportion as the condition of any pauper class is elevated above the condition of independent labourers, the condition of the independent class is depressed; their industry is impaired, their employment becomes unsteady, and its remuneration in wages is diminished. Such persons, therefore, are under the strongest inducements to quit the less eligible class of labourers and enter the more eligible class of paupers. The converse is the effect when the pauper class is placed in its proper position, below the condition of the independent labourer. Every penny bestowed, that tends to render the condition of the pauper more eligible than that of the independent labourer, is a bounty on indolence and vice. We have found, that as the poor's-rates are at present administered, they operate as bounties of this description, to the amount of several millions annually.

Source: Reprinted in M. W. Flinn (ed.), *Readings in Economic and Social History* (London: Macmillan, 1964), pp. 364–65.

Document 21   A CORNISH BREAD RIOT, 1773

From a letter written by a gentleman in Bodmin, explaining collective action by Cornish tinners against the exportation of corn at high prices when there was a strong local demand for corn.

We had the devil and all of a riot at Padstow. Some of the people have run to too great lengths in exporting of corn, it being a great corn country. Seven or eight hundred tinners went thither, who first offered the corn factors seventeen shillings for twenty-four gallons of wheat; but being told they should have none, they immediately broke open the cellar doors, and took away all in the place without money or price. About sixteen or eighteen soldiers were called out to stop their progress, but the Cornishmen rushed forward and wrested the firelocks out of the soldiers' hands: from thence they went to Wadebridge, where they found a great deal of corn cellared for exportation, which they also took and carried away . . . We think 'tis but the beginning of a general insurrection, because as soon as the corn which they have taken away is expended, they will assemble in greater numbers armed, for 'tis an old saying 'The belly has no ears.'

Source: John Sherratt to the Earl of Rochford, 24 January 1773, in R. A. Roberts (ed.), *Calendar of Home Office Papers of the Reign of George III . . . preserved in Her Majesty's Public Record Office. Volume IV: 1773–1775* (London, 1899), pp. 8–9.

PARLIAMENT AGAINST TRADE UNIONISM, 1799 **Document 22**

Extract from debates in Parliament concerning trade unionism just prior to the passing of the Combination Act of 1799.

8 April: Sir John Anderson brought up a Report of a Select Committee, to whom the Petition of the master millwrights was referred. The substance of the Report was that there existed among the journeymen millwrights, within certain districts in and about the metropolis, a combination which was dangerous to the public, and which the masters had not sufficient power to repress.

The Report being read, Sir John Anderson moved 'That leave be given to bring in a Bill to prevent unlawful combination of workmen employed in the millwright business, and to enable the magistrates to regulate their wages within certain limits.'

Mr. Wilberforce said he did not object to the principle of this motion . . . but he [asked] whether it might not be advisable to extend the principle of this motion, and make it general against combinations of all workmen. These combinations he regarded as a general disease in our society.

17 June: Mr. Chancellor Pitt said it was his intention to endeavour to provide a remedy to an evil of very considerable magnitude; he meant that of unlawful combination among workmen in general – a practice which had become much too general, and was likely, if not checked, to produce very serious mischief. He could not state particularly the nature of the Bill which he intended to move for leave to bring in; but it would be modelled in some respect on that of the Bill for regulating the conduct of the paper manufacturers . . . He then moved that leave be given to bring in a Bill to prevent unlawful combinations of workmen.

Source: Debate in the House of Commons, 1799, *Debrett*, vols LIII–LIV.

Document 23   A WARNING FROM NED LUDD, 1812

An example of an anonymous threatening Luddite letter sent to a Huddersfield master in the woollen industry in 1812.

Sir,

Information has just been given in, that you are a holder of those detestable Shearing Frames, and I was desired by my men to write to you, and give you fair warning to pull them down, and for that purpose I desire that you will understand I am now writing to you, you will take notice that if they are not taken down by the end of next week, I shall detach one of my lieutenants with at least 300 men to destroy them, and further more take notice that if you give us the trouble of coming thus far, we will increase your misfortunes by burning your buildings down to ashes, and if you have the impudence to fire at any of my men, they have orders to murder you and burn all your Housing. You will have the goodness to go to your neigbours to inform them that the same Fate awaits them if their Frames are not taken down, as I understand there are several in your neighbourhood Frame Holders, and as the views and intentions of me and my men have been so misrepresented, I will take this opportunity of stating them, which I desire you will let all your Brethren sir know of, I would have the Merchant Master Drapers, the Government and the Public know that the grievances of such a number of men is not to be made sport of, for by the last returns there were 2782 sworn Heroes bound in a Bond of necessity, either to redress their grievances or perish in the attempt, in the army of Huddersfield alone, nearly double sworn men in Leeds, by the latest Letters from our Correspondents, we learn that the Manufacturers of the following Places are going to rise and join us in redressing their wrongs viz Manchester, Wakefield, Halifax, Bradford, Sheffield, Oldham, Rochdale and all the Cotton Country, where the Brave Mr Hanson will lead them on to victory, the weavers in Glasgow and many Parts of Scotland will join us, the Papists in Ireland are rising to a Man, so that they are likely to find the soldiers something else to do than idle in Huddersfield, and then woe to be to the Places now guarded by them, for we have come to the easier way of burning them to ashes, which will most assuredly be their Fate either sooner or later – the immediate cause of us beginning when we did was that Rascally Letter of the Prince Regent to Lords Grey and Grenville which left us no hope of a change for the better, by his falling in with that damned set of Rogues Perceval & Co to whom we attribute all the miseries of our country but we hope for assistance from the French Emperor in shaking off the Yoke of the Rottenest, wickedest and most Tyrannical Government that ever existed, then down comes the Hanover Tyrants and all our tyrants from the greatest to the smallest, and we will be governed by a just Republic, and may the Almighty hasten those happy times is the wish and prayer of Millions in this Land, but we wont only pray but we will fight, the Red Coats shall know when the proper times come, we will never lay down our arms till the House of Commons passes an act to put down all the machinery hurtfull to the Commonality and repeal that to the Frame Breakers – but we petition no more, that wont do, fighting must,

   Signed by the General of the Army of Redressers
   NEDD LUDD
   Clerk.

Source: National Archives, Kew, Home Office Papers, 40/41, quoted in G. D. H. Cole and A. W. Filson (eds), *British Working Class Movements* (London: Macmillan & Co., 1951), pp. 114–15.

THE PETERLOO MASSACRE, 1819   **Document 24**

An eyewitness account of the mass meeting held at St Peter's Fields, Manchester, on 16 August 1819. Written by Robert Mutrie, a special constable on duty for the day, to his brother-in-law, Archibald Moore, the document comments on armed radicals and the concerted action by the authorities.

MANCHESTER
THURSDAY EVENING
too late for post

My Dear Sir,

. . . It was a dreadful day Monday – I was at my post with them keeping an open passage betwixt the House where the magistrate was stationed and the Hustings from which the *Great men* addressed the people – In witnessing such a multitude of poor deluded people coming on the green in regular military order with monstrous clubs over their shoulders I felt much for them, for I was well aware that if not dispersed by the Military from that green, then, when dispersed of their own accord they would end their days work by murder and expire at night on the way home when perhaps many more lives would have been lost.

   As it was, the Yeomanry came on the grounds gave three cheers and charged – not very quick, and using only the backs of their sabres – the constables were close behind them when the 15th Dragoons made their appearance and without previous knowledge of what was done they mistook us constables with our batons for the Reformers with pistols (I suppose) for in one moment upwards of 100 of us are laid on our backs – I was down but got up by laying hold a horses rein without being hurt – I was afterwards, struck on the head with a sabre of the 15th and then by the Cheshire Troop. Fortunately neither of them hurt me much – I got to the Hustings and in the scuffle for plunder I got hold of a very grand cap of liberty from off one of the standards – I thought I could have secured this in my pocket, but unluckily it was red cloth lined with Tin so I could not squeeze it together.

After the rough usage I had received I did not much like the idea of trusting myself on foot among the soldiers again, so I ordered my charger whose back I never left from 2 o'clock afternoon till 3 o'clock next morning. – being employed riding up and down the streets all the time with Mr. Norris the Magistrate and the Military – whereon the Military went and constable Mr. [illeg.] with them – I got one troop of the 15th to attend to with some foot soldiers – if you look at your map you will find that the most notorious part of the Town New Cross is in your neighbourhood – well on this delight-ful station I took my place – we charged and cleared the streets 50 times without using either swords or guns, but all to no purpose for the people came out again as soon as we retreated to the Cross.

The officer, Capt. Booth who commanded the troop of the 15th after we had been exposed to the pelting of stones for an hour or two got into the most furious passion and swore to Mr. Norris if he did not immediately read the riot act he would order his men to their quarters.

Mr. Norris was very averse that we should commence hostilities and with great reluctance gave his consent that it should be read. The moment it was read Capt. B. ordered the Infantry officer to form a hollow square in the centre of the Cross, we all took shelter in the square when the word was given to fire in all directions – the square then opened and the horse charged every way upon the crowd – my mare grew quite mad and carried me over the back of many a poor Devil. – two people were shot in the first charge just opposite my room window. You may be sure I was (as well as my Mare) very thankful to get relieved at 3 o'clock in the morning. I got very little sleep at all that week, as being in the very heart of the disturbances, I was liable to be called on every hour in the night. Hunt has got out on bail and returned from Lancaster here the night before last – he has taken up his residence at his friend Mr. Johnston's cottage. I think he will not venture to call another meeting but I am much afraid we shall have more disturbances in the neighbourbood – there is a very bad disposition yet left in the people which nothing but blood will satisfy – they continue to meet in the night-time for Military Exercise – this does not look like peace.

Source: Philip Lawson, 'Reassessing Peterloo', *History Today*, 38 (March 1988), p. 26.

————◀●▶————

THE 'SWING' PROTESTS IN NORFOLK, 1830   **Document 25**

The 'Swing' riots occurred in numerous counties in late 1830 as a result of low wages for skilled agricultural workers and competition from the introduction of threshing machines at harvest time.

The *Magistrates* in the Hundreds of *Tunstead* and *Happing*, in the county of Norfolk, having taken into consideration the disturbed state of the said Hundreds and the Country in general, wish to make it publicly known *that it is their opinion* that such disturbances principally arise from the use of Threshing machines, and to the insufficient Wages of the Labourers. The Magistrates therefore beg to *recommend* to the Owners and Occupiers of Land in these Hundreds to *discontinue the use of Threshing Machines, and to increase the Wages of Labour* to Ten Shillings a week for able bodied men, and that when task work is preferred, that it should be put out at such a rate as to enable an industrious man to earn Two Shillings per day.

The Magistrates are determined to enforce the Laws against all tumultuous Rioters and Incendiaries, and they look for support to all the respectable and well disposed part of the Community; at the same time they feel a full conviction that *no severe measures will be necessary*, if all the proprietors of Land will give proper employment to the Poor on their own Occupations, and encourage their Tenants to do the same.

Source: The National Archives, Kew, The magistrates of North Walsham, 24 November 1830, HO 52/9, in Eric Hobsbawm and George Rudé, *Captain Swing* (London: Lawrence and Wishart, 1969), p. 156.

THE CHARTIST LAND PLAN   **Document 26**

An extract from the autobiography of a former Chartist, Benjamin Wilson, who lived in Salterhebble, near Halifax, Yorkshire, and had various occupations, finally becoming a gardener.

The Chartists were called ugly names, the swinish multitude unwashed and levellers. I never knew levelling advocated amongst the Chartists, neither in public nor private, for they did not believe in it, nor have I known a case of plunder in the town, though thousands have marched through its streets to meetings in various places. What they wanted was a voice in making the laws they were called upon to obey; they believed that taxation without representation was tyranny, and ought to be resisted; they took a leading part in agitating in favour of the ten hours question, the repeal of the taxes on knowledge, education, co-operation, civil and religious liberty and the land question, for they were true pioneers in all the great movements of their time. Feargus O'Connor tried to grapple with the land question. He formed a company on the small farm system and purchased several large estates and a great many thousands became members, including several of my friends, and although trade was bad, they cheerfully made great sacrifices to raise the money. Feargus had a great many difficulties to contend against, for he had nearly all the press in the country against him, whilst a great many got on to the land who had no knowledge of it, and what with the opposition outside and the dissatisfaction within, the company was thrown into Chancery.

Source: Benjamin Wilson, *The Struggles of an Old Chartist* ... (Halifax, 1887), reprinted in David Vincent (ed.), *Testaments of Radicalism: Memoirs of Working Class Politicians 1790–1885* (London: Europa Publications, 1977), p. 210.

Document 27   CHARTISM AND A TRIAL FOR SEDITION, 1840

Evidence given at the trial for sedition of Robert Peddie, a Scottish Chartist who had come to Bradford to lead the local Chartists. Emphasises physical force protest in a plan to form an insurgent force of Bradford Chartists.

The further examination of James Harrison of Bradford in the said Riding Labourer taken on Oath in the presence and hearing of the Prisoner Robert Peddie the twenty first Day of February 1840.

Who says On Saturday the 25th of January last the Charter and its final object was mentioned at Hargreaves Beer Shop at a Chartist Meeting by the Prisoner George Flinn and Isaac Holloway, John Turner, William Brook and Marsden and others – Peddie said that if they brought up half the quantity of men they said they had he could beat the soldiers and establish the Charter – he could insure the people that they could have the Charter in two or three days – that it could not be obtained without physical force and that they would use physical force – after taking Bradford they would go and take Dewsbury and after taking Dewsbury they would take all the places on their way to London – after they got to London they would upset the Government, and do all this in three or four days – Peddie said that when they came from Low Moor down to Bradford they would have the piece-hall as a depot for ammunition and the news room as a depot for the men the pillage of different places bread clothes and provisions were to be taken to the newsroom and when they left Bradford to be taken in the baggage wagons – Peddie said we'll have the miners agate with their picks and make port holes thro' the walls we can soon do it – Peddie and the others said that they wanted annual parliaments universal suffrage – no qualification – vote by ballot, that there should be an equal division of property thro' the Country – take all and sweep all before them – especially the money – that they would upset the Government by physical force when they got to London as nothing else would do – that when they had upset the Government they would establish the Charter – that he Peddie would have the management of every thing – that there was to be a national convention – to give every poor man his own rights and that they could do nothing without it – these subjects were agitated both on the Saturday night and Sunday night the 26th of January – on the Sunday at Turner's and they all agreed to what Peddie said – Peddie and Marsden, George Flinn, Isaac Holloway and myself William Brook, Thomas Drake and John Turner were all at his Turners house – Peddie was to be the head Leader and all were Leaders . . . On the Saturday night a little after seven I went with Marsden as far as the Junction Inn on the Leeds New Road in Bradford on his way to Leeds to set fire to the magazine at Leeds and then bring the Leeds Chartists to Bradford – he said he should bring a hundred men from Leeds . . . on Peddie stating what his object was they said they were all ready to join him – they approved of his plans – I had heard physical force and the Charter talked about very often by all the parties – I have named at different times and places – and all agreed to join Peddie in his plans –

James Harrison

Sworn before us

H. W. Hird

B. Hague

Source: The National Archives, Kew, TS 11/814/2678, in Dorothy Thompson (ed.), *The Early Chartists* (London and Basingstoke: Macmillan, 1971), pp. 282–83.

ATTITUDES TOWARDS THE GAME LAWS — **Document 28**

Taken from a parliamentary inquiry into the Game Laws, 1845, this extract illustrates different attitudes towards theft in the countryside.

I had some sheep in the neighbourhood of Luton, just by the town, and I frequently missed stakes, pulled up of a night and hurdles pulled up, and the sheep were let out over the fresh turnips; the consequence was, that one evening my shepherd went and took a person that had taken a hurdle and broken it up. I went down and found the hurdle underneath a heap of stubble. The man was found guilty? Yes; the punishment was about 6s or 7s, and he had a fortnight to pay it in; . . . Was the charge against the man before the magistrates a charge of stealing? – It was for stealing; it was not for letting out the sheep, but for taking a hurdle out of the field, and breaking it up for firewood. Was it malicious damage that you complained of, or felony? I did not consider it felony; it was taking the hurdle, and breaking it up for firewood.

Source: Parliamentary Papers, report from the Select Committee on the Game Laws, 1845, Pt. 1, qus. 448–54.

Document 29   OLD BAILEY PROCEEDINGS, 1764

Summary of the trial of Richard Smith at the Old Bailey, London, 17 October 1764. He was indicted twice for the general theft of simple grand larceny and the specific theft of pickpocketing. He was found guilty and sentenced to convict transportation to North America.

Richard Smith was indicted for stealing a silver watch, value 40s. the property of William Slee, privately from his person, August 12.

William Slee. On the 12th of August, I was at St. James's, with a country friend that wanted to see his Majesty: I lost my watch in the crowd; I don't know who took it; it was taken out of my pocket. I went to Sir John Fielding, and got it advertised. About a fortnight after, Sir John's clerk wrote to me, to let me know they had found my watch. I went there; they sent me to a pawnbroker, who is here; there I found it to be my watch.

John Ashbener. I live at Lower Featherstone-buildings; I am a pawnbroker. A day or two after this watch was advertised, the prisoner brought it to me to pledge; I seeing such a watch advertised, stopped it. (*Produced in court, and deposed to by prosecutor*). The prisoner was taken up for an offence of the like nature: Sir John Fielding sent for me, and I knew him to be the man that brought it.

Prisoner's Defence

I had been up the Strand, and returning back, I met a young woman that I keep company with, she is a woman of the town. I came down as far as Butcher row with her, and went in at the Thatch'd-house: I gave her part of a pint of beer: she told me, a young man that she used to live with, was gone to sea, and she had a watch of his in pawn, that I might have, if I would fetch it out: she asked me for the money to fetch it out, and I gave it her. I was for going with her to the pawnbroker, being afraid to trust her with the money, but she would not let me go with her. I gave her a guinea and a half, and 5s.

she gave the guinea and half, and put the rest in her pocket. In a day or two after, I had occasion for money, so I went to pawn it, and the man stopt it. I went in search of her and the young fellow, but could not hear any thing of them. The pawnbroker knows I offered it in my own name, that shows I did not steal it.

Ashbener. He said his name was Smith, and it was his own; that he had had it some time. I asked him how many months he had had it? he said, he had had it some months. After that, he said, he had it of a young woman, whom he kept company with a few days ago.

Guilty of stealing, but not privately from his person. Transported.

(**L.**) He was a second time indicted for stealing a silver watch, value 3*l*. a metal watch-key, value 6*d*. and a silver seal, value 12*d*. the property of William Proudfoot, September 21.

William Proudfoot. I was going through the Blue-coat-school, near Christ-church, on the 21st of September. There were a parcel of people assembled together to see my Lord Mayor; I had not stood there above five minutes, before I found somebody taking my watch out of my pocket; I put my hand down, and it was very near out; the prisoner was standing with his face towards me. I looked round, lest I should accuse him wrongfully, and saw no other person could possibly take it out but him, their backs were towards me: he seeing me put my hand down, turned away from me, and was gone for five or six minutes: then he came again and stood as before, just before me. I had a notion he would attempt it a second time, and was desirous of detecting him. I took notice of all the people, and saw it was impossible, as they stood, for any to take it but the prisoner; he had his hand down just by my fob: I found my watch move again in my pocket, he gave me a shove with his arm: I put my hand down immediately, and said my watch was gone; he had it in his right hand; I catched hold of his left hand; there was a man stood behind him; I was a little fearful he should deliver it to him. I took hold of that man, and immediately my watch fell to the ground, just by the prisoner's foot; the prisoner desired me to say no more about it, but to go into a house, and he would speak to me about it: I gave the constable charge of him immediately, and he was taken to Guildhall; there he was examined.

Q. Did you get your watch again?

Proudfoot. I did.

Prisoner's Defence

He had hold of another person, and a little boy came and said, Sir, here is your watch.

Proudfoot. I saw the watch moving just at his toe, and heard it fall; but did not see it drop out of his hand; it was impossible it should fall from any body else.

Guilty. Transported.

Source: Robert B. Shoemaker and Tim Hitchcock (eds), *The Old Bailey Proceedings 1674–1834*, 2002–4 (available online at www.oldbaileyonline.org, ref: t17641017-4).

Document 30   THE STATE OF THE PRISONS IN ENGLAND AND WALES, 1777

John Howard, prison reformer (?1726–90), describes the terrible conditions prevailing in prisons and suggests remedies for their improvement.

There are prisons, into which whoever looks will, at first sight of the people confined there, be convinced, that there is some great error in the management of them: the sallow meagre countenances declare, without words, that they are very miserable: many who went in healthy, are in a few months changed to emaciated dejected objects. Some are seen pining under diseases, '*sick and in prison*;' expiring on the floors, in loathsome cells, of pestilential fevers, and the confluent small-pox: victims, I must not say to the cruelty, but I will say to the inattention, of sheriffs, and gentlemen in the commission of the peace.

The cause of this distress is, that many prisons are scantily supplied, and some almost totally unprovided with the necessaries of life.

There are several Bridewells (to begin with them) in which prisoners have no allowance of *Food* at all. In some, the keeper farms what little is allowed them: and where he engages to supply each prisoner with one or two pennyworth of bread a day, I have known this shrunk to half, sometimes less than half the quantity, cut or broken from his own loaf.

It will perhaps be asked, does not their work maintain them? for every one knows that those offenders are committed to *hard labour.* The answer to that question, though true, will hardly be believed. There are very few Bridewells in which any work is done, or can be done. The prisoners have neither tools, nor materials of any kind; but spend their time in sloth, profaneness and debauchery, to a degree which, in some of those houses that I have seen, is extremely shocking.

Some keepers of these houses, who have represented to the magistrates the wants of their prisoners, and desired for them necessary food, have been silenced with these inconsiderate words, *Let them work or starve.* When those gentlemen know the former is impossible, do they not by that sentence, inevitably doom poor creatures to the latter?

I have asked some keepers, since the late act for preserving the health of prisoners, why no care is taken of their sick: and have been answered, that the magistrates tell them *the act does not extend to Bridewells.*

In consequence of this, at the quarter sessions you see prisoners, covered (hardly covered) with rags; almost famished; and sick of diseases, which the discharged spread wherever they go, and with which those who are sent to the County-Gaols infect these prisons.

The same complaint, *want of food,* is to be found in many *County-Gaols.* In about half these, debtors have no bread; although it is granted to the high-wayman, the house-breaker, and the murderer; and medical assistance, which is provided for the latter, is withheld from the former. In many of these Gaols, debtors who would work are not permitted to have any tools, lest they should furnish felons with them for escape or other mischief. I have often seen those prisoners eating their water-soup (bread boiled in mere water) and heard them say, 'We are locked up and almost starved to death' . . .

To their wanting necessary food, I must add not only the demands of gaolers, etc. for fees; but also the extortion of bailiffs. These detain in their houses (properly enough denominated *spunging-houses*) at an enormous expence, prisoners who have money. I know there is a legal provision against this oppression; but the mode of obtaining redress (like that of recovering the groats) is attended with difficulty: and the abuse continues. The rapine of these extortioners needs some more effectual and easy check: no bailiff should be suffered to keep a public house; the mischiefs occasioned by their so doing, are complained of in many parts of the kingdom.

Here I beg leave to mention the hard case of prisoners confined on exchequer processes; and those from the ecclesiastical courts: the latter are excluded from the privilege of bail; and the former from the benefit of insolvent acts.

Felons have in some Gaols two pennyworth of bread a day; in some three halfpennyworth; in some a pennyworth; in some a shilling a week: the particulars will be seen here-after in their proper places. I often weighed the bread in different prisons, and found the penny loaf $7^1/2$ to $8^1/2$ ounces, the other loaves in proportion. It is probable that when this allowance was fixed by its value, near double the quantity that the money will now purchase, might be bought for it: yet the allowance continues unaltered: and it is not uncommon to see the whole purchase, especially of the smaller sums, eaten at breakfast: which is sometimes the case when they receive their pittance but once in two days; and then on the following day they must fast.

This allowance being so far short of the cravings of nature, and in some prisons lessened by farming to the gaoler, many criminals are half starved: such of them as at their commitment were in health, come out almost famished, scarce able to move, and for weeks incapable of any labour.

Many prisons have *No Water*. This defect is frequent in Bridewells, and Town-Gaols. In the felons courts of some County-Gaols there is no water: in some places where there is water, prisoners are always locked up within doors, and have no more than the keeper or his servants think fit to bring them: in one place they are limited to three pints a day each – a scanty provision for drink and cleanliness! . . .

Air which has been breathed, is made poisonous to a more intense degree by the effluvia from the sick; and what else in prisons is offensive. My reader will judge of its malignity, when I assure him, that my cloaths were in my first journeys so offensive, that in a post-chaise I could not bear the windows drawn up: and was therefore often obliged to travel on horseback. The leaves of my memorandum-book were often so tainted, that I could not use it till after spreading it an hour or two before the fire: and even my antidote, a vial of vinegar, has after using it in a few prisons, become intolerably disagreeable. I did not wonder that in those journies many gaolers made excuses; and did not go with me into the felons wards.

Source: John Howard, *The State of the Prisons in England and Wales, with Preliminary Observations, and an Account of some Foreign Prisons* (1777), reprinted in Joel H. Wiener (ed.), *Great Britain: The Lion at Home: A Documentary History of Domestic Policy 1689–1973*, 4 vols (New York: Chelsea House, 1974), vol. 1, pp. 502–5.

Further Reading

Numerous anthologies provide a good selection of primary documents dealing with social change in early industrial Britain. Examples include J. T. Ward (ed.), *The Age of Change, 1770–1870* (London: A. & C. Black, 1975); Alasdair Clayre (ed.), *Nature and Industrialisation: An Anthology* (Oxford: Oxford University Press in association with the Open University, 1977); E. Royston Pike (ed.), *Human Documents of the Industrial Revolution in Great Britain* (London: Allen and Unwin, 1966); and Roy Porter and Edward Royle (eds), *Documents of the early Industrial Revolution* (Cambridge: University of Cambridge Local Examinations Syndicate, 1983). Foreign travellers wrote extensively on the process of industrialisation in Britain. For one such commentary, see Kenneth Morgan (ed.), *An American Quaker in the British Isles: The Travel Journals of Jabez Maud Fisher, 1775–1779* (Oxford: Oxford University Press, 1992).

Original material written by working class people who experienced the social changes of industrial Britain is available in John Burnett (ed.), *Useful Toil: Autobiographies of Working People from the 1820s to the 1920s* (London: Routledge, 1994 edn.) and Thomas Sokoll (ed.), *Essex Pauper Letters 1731–1837* (Oxford: Oxford University Press, 2001). Extensive original material on the Luddites and the Chartists is included respectively in Kevin Binfield (ed.), *Writings of the Luddites* (Baltimore: Johns Hopkins University Press, 2004) and Gregory Claeys (ed.), *The Chartist Movement in Britain 1838–50*, 6 vols. (London: Pickering & Chatto, 2001). Documents on social change in industrial Britain can also be found in B. W. Clapp (ed.), *Documents in English Economic History: England since 1760* (London: G. Bell, 1976). Matlthus's *An Essay on the Principle of Population* (1798) has been reprinted many times; the easiest-to-find edition is published by Penguin Classics with an introduction by Antony Flew (New York: Penguin Books, 1986).

To understand social change in early industrial Britain it is first necessary to appreciate the main shifts in people's economic and material circumstances from *c*.1750 to 1850. A brief introduction is available in Kenneth

Morgan, *The Birth of Industrial Britain: Economic Change 1750–1850* (Harlow: Pearson Education, 1999). This *Seminar Study in History* is the companion volume to the current book. The classic economic history of Britain in the Georgian, Victorian and Edwardian periods is Peter Mathias, *The First Industrial Nation: An Economic History of Britain 1700–1914*, 3rd edn (1969; London: Routledge, 2001). Contrasting studies of the economic history of the British Industrial Revolution can be found in essays by a team of scholars in Robert C. Allen, *The British Industrial Revolution in Global Perspective* (Cambridge: Cambridge University Press, 2009) and Joel Mokyr, *The Enlightened Economy: An Economic History of Britain 1700–1850* (New Haven: Yale University Press, 2009). Other helpful studies on the economic background to social change in eighteenth- and nineteenth-century Britain are R. C. Floud, *The People and the British Economy, 1830–1914* (Oxford: Oxford University Press, 1997); M. J. Daunton, *Progress and Poverty: An Economic and Social History of Britain, 1700–1850* (Oxford: Oxford University Press, 1995); Charles More, *The Industrial Age: Economy and Society in Britain 1750–1985*, 2nd edn (1989; Harlow: Longman, 1997); and Steven King and Geoffrey Timmins, *Making Sense of the Industrial Revolution: English Economy and Society 1700–1850* (Manchester: Manchester University Press, 2001). The experience of industrialisation north of the border is analysed in Christopher A. Whatley, *The Industrial Revolution in Scotland* (Cambridge: Cambridge University Press, 1997).

Many books trace the main themes of English social history in the century before 1850, though only in recent years have historians attempted to integrate the Scottish experience of industrialisation with that of England and Wales. Asa Briggs, *The Age of Improvement*, 2nd edn (1959; Harlow: Longman, 1999) is still a vigorous introductory account of Britain's development from the time of the Younger Pitt to the era of Gladstone and Disraeli. E. P. Thompson, *The Making of the English Working Class* (London: Gollancz, 1963) is a landmark study of the formation of working-class consciousness between the French Revolution and the Great Reform Act. Harold Perkin, *The Origins of Modern English Society* (London: Routledge & Kegan Paul, 1969) remains a stimulating study. More recent overviews of the social history of British industrialisation are Eric J. Evans, *The Forging of the Modern State: Early Industrial Britain 1783–1870*, 3rd edn (1983; Harlow: Longman, 2001); Patrick K. O'Brien and Roland Quinault (eds), *The Industrial Revolution and British Society* (Cambridge: Cambridge University Press, 1993); Edward Royle, *Modern Britain: A Social History, 1750–1997*, 2nd edn (1987; London: Edward Arnold, 1997); John Belchem, *Industrialization and the Working Class: The English Experience, 1750–1900* (Aldershot: Scolar Press, 1990); and F. M. L. Thompson (ed.), *The Cambridge Social History of Britain 1750–1850*, vol. 1: *Regions and Communities*; vol. 2: *People and their*

Environment; vol. 3: *Social Agencies and Institutions* (Cambridge: Cambridge University Press, 1990).

Essential material on demographic history is contained in two magisterial tomes associated with the Cambridge Group for the History of Population and Social Structure: E. A. Wrigley and R. S. Schofield, *The Population History of England, 1541–1871: A Reconstruction* (Cambridge: Cambridge University Press, 1981) and E. A. Wrigley, R. S. Schofield and J. Oeppen, *English Population History from Family Reconstitution, 1580–1837* (Cambridge: Cambridge University Press, 1997). The starting point for consideration of urban development in early industrial Britain is Peter Clark (ed.), *The Cambridge Urban History of Britain, vol. 2: 1540–1840* (Cambridge: Cambridge University Press, 2000). Developments in Scotland are traced in T. M. Devine, *The Scottish Nation, 1700–2000* (Harmondsworth: Allen Lane, 1999). Social administration and social policy have attracted good general surveys, such as U. R. Q. Henriques, *Before the Welfare State: Social Administration in Early Industrial Britain* (London: Longman, 1979) and Derek Fraser, *The Evolution of the British Welfare State*, 4th edn (1973; Basingstoke: Palgrave Macmillan, 2009). An increased interest in women's history over the past two generations has resulted in more attention to women's role in industrialisation. For surveys on this subject see Jane Rendall, *Women in Industrializing Society: England 1750–1880* (Oxford: Blackwell, 1990); Deborah Valenze, *The First Industrial Woman* (Oxford: Oxford University Press, 1995); Katrina Honeyman, *Women, Gender and Industrialization in England, 1700–1870* (Basingstoke: Macmillan, 2000); and Robert B. Shoemaker, *Gender in English Society 1650–1850: The Emergence of Separate Spheres?* (Harlow: Longman, 1998).

Discussions of labour practices in manufacturing outside factories can be found in John Rule, *The Experience of Labour in Eighteenth Century Industry* (London: Croom Helm, 1981); Maxine Berg, *The Age of Manufactures 1700–1820*, 2nd edn (1985; London: Routledge, 1994); and Duncan Bythell, *The Sweated Trades: Outwork in Nineteenth-Century Britain* (London: Batsford, 1978). An older study containing much useful information on urban work is Malcolm I. Thomis, *The Town Labourer and the Industrial Revolution* (London: Batsford, 1974). E. P. Thompson's famous article on the time discipline of the factories is reprinted in his *Customs in Common* (London: Merlin Press, 1991). The rewards and punishments associated with factory work, and the growth of factory villages, are discussed in the republished essays found in Sidney Pollard, *Essays on the Industrial Revolution in Britain* (Aldershot: Ashgate Variorum, 2000). An important reminder that most manufacturing sectors of Britain *c.*1850 were not dominated by factory employment comes in Eric Hopkins, 'Working hours and conditions during the industrial revolution: a reappraisal', *Economic History Review*, 35 (1982). For women's work see Nigel Goose (ed.), *Women's Work in Industrial England; regional and local perspectives* (Hatfield: Local Population Studies, 2007). For child labour see Peter Kirby, *Child Labour in Britain, 1750–1870* (Basingstoke: Palgrave Macmillan, 2003). Working-class leisure in industrial England has attracted several readable histories, notably Robert W. Malcolmson, *Popular Recreations in English Society, 1700–1850* (Cambridge: Cambridge University Press, 1973); Bob Bushaway, *By Rite: Custom, Ceremony and Community in England 1700–1880* (London: Junction Books, 1982); Emma Griffin, *England's Revelry: A History of Popular Sports and Pastimes, 1660–1830* (Oxford: Oxford University Press, 2005); and Adrian Harvey, *The Beginnings of a Commercial Sporting Culture in Britain, 1793–1850* (Aldershot: Ashgate, 2004).

Classic discussions of the standard of living controversy are Eric J. Hobsbawm, 'The standard of living during the industrial revolution: a discussion I' and R. M. Hartwell, 'The standard of living during the industrial revolution: a discussion II', both published in the *Economic History Review*, 16 (1963–64). Quantitative studies of living standards include Peter H. Lindert and Jeffrey G. Williamson, 'English workers' living standards during the industrial revolution: a new look', *Economic History Review*, 36 (1983) and Sara Horrell and Jane Humphries, 'Old questions, new data and alternative perspectives: families' living standards in the industrial revolution', *Journal of Economic History*, 52 (1992). Other important contributions to the debate on living standards during British industrialisation are C. H. Feinstein, 'Pessimism perpetuated: real wages and the standard of living in Britain during and after the industrial revolution', *Journal of Economic History*, 58 (1998) and Hans-Joachim Voth, 'Living Standards and the Urban Environment', in Roderick Floud and Paul Johnson (eds), *The Cambridge Economic History of Modern Britain. Volume 1. Industrialisation, 1700–1860* (Cambridge: Cambridge University Press, 2004). The use of anthropometric measures to estimate living standards is deployed in Roderick C. Floud, Kenneth Wachter and Annabel Gregory, *Height, Health and History: Nutritional Status in the United Kingdom, 1750–1980* (Cambridge: Cambridge University Press, 1990). Overviews of diet and housing are provided in John Burnett, *Plenty and Want: A Social History of Diet in England from 1815 to the Present Day* (Harmondsworth: Penguin, 1983) and *A Social History of Housing, 1815–1985*, 2nd edn (1978; London: Methuen, 1986).

The religious dimension of early industrial Britain is covered in W. R. Ward, *Religion and Society in England, 1790–1850* (London: Batsford, 1972); Alan D. Gilbert, *Religion and Society in Industrial England: Church, Chapel and Social Change, 1740–1914* (London: Longman, 1976); William Gibson, *Church, State and Society, 1760–1850* (Basingstoke: Macmillan, 1994); and C. G. Brown, *Religion and Society in Scotland since 1707* (Edinburgh: Edinburgh University Press, 1997). A magisterial study of nonconformity appears in Michael Watts, *The Dissenters, vol. 1: from the Reformation to the French Revolution; vol. 2: The Expansion of Evangelical Nonconformity* (Oxford: Clarendon Press, 1978, 1995). Contrasting studies of the Church of England are found in Peter Virgin, *The Church in an Age of Negligence 1700–1840* (Cambridge: James Clarke, 1989) and John Walsh, Colin Haydon and Stephen Taylor (eds), *The Church of England c.1689–1833* (Cambridge: Cambridge University Press, 1994). The Halévy thesis on Methodism as an antidote to Jacobinism is outlined in Elie Halévy, *A History of the English People in 1815* (1913; repr. New York: Barnes & Noble, 1968). For Methodism see David Hempton, *Methodism and Politics in British Society, 1750–1850* (London: Hutchinson, 1984) and *The Religion of the People: Methodism and Popular Religion, c.1750–1900* (London: Routledge, 1996). The best detailed study of attitudes towards Catholicism is Colin M. Haydon, *Anti-Catholicism in Eighteenth-Century England c.1714–80: A Political and Social Study* (Manchester: Manchester University Press, 1993).

Religion had an important impact on educational developments in early industrial Britain. This is outlined in J. S. Hurt, *Education in Evolution: Church, State, Society and Popular Education, 1800–1870* (London: Paladin, 1972) and Thomas W. Laqueur, *Religion and Respectability: Sunday Schools and Working-Class Culture* (New Haven: Yale University Press, 1976). For the motives behind state involvement in educational provision see Richard Johnson, 'Educational policy and social control in early Victorian England', *Past and Present*, 49 (1970). See also the essays in P. McCann (ed.), *Popular Education and Socialization in the Nineteenth Century* (London: Methuen, 1977). Good overviews of elementary education in relation to other educational developments in industrialising Britain are available in Michael Sanderson, *Education, Economic Change and Society in England, 1780–1870*, 2nd edn (1983; Cambridge: Cambridge University Press, 1991); E. G. West, *Education and the Industrial Revolution* (London: Batsford, 1975); Anne Digby and Peter Searby (eds), *Children, School and Society in Nineteenth-Century England* (London: Macmillan, 1981); R. D. Anderson, *Education and the Scottish People, 1750–1918* (Oxford: Oxford University Press, 1995); and W. B. Stephens, *Education in Britain 1750–1914* (Basingstoke: Macmillan, 1998).

A number of excellent studies trace the evolution of the poor law in England and Wales: Anthony Brundage, *The English Poor Laws, 1700–1930* (Basingstoke: Palgrave Macmillan, 2002); Tim Hitchcock, Peter King and Pamela Sharpe (eds), *Chronicling Poverty: The Voices and Strategies of the English Poor 1640–1840* (Basingstoke: Macmillan, 1997); Alan J. Kidd, *State, Society and the Poor in Nineteenth-Century England* (Basingstoke: Macmillan, 1999); M. A. Crowther, *The Workhouse System, 1834–1929: The History of an English Social Institution* (London: Batsford, 1981); David Englander, *Poverty and Poor Law Reform in Nineteenth-Century Britain: From Chadwick to Booth,*

1834–1914 (Harlow: Longman, 1998); and K. D. M. Snell, *Parish and Belonging: Community, Identity and Welfare in England and Wales, 1700–1950* (Cambridge: Cambridge University Press, 2006). The best study on the changing ideas of the Old Poor Law in a period when its finances were strained is J. R. Poynter, *Society and Pauperism: English Ideas on Poor Relief 1795–1834* (London: Routledge & Kegan Paul, 1969). For Wales see David W. Howell, *The Rural Poor in Eighteenth-Century Wales* (Cardiff: University of Wales Press, 2000). For Scotland, which had a different poor law tradition than England and Wales, the best study is Rosalind Mitchison, *The Old Poor Law in Scotland* (Edinburgh: Edinburgh University Press, 2000). Collective self-help is the theme of Simon Cordery, *British Friendly Societies, 1750–1914* (Basingstoke: Palgrave Macmillan, 2003).

Popular protest in early industrial Britain has spawned innumerable studies. John Stevenson provides a middle-of-the-road overview in *Popular Disturbances in England 1700–1832*, 2nd edn (1979; Harlow: Longman, 1992). Andrew Charlesworth (ed.) *An Atlas of Rural Protest in Britain, 1548–1900* (London: Croom Helm, 1983) is a helpful contribution by a historical geographer. A short, useful synthesis appears in John E. Archer, *Social Unrest and Popular Protest in England 1780–1840* (Cambridge: Cambridge University Press, 2000). Food riots are documented, along with other popular disturbances, in Adrian Randall, *Riotous Assemblies: Popular Protest in Hanoverian England* (Oxford: Oxford University Press, 2006). R. M. Hartwell offers a sceptical view of the impact of political radicalism on protest in 'La révolution manquée' in D. C. Coleman and Peter Mathias (eds), *Enterprise and History: Essays in Honour of Charles Wilson* (Cambridge: Cambridge University Press, 1984). For the Wilkite movement see John Brewer, *Party Ideology and Popular Politics at the Accession of George III* (Cambridge: Cambridge University Press, 1976) and George Rudé, *Wilkes and Liberty: A Social Study of 1763 to 1774* (Oxford: Clarendon Press, 1962). For the impact of the French Revolution on radical protest see H. T. Dickinson, *British Radicalism and the French Revolution 1789–1815* (Oxford: Blackwell, 1985) and the studies collected in J. R. Dinwiddy, *Radicalism and Reform in Britain, 1780–1850* (London: Hambledon, 1992). The Luddite movement is analysed in J. R. Dinwiddy, *From Luddism to the First Reform Bill* (Oxford: Blackwell, 1986) and Malcolm I. Thomis, *The Luddites: Machine-Breaking in Regency England* (Newton Abbot: David & Charles, 1970). Helpful guides to Chartism include D. J. V. Jones, *Chartism and the Chartists* (Harmondsworth: Allen Lane, 1975); Dorothy Thompson, *Chartists: Popular Politics in the Industrial Revolution* (Aldershot: Wildwood House, 1986); Edward Royle, *Chartism*, 3rd edn (1987; Harlow: Longman, 1996); and Malcolm Chase, *Chartism: A New History* (Manchester: Manchester University Press, 2007).

Synthetic studies dealing with crime, justice and punishment in early industrial Britain include Clive Emsley, *Crime and Society in England 1750–1900*, 2nd edn (1987; Harlow: Longman, 1996) and *The English Police: A Political and Social History*, 2nd edn (1991; Harlow: Longman, 1996); David Taylor, *Crime, Policing and Punishment in England, 1750–1914* (Basingstoke: Macmillan, 1998); and D. J. V. Jones, *Crime, Protest, Community and Police in Nineteenth-Century Britain* (London: Routledge, 1982). An important statement on the ideology of the law appears in Douglas Hay, 'Property, authority and the criminal law', in Douglas Hay, Peter Linebaugh, John Rule, E. P. Thompson and Cal Winslow (eds), *Albion's Fatal Tree: Crime and Society in Eighteenth-Century England* (Harmondsworth: Allen Lane, 1975). For sentencing practices see Peter King, *Crime, Justice, and Discretion in England, 1740–1820* (Oxford: Oxford University Press, 2000). For public hangings see Peter Linebaugh, *The London Hanged: Crime and Civil Society in the Eighteenth Century*, 2nd edn (1991; London: Verso, 2006) and V. A. C. Gatrell, *The Hanging Tree: Execution and the English People, 1770–1868* (Oxford: Oxford University Press, 1994). For transportation see A. Roger Ekirch, *Bound for America: The Transportation of British Convicts to the Colonies, 1718–1775* (Oxford: Oxford University Press, 1987) and Simon Devereaux, 'In place of death: transportation, penal practices, and the English state, 1770–1830', in Carolyn Strange (ed.), *Qualities of Mercy: Justice, Punishment, and Discretion* (Vancouver: University of British Columbia Press, 1996). Changes in the provision of prisons are explained in Michael Ignatieff, *A Just Measure of Pain: The Penitentiary in the Industrial Revolution 1750–1850* (London: Macmillan, 1978).

References

Allen, Robert C. (2009) *The British Industrial Revolution in Global Perspective*. Cambridge: Cambridge University Press.

Bushaway, Bob (1982) *By Rite: Custom, Ceremony and Community in England 1700–1880*. London: Junction Books.

Chase, Malcolm (2007) *Chartism: A New History*. Manchester: Manchester University Press.

Clapp, B. W. (1994) *An Environmental History of Britain since the Industrial Revolution*. Harlow: Longman.

Clark, J. C. D. (2000) *English Society 1688–1832: Ideology, Social Structure and Political Practice during the Ancien Regime*, 2nd edn. Cambridge: Cambridge University Press.

Corfield, P. J. (1995) 'Georgian England: one state, many faiths', *History Today*, 45, April.

Daunton, M. J. (1995) *Progress and Poverty: An Economic and Social History of Britain, 1700–1850*. Oxford: Oxford University Press.

De Vries, Jan (1994) 'The industrial revolution and the industrious revolution', *Journal of Economic History*, 54.

Devereaux, Simon (1996) 'In place of death: transportation, penal practices, and the English state, 1770–1830', in Carolyn Strange (ed.) *Qualities of Mercy: Justice, Punishment, and Discretion*. Vancouver: University of British Columbia Press.

Digby, A. and Searby, P. (eds) (1981) *Children, School and Society in Nineteenth-Century England*. London: Macmillan.

Evans, Eric J. (1983) *The Forging of the Modern State: Early Industrial Britain 1783–1870*, 3rd edn. Harlow: Longman, 2001.

Feinstein, C. H. (1998) 'Pessimism perpetuated: real wages and the standard of living in Britain during and after the industrial revolution', *Journal of Economic History*, 58.

Floud, Roderick C., Wachter, Kenneth and Gregory, Annabel (1990) *Height, Health and History: Nutritional Status in the United Kingdom, 1750–1980*. Cambridge: Cambridge University Press.

Gilbert, Alan D. (1976) *Religion and Society in Industrial England: Church, Chapel and Social Change 1740–1914*. London: Longman.

Goldstrom, J. M. (ed.) (1972) *Education: Elementary Education 1780–1900*. Newton Abbot: David & Charles.

Griffin, Emma (2005) *England's Revelry: A History of Popular Sports and Pastimes*. Oxford: Oxfod University Press.

Halévy, Elie (1913) *A History of the English People in 1815*. New York: Barnes & Noble reprint, 1968.

Hartwell, R. M. (1963–4) 'The standard of living during the industrial revolution: a discussion II', *Economic History Review*, second series, 16.

Hartwell, R. M. (1984) 'La révolution manquée' in Coleman, D. C. and Mathias, Peter (eds) *Enterprise and History: Essays in Honour of Charles Wilson*. Cambridge: Cambridge University Press.

Hay, Douglas (1975) 'Property, authority and the criminal law', in Douglas Hay, Peter Linebaugh, John Rule, E. P. Thompson and Cal Winslow (eds) *Albion's Fatal Tree: Crime and Society in Eighteenth-Century England*. Harmondsworth: Allen Lane.

Hempton, David (2002) 'Enlightenment and faith', in Paul Langford (ed.) *The Short Oxford History of the British Isles: The Eighteenth Century*. Oxford: Oxford University Press.

Hilton, Boyd (1988) *The Age of Atonement: The Influence of Evangelicalism on Social and Economic Thought, 1795–1865*. Oxford: Clarendon Press.

Ignatieff, Michael (1978) *A Just Measure of Pain: The Penitentiary in the Industrial Revolution 1750–1850*. London: Macmillan.

Johnson, Richard (1970) 'Educational policy and social control in early Victorian England', *Past and Present*, 49(1).

Jones, D. J. V. (1975) *Chartism and the Chartists*. Harmondsworth: Allen Lane.

King, Peter (2000) *Crime, Justice and Discretion in England, 1740–1820*. Oxford: Oxford University Press.

Malcolmson, Robert W. (1973) *Popular Recreations in English Society, 1700–1850*. Cambridge: Cambridge University Press.

Nicholas, Stephen and Steckel, Richard H. (1991) 'Heights and health of English workers during the early years of industrialisation, 1770–1815', *Journal of Economic History*, 51.

O'Brien, Patrick K. and Engerman, Stanley L. (1981) 'Changes in income and its distribution during the industrial revolution', in R. C. Floud and D. N. McCloskey (eds) *The Economic History of England, vol. 1: 1700–1860*. Cambridge: Cambridge University Press.

Philips, David (1993) 'Crime, law and punishment in the industrial revolution', in Patrick K. O'Brien and Roland Quinault (eds) *The Industrial Revolution and British Society*. Cambridge: Cambridge University Press.
Plumb, J. H. (1950) *England in the Eighteenth Century*. Harmondsworth: Penguin.
Porter, Roy (1982) *English Society in the Eighteenth Century*. Harmondsworth: Penguin.

Reid, Douglas A. (1980) 'Review article: Leisure and recreation', *History*, 65.
Richards, Eric (1974) 'Women and the British economy since about 1700: an interpretation', *History*, 59.
Rule, John (1986) *The Labouring Classes in Early Industrial England, 1750–1850*. Harlow: Longman.

Thomis, Malcolm I. and Holt, Peter (1977) *Threats of Revolution in Britain 1789–1848*. London: Macmillan.
Thompson, E. P. (1963) *The Making of the English Working Class*. London: Gollancz.
Thompson, E. P. (1991) *Customs in Common*. London: Merlin Press.

Valenze, Deborah (1985) *Prophetic Sons and Daughters: Female Preaching and Popular Religion in Industrial England*. Princeton, NJ: Princeton University Press.
Virgin, Peter (1989) *The Church in an Age of Negligence 1700–1840*. Cambridge: James Clarke.
Voth, Hans-Joachim (2004) 'Living standards and the urban environment', in Roderick Floud and Paul Johnson (eds) *The Cambridge Economic History of Modern Britain. Volume 1: Industrialisation, 1700–1860*. Cambridge: Cambridge University Press.

Walsh, John, Haydon, Colin and Taylor, Stephen (eds) (1994) *The Church of England c.1689–1833*. Cambridge: Cambridge University Press.

Index